Designing Tomorrow

Designing Tomorrow
America's World's Fairs of the 1930s

Edited by Robert W. Rydell and Laura Burd Schiavo

With contributions by Robert Bennett, Matthew Bokovoy, Robert A. González, Neil Harris, Lisa D. Schrenk, Kristina Wilson, and Richard Guy Wilson

Yale University Press New Haven and London

Front-matter and chapter-opening illustrations: page i (plate 34, p. 114); page ii (detail of plate 49, p. 130); page vi (plate 50, p. 131); page viii (fig. 9, p. 17); page x (detail of fig. 2, p. 181); pages xii–xiii (detail of plate 57, pp. 138–139); page xiv (detail of fig. 2, p. 4); page 22 (detail of fig. 6, p. 34); page 40 (detail of fig. 2, p. 46); page 56 (fig. 2, p. 63); page 76 (plate 56, p. 137); page 140 (detail of fig. 1, p. 144); page 158 (detail of fig. 5, p. 169); page 176 (detail of fig. 3, p. 182); page 192 (fig. 3, p. 196); page 200 (detail of plate 37, p. 117).

Designed by Jena Sher
Set in Univers type by Amy Storm
Printed in Singapore by CS Graphics

Library of Congress Cataloging-in-Publication Data
Designing tomorrow: America's world's fairs of the 1930s / edited by Robert W. Rydell and Laura Burd Schiavo; with contributions by Robert Bennett . . . [et al.].
    p. cm.
  Based on an exhibition held at the National Building Museum, Washington, DC, October 2010–July 2011.
  Includes bibliographical references and index.
  ISBN 978-0-300-14957-9 (cloth : alk. paper) 1. Trade Shows—United States—History—20th century—Exhibitions. I. Rydell, Robert W. II. National Building Museum (U.S.). III. Title: America's world's fairs of the 1930s.
  T395.5.U6D48 2010
  907.4'73—dc22
                                    2009051023

A catalogue record for this book is available from the British Library.

This paper meets the requirements of ANSI/NISO Z39.48-1992 (Permanence of Paper).

10 9 8 7 6 5 4 3 2 1

To our families Stephen, Hannah, and Leah Burd, and Kiki, Claire, and Johanna Rydell

Contents

Foreword

Seventy years ago, the New York World's Fair and San Francisco Golden Gate International Exposition were entering their second season of operation, bringing to culmination the decadelong run of America's Depression-era world's fairs. Few expositions since have so engaged the American public. The population that witnessed the Depression-era fairs is aging, and as memories fade and the fairs are lost to nostalgia, expositions are often dismissed as mere escapism. The essays in *Designing Tomorrow: America's World's Fairs of the 1930s* challenge us to explore what that "escape" looked like—to engage critically with these masterful built environments and the cultural work they performed in helping to introduce modernism into the American popular imagination. Although by no means stylistically monolithic, the architects and designers conceived the worlds they created as modern, linked their design to a better future, and in the process helped fairgoers envision the future of the United States. In the midst of the Great Depression, it would have been just as reasonable to escape into the past. Instead, they imagined tomorrow.

World's fairs are ideal subjects for the National Building Museum, encompassing as they do disciplines integral to the Museum's mission—architecture, design, engineering, and landscape. And the Museum and the expositions share another characteristic—an engagement with the public. This book and the accompanying National Building Museum exhibition of the same name reach the public thanks to the work of more people than can be named here, but some words of appreciation are due to the following contributors. The world's fair historian Robert W. Rydell was asked to consult on this project when it was only the germ of an idea. Bob has stuck by it, and by the Museum, driven by his love of the material and his enthusiasm for sharing it. Designing Tomorrow was curated with admirable dedication and passion by Laura Burd Schiavo in partnership with assistant curator Deborah Sorensen and with encouragement and support from Vice President for Exhibitions and Collections Catherine Frankel. The National Building Museum is pleased to join for the first time with Yale University Press on this important contribution to American architectural and design history.

The Museum's programs depend on the generosity of its friends and supporters. The publication *Designing Tomorrow: America's World's Fairs of the 1930s* was made possible by the Graham Foundation for Advanced Studies in the Fine Arts. Support for the exhibition and publication was provided in part by a major grant from the National Endowment for the Humanities: Because democracy demands widsom. (Any views, findings, conclusions, or recommendations expressed in this publication do not necessarily represent those of the National Endowment for the Humanities.) Additional support was provided by the National Endowment for the Arts, and Jean S. and Frederic A. Sharf. We are grateful to all of them for their commitment.

Chase W. Rynd
Executive Director

ix

Acknowledgments

Like the world's fairs it explores, this book was a true collaboration. And like some of the best intellectual endeavors, it was made possible only through the willingness of scholars to share—to share their ideas, their research, their knowledge, and their time. We would therefore like to thank, first and foremost, the contributors: Robert Bennett, Matthew Bokovoy, Robert González, Neil Harris, Lisa Schrenk, Kristina Wilson, and Richard Guy Wilson. Our interview with Richard Guy Wilson was a particular delight. His willingness to contribute his thoughts and reflections allowed us to bring a distinctive finale to this volume. Many of the contributors have served on the advisory committee for the larger National Building Museum exhibition project for many years. It is a pleasure to help bring their original scholarship to publication.

At the National Building Museum, we would like to thank Deborah Sorensen for her expert managing of the illustrations, and Stephanie Anderson and Diane Riley for their able assistance with the preparation of the manuscript. Vice President for Exhibitions and Collections Catherine Frankel and Director Chase Rynd supported this project from its inception. At Yale we thank Michelle Komie, whose initial enthusiasm gave the project a timely boost, and Dan Heaton for his excellent editing eye. Across the country a number of people championed the cause: Paul Greenhalgh, Tammy Lau, Jack Masey, and Golden Gate International Exposition advocates Claire Isaacs, Anne Schoebelen, and Richard and Shirley Hansen.

The illustrations presented here come from an array of museums, historical societies, university special collections, corporate and state archives, and private collectors, all credited at the back of the volume. The assistance of the staffs of these organizations made our use of the illustrations possible, and thus made the book better. But a few individuals must be called out for special recognition of a commitment that rises beyond the call of duty: James Boufford (Albert Kahn Associates), Eric Longo, Lindsey MacAllister (formerly at the Museum of Science and Industry), Amy Sanderson (The Charles Rand Penney Collection and Research Facility), and Tammy Lau (University of California, Fresno).

The origins of this exhibition date to conversations between then National Building Museum Chief Curator Howard Decker and Fred Sharf, who backed the idea with financial support. This book, as well as the exhibition by the same name, is the final result.

Robert W. Rydell
Bozeman, Montana

Laura Burd Schiavo
Washington, D.C.

Designing Tomorrow

Introduction
Making America (More) Modern
America's Depression-Era World's Fairs

Robert W. Rydell

[As General Ferdinand Foch said at the Battle of the Marne], "my center yields, my right gives ground, the situation is excellent, I shall attack." . . . [Today], civilization with its back against the wall, fighting a mysterious and baffling foe, awaits another Battle of the Marne. What if the Century of Progress should break through? Might it not outflank the army of Depression? Might it not mean not only the deliverance of Chicago, but of the whole world?

Architect Thomas E. Tallmadge, *Vanity Fair*, September 1932

Between 1933 and 1940 an upthrust of modernist world's fairs broke through the crust of Depression-era America and transformed Chicago, San Diego, Dallas, Cleveland, San Francisco, and New York into blazing beacons of light and hope in a world mired in grim economic news and sad tidings of wars already under way and about to come. Today, these fairs are receding in memory. And with lapses in memory come distortions. For instance, to the extent any of these fairs are remembered, the 1939–1940 New York World's Fair gets most of the attention. Chicago's 1933–1934 Century of Progress Exposition, the world's fair that made the rest possible, is barely an afterthought, except in Chicago, and the fairs hosted by the other cities are recalled only as curiosities. To argue whether one fair or another was most important misses the point. These fairs, individually and collectively, helped Americans find their way out of the Great Depression. They did so not by accident, but by design. Attended by some one hundred million visitors, these fairs left in their wake a vision of the United States emerging from the Great Depression as a consumer-centered, corporation-driven nation-state powered forward by science and technology and governed by a federal system made newly attentive by the circumstances of the 1930s to the welfare of its citizens.[1] The fairs of the 1930s sustained and remade the American nation at a time of crisis second only to the Civil War.[2]

To understand the importance of world's fairs to the national recovery of the United States in the 1930s, it is best to begin at the top—with President Franklin Roosevelt. When word reached him in 1935 about plans developing in New York City to hold a fair that would surpass the just completed 1933–1934 Century of Progress Exposition, FDR wasted no time cabling his friend the architect Francklyn Paris: "I have been much interested in hearing of the possibility of an exposition to be held in New York in 1939 in commemoration of the inauguration of George Washington as First President." Then, FDR added: "I hope you will keep me in touch with the decisions and plans."[3] Make no mistake: world's fairs were anything but sideshows. Between 1933 and 1940 scarcely a year went by in the United States without a world's fair that required close collaboration between the federal government and state and local political and business leaders. At once nostalgic and utopian, these spectacles attracted tens of millions of visitors looking for some hope that America's star might rise again.[4]

Why all of this interest in world's fairs? Why would FDR be so eager to promote, of all things, a world's fair in New York City in 1939 in the midst of the Great Depression? The short answer is that the idea of holding a world's fair to promote economic growth and inspire feelings of nationalism during a time of national crisis came as naturally to FDR as the idea of throwing out the first ball on opening day of the baseball season.

Like his predecessor in the presidency, Herbert Hoover, and like most Americans, FDR had grown up in a world replete with world's fairs, sometimes called international exhibitions or universal expositions, which, with their palatial Beaux-Arts exhibition palaces and midways, had always functioned as antidotes to cycles of economic depression and panic (figs. 1, 2).[5] Indeed, both Hoover and FDR had worked to promote the 1915 San Francisco Panama-Pacific International Exposition as a launching pad for America's economic expansion across the Pacific Rim.[6]

During the 1920s, however, with the economy booming, it seemed to many that world's fairs had outlived their usefulness. The British Empire Exhibition held outside of London in 1924–1925 suffered from poor attendance, and Philadelphia's 1926 Sesquicentennial Exhibition suffered disastrous attendance, the result of poor weather and generally boring exhibits. By the close of the 1926 exposition, some cultural critics were declaring that world's fairs had become cultural dinosaurs and had lost their relevance for American life.[7]

But that was not the case in Chicago. Because they understood that America's postwar prosperity would not last forever, Rufus Dawes, an oil baron and banker, and his brother, Charles, Calvin Coolidge's vice president and ambassador to England, determined to hold a world's fair in Chicago to commemorate the founding of the city and the fortieth anniversary of the 1893 World's Columbian Exposition. The 1929 stock market crash only underscored the urgency of the task. With unemployment worsening and anxieties deepening about the import of the 1917 Russian Revolution for capitalist nation-states, the Dawes brothers wasted no time pushing forward plans to hold another great Chicago fair that would remind Americans of the nation's progress over the preceding century and shore up popular faith in America's political economy and future.[8]

In their early assessments of the failure of the Philadelphia exposition, the Dawes brothers concluded that the Chicago fair would have to be different. It would have to have both a novel theme and a new look that would distinguish it from its predecessor and give new meaning to modernity. The theme developed quickly at the suggestion of the astrophysicist George Hale and the engineer Michael Pupin. Both understood that the First World War, with its vast destruction, had undercut popular trust in science and technology, and they saw an opportunity to use the Chicago fair to rebuild popular support for both enterprises. Hale, in particular, had excellent contacts with the National Research Council and persuaded its leadership to develop a theme for the fair. It was nothing short of brilliant: "Science finds, industry applies, man conforms" (fig. 3). From the start, many of the nation's leading scientists and engineers began working on exhibits to get across the message that science and technology could usher in a new utopian age. Their efforts would culminate in the fair's theme center, the Temple of Science, later rechristened as the Hall of Science.[9]

Robert W. Rydell

2

fig. 1 Court of Honor, World's
Columbian Exposition, Chicago,
1893. James W. Shepp and Daniel
B. Shepp, *Shepp's World's Fair
Photographed* (Chicago: Globe Bible
Publishing, 1893). Collection of
Deborah Sorensen.

fig. 2 Paul Cret's Hall of Science at the Century of Progress Exposition, with John Storrs's sculpture *Knowledge Combating Ignorance*. Kaufmann and Fabry Co. *Official Pictures of A Century of Progress Exposition* (Chicago: Reuben H. Donnelley, 1933). National Building Museum.

The bigger problem confronting exposition organizers was the look of the fair. No doubt it had to be modern. But what exactly did this mean? Hadn't the earlier generation of fairs with their grand neoclassical designs seemed modern to the people who had visited them? Complicating any answer to these questions was another exposition, the 1925 Paris Exposition internationale des arts décoratifs et industriels moderne. The Paris exposition, which reframed design syntax across architecture and the arts on both sides of the Atlantic, had been without an official U.S. government exhibit. Secretary of Commerce Herbert Hoover had declined an invitation from the French government to participate.[10]

Hoover obviously bore no hostility to the exposition medium. His objection to U.S. participation in the Paris event stemmed from the French requirement that "reproductions, imitations and counterfeits of ancient styles will be prohibited," and from his conviction that modernism did not really exist in the United States, and that, if it did, it certainly did not reflect American culture.[11] The reaction from American artists, architects, and designers came swiftly. What about the architects Frank Lloyd Wright and Richard Neutra? What about the artists Man Ray and

Joseph Stella? In response to his critics, Hoover agreed to appoint an official U.S. commission to visit the Paris fair and report back on its content. This *Report of Commission Appointed by the Secretary of Commerce to Visit and Report upon the International Exposition of Modern Decorative and Industrial Art in Paris* did not impress anyone with its catchy title. But it was written less as a report than a manifesto, and its far-reaching conclusions set the stage for much of the thinking that fed the modernist designs of America's Depression-era world's fairs.

Led by the industrial art specialist Charles R. Richards, Arts-in-Industry medal winner Henry Creange, and the Lenox Ceramics designer Frank Graham Holmes, the commission defended the secretary's reasons for not participating in the Paris exposition. "As a nation we now live artistically largely on warmed-over dishes," they declared in the introduction to the report. Put simply, the problem with American design was that it was too historicist in nature. This was unfortunate for two reasons. First, it posed a problem for the standing of American art in Europe. Second, and more important, it posed a problem for American industry. What the Paris exposition taught above all, the commissioners observed, was that the application of

5

art to industry could improve both domestic and international markets for American manufacturers in the same way art had led the way in France. "Had the French waited for the initiative of industry to renew itself and break away from the beaten paths in which world competition had forced them to enter, . . . French commerce might have suffered irreparable damage." In France, the commissioners insisted, artists led the way. "Industry followed."[12]

For the United States, the take-away message was clear. First, the commissioners insisted, "the modern movement in applied art is destined to play a large part in the near future in many important fields of production throughout the western world." Second, they emphasized, "the nation which most successfully rationalizes the movement and brings its expression into terms acceptable and appropriate to modern living conditions and modern taste will possess a distinct advantage both as to its domestic and its foreign trade." Third, they warned of becoming "entirely dependent . . . upon foreign talent." And finally, they made this telling observation: because of costs associated with mass production, American manufacturers tended to be conservative about experimenting with new designs. "This conservatism," they lamented, "is increased by lack of confidence on the part of American manufacturers as to the willingness of our public to accept new forms." But hope lay at hand because, as the commissioners made clear, "in no other nation are the facilities for transmitting new ideas to the mass of the people so highly developed, and in no other nation is the response immediate when interest is aroused."[13]

What exactly did this mean for design? The authors of the report were explicit. "To blend the old with the new, to embody some element that has already been accepted by the public, is to start that creation with a very fair chance of life. Creation that departs too radically from the past; that throws into the discard all that has gone before, is apt to be short-lived."[14] Although scholars have not paid much attention to the manifesto laid down by Hoover's Paris commissioners, theirs was exactly the message that took hold in the minds of the men who planned the 1933 Chicago fair and produced a distinctive American modern style that would course through America's Depression-era world's fairs.[15]

To put this in slightly different terms, the history of American modernism revealed through America's world's fairs is rather different from the one that takes as its starting point the high modernist, museum-based exhibitions that hit with full force between 1926 and 1932. These exhibitions—the 1926 American Association of Museums exhibit at the Museum of Modern Art (MoMA), based on selected objects from the 1925 Paris Exposition, the 1927 Machine-Age Exposition organized by Jane Heap in a New York warehouse with works by Le Corbusier and Walter Gropius, and the International Exhibition of Modern Architecture organized in 1932 at MoMA by Henry-Russell Hitchcock and Philip Johnson—put to rest the notion that American design was not sufficiently modern to share the world stage with European designers. On an aesthetic level, these were landmark events, and the thirty-three thousand visitors to the 1932 MoMA show doubtless included many influential designers.[16] But world's fairs attracted tens of millions of visitors. As showcases of modern design and of the application of modern design to immediate social problems, these fairs arguably had more influence on the general public than any of the museum-based exhibitions. Precisely because they were about more than aesthetics, world's fairs revealed something else about American modernism between the wars. No less than in Europe, the modernists who designed America's fairs conceived their work in ideological terms, but with this difference: where many Europeans harbored ideas of social and political revolution, American modernists who hopped on the world's fair bandwagon sought to head off revolution.[17]

Really, one might ask, how much of a concern in America was political revolution during the Great Depression? Reflect for a moment on the setting. Given the severity of the worldwide crisis in capitalist economies that fueled the rise of fascism in Europe and home-rule movements throughout many of Europe's overseas colonies, not to mention the gravity of soaring unemployment rates in the United States, it is easy to understand Ford Motor Company executive Fred L. Black's recollection of the impact of the Great Depression on the American political landscape. "There was," he recalled, "the possibility of revolution." Secretary of Commerce Daniel Roper similarly remembered "riots and threats of riots throughout the country." John Stephen Sewell, who became director of exhibits at the 1933 fair, declared that the government

6

Robert W. Rydell

and business would have to cooperate or "the country will go Bolshevik." They were not alone in their fears. Inspired by the creation of a special "Red Squad" within the Chicago Police Department, police forces across the nation stepped up intelligence-gathering activities and pre-emptive interventions to head off efforts by left-leaning political organizations to gain the support of the unemployed.[18] What kept the United States from going under? President Franklin D. Roosevelt's New Deal reforms certainly helped; so did the world's fairs, themselves products of collaboration between the federal government and the private sector. As I have argued elsewhere, the fairs—and remember there were several, organized in Dallas, San Diego, Cleveland, New York, and San Francisco in addition to Chicago—outfitted the United States with a lifebuoy that prevented the American political economy from sinking.[19]

Becoming (More) Modern

The fairs that erupted across the American landscape were at once carefully planned responses to the Great Depression and blueprints for building a better future that never lost sight of the past. Chicago's Century of Progress took its name from the hundred years that had passed from Chicago's founding in 1833 to the fair's opening in 1933. San Diego's California-Pacific Exposition took its inspiration from the romance of southern California's past. Dallas looked to the founding of the Republic of Texas in 1836 as its point of departure for measuring progress toward the present and future. Cleveland's historical peg was the centennial of the city's incorporation. San Francisco's exposition promoters excavated the Pacific Rim's deep past and constantly evoked historicized and romanticized ideas about the "primitive" cultures that had gone before. And even New York's exposition organizers, who would always be remembered for planning a fair that took as its theme "the world of tomorrow," began by imagining a spectacle that would commemorate a historical event—George Washington's inauguration in New York City in 1789—and toyed with calling their fair the Liberty Exposition.

When we reflect on the history of modernism, we sometimes become so infatuated with the cutting edge and avant-garde that we cut out portions of the story that don't quite fit our expectations. This is the point that Neil Harris

underscores in his essay that follows about the major art exhibitions organized for several of the world's fairs. Harris asks us to think about the art exhibits that we would expect to find at the modernist world's fairs of the 1930s. And the works of contemporary artists like Lyonel Feininger and Aaron Douglas were certainly on display around the fairgrounds. But what excited the organizers of the art exhibitions—and the audiences who stood in line to gain entrance to galleries—were the works of the old masters. At Chicago's Art Institute, which was reorganized for the 1933–1934 Century of Progress Exposition, masterworks by Titian, Rembrandt, and El Greco drew tens of thousands of visitors. The unexpected success of this show inspired the organizers of the New York and San Francisco fairs to follow suit. At both fairs, as Harris points out, it was works by the old masters—including Botticelli's *Birth of Venus,* which traveled to the San Francisco exposition—that stole the show.[20]

What was going on here? Why not follow the precedent set by the 1925 Paris exposition and exclude historicist designs of all kinds? An important clue comes from the 1925 U.S. government report on that exposition. Remember that the authors of the report had insisted: "To blend the old with the new, to embody some element that has already been accepted by the public, is to start that creation with a very fair chance of life."[21] This is precisely how the old masters fit into these expositions—as bedrock for one of the fundamental messages that ran throughout these fairs, namely, that modern American design would build upon, not undermine, the underpinnings of what most Americans regarded as cornerstones of their own nation and of Western civilization more generally. Modernism might be bold. It might be unsettling. But because it built on the past, modernism in its American guise would only enhance the possibilities for Americans to make progress out of the Depression and toward a better future. To make this case, exposition planners took another page out of the 1925 report on the Paris exposition that declared in no uncertain terms that "the nation which most successfully rationalizes the [modern movement in applied art] and brings its expression into terms acceptable and appropriate to modern living conditions and modern taste will possess a distinct advantage both as to its domestic and its foreign trade."[22] The United States could lead or follow. For American industrial designers, the choice was clear.

Industrial design came of age with the fairs of the 1930s. As the historian Richard Guy Wilson has observed, the term *industrial design* has roots back at least in the 1910s, but began to coalesce only in the late 1920s and early 1930s, when several talented artists and theater set designers, many of whom had backgrounds in advertising, began applying their talents to altering—modernizing — the appearance of machine-age products and machine-age fashions. Some even went so far as to propose engineering women's bodies to make them more efficient. By the close of the 1930s, due largely to their work at world's fairs, Norman Bel Geddes, Walter Dorwin Teague, Henry Dreyfuss, Donald Deskey, and Raymond Loewy had become household names, and their designs had become synonymous with modern American life.[23]

Bel Geddes sounded the clarion call for industrial design in his book *Horizons,* which he wrote just before the opening of the 1933 Chicago exposition. Intended as a manifesto on behalf of the power of design to reinvent America as one vast "industrial organism," Bel Geddes proclaimed: "We are entering an era which, notably, shall be characterized by *design* in four specific phases: Design in social structure to insure the organization of people, work, wealth, leisure. Design in machines that shall improve working conditions by eliminating drudgery. Design in all objects of daily use that shall make them economical, durable, convenient, congenial to every one. Design in the arts, painting, sculpture, music, literature, architecture, that shall inspire the new era." What would drive this vision toward the future? Bel Geddes had a ready answer: "Tomorrow," he declared, "we will recognize that in many respects progress and combination are synonymous." Corporate consolidation wedded to modern design— here was a vision of a marriage that would be made not in heaven but at the Chicago Century of Progress Exposition and celebrated at each of America's succeeding Depression-era fairs.[24]

In many respects, the auto industry led the way. Some of the most memorable buildings from the fairs of the 1930s were Albert Kahn's gearlike Ford Building at the Chicago exposition (designed with Walter Dorwin Teague) and his General Motors Futurama complex (designed

with Norman Bel Geddes) for the 1939 New York World's Fair. But the interesting thing about these fairs is that multiple industries marched to the new music of modernism. And they were joined by the U.S. government, which deployed architects and designers to make the machinery of the federal government seem as relevant to people's lives as the machine age itself. There is good reason to concentrate on the works of important corporate pavilions, but to do so exclusively is to miss the forest for trees, in an almost literal sense. Manufacturers represented at the fairs produced a forest of paper products in the form of advertising pamphlets that tried to convince fairgoers that, through the consumption of newly stylized goods, they could be become as modern as their toasters and roadsters, or, for that matter, their countertops and commodes.[25] And the designers did not rest there. For some, the goal of modern design was nothing less than redesigning the human body. If a fair could be an "industrial organism," so could a body. If a building or pen could be streamlined, so could a human being. American modernism, in short, was not just about style or a way of living; it was not just about surfaces. It was about the substance and meaning of modern life itself.

If this sounds like an exaggeration, it is important to understand that the designers of the fairs never thought in small terms. Indeed, they pumped steroids into the aphorism attributed to Daniel H. Burnham, director of works of the 1893 fair: "Make no little plans, for they have not the power to stir men's minds." As Bel Geddes informed Burnham's sons before the 1933 Chicago fair opened: "I want you to know that there is a second office which bears the visionary statement of your great father over its fireplace."[26]

Industrial designers and architects did not stop with stylizing buildings. Exposition designers understood that to make America more modern, Americans would have to change their habits from the way they prepared food and dressed to way they thought about transportation, work, and leisure.[27] This emphasis is developed by Lisa Schrenk in her contribution to this volume, where she underscores how designers from major industries joined exposition teams and did so with a fervor and commitment to saturation advertising that is astounding to behold.

In 1939 several industrial designers who crafted showpiece pavilions at the New York fair responded to an invi-

fig. 4 "Radically New Dress System for Future Women, Prophesies Donald Deskey." Anton Bruehl, photographer. *Vogue*, February 1, 1939. Anton Bruehl/*Vogue* © Condé-Nast Publications.

tation from *Vogue* magazine to put their imaginations to work on creating fashions for "the woman of the Future." Their modern designs for—and on—women bear close scrutiny, especially for the influence of eugenics, the popular "science" of race betterment. Donald Deskey, the renowned designer of New York's Radio City Music Hall and several New York World's Fair exhibits, made this prediction: "Medical Science will have made [the woman of the future's] body Perfect. She'll never know obesity, emaciation, colds in the head, superfluous hair, or a bad complexion—thanks to controlled diet, controlled basal metabolism. Her height will be increased, her eyelashes lengthened—with some X-hormone." Consequently, women would only need to have "a system of clothes units," machinelike interchangeable parts that could, of course, be mass produced (fig. 4).[28]

Raymond Loewy, who had established his reputation for railroad car and airplane interiors before being selected to design the Focal Exhibit of the Transportation Zone at the 1939 fair, made the explicit link with eugenics when he extended the theme of transportation to women's travel wear and his design for a garment that could be converted from casual to formal dinner dress. The larger problem for designers, he implied, wasn't coming up with the designs for the dress. Rather, the problem lay with the unsatisfactory physique of women. "But," he told readers, there was no reason to worry, because "eugenic selection may bring generations so aesthetically correct that such clothes will be in order." Little wonder that this same issue of *Vogue* included a piece entitled "To-Morrow's Daughter," which peered into the future and concluded: "To-morrow's American Woman may be the result of formulae—the tilt of her eyes, the curve of her chin, the shade of her hair ordered like crackers from the grocer. She may be gentle, sympathetic, understanding—because of a determinable combination of genes. She may be part of America, the world-power; or of America, the absorbed state. A little wistfully, we play with possibilities."[29] Streamlining, in other words, had as much to do with ideology—in this case, the ideology of creating a race of near-perfect human beings—as with style.[30] Or, to put it a bit differently, the version of modernism that Hitchcock and Johnson spun for MoMA-goers as being primarily about aesthetics, and not about ideology, stood at some remove

9

from the ideologically inflected, wrap-around presentation of modernism through the world's fairs.

At the fairs, unlike at the MoMA exhibition, designers embraced all of American life—right down to the biology and psychology of life itself—and insisted that modern styles were helpmates of economic recovery. The striking aspect of the expositions, according to the historian Roland Marchand, was how industrial designers first took it upon themselves to assert knowledge of consumers' desires and, second, relied on entertainment as a wedge for driving modern designs into spaces where people lived.[31] Unlike industrial exhibits at Victorian-era fairs that stressed putting industrial processes on view, exhibits at the fairs of the 1930s increasingly stressed showmanship to win fairgoers over to particular corporate brands. At the 1939 New York World's Fair, for instance, Norman Bel Geddes linked images of better living in the present to an American future of unbounded prosperity. In the Futurama ride he designed for General Motors, twenty-eight thousand visitors a day traveled over a miniaturized landscape of America in 1960. This vision of clustered, high-rise cities, joined by a superhighway system, implied that time and space could be utterly reconfigured by technology if new ideas in infrastructure and planning were backed by federal dollars. America in the 1930s seemed poised to become a modern powerhouse if only people would place their faith in experts like those who turned an ash dump in Flushing, Queens, into a model for creating a better world of tomorrow.

What could one expect the future to be like? At the New York World's Fair, beyond Futurama, visitors could find answers that included demonstrations of the RCA television, FM radio, and the Westinghouse robot Elektro. At the Texas Centennial Exposition, visitors could experience the most extensive use of air conditioning to date and be dazzled by the Wonder World of Chemistry exhibits in the Du Pont Pavilion. No less revealing of the future about to unfold were exposition gardens.

For the 1939 New York fair, twenty-nine-year-old landscape architect Garrett Eckbo gave the shrubbery outside the General Motors Building a streamlined look (fig. 5). (Eckbo would go on to design Alcoa's innovative "aluminum" garden in the 1950s.)[32] Elsewhere, in the Gardens on Parade exhibit at the 1940 version of the same fair, visitors could find echoes of the GM landscaping in the

"Garden of the Future," where a glass fence enclosed "bold mass plantings" bisected by a "sharply curved pathway." For those interested in protecting their gardens from disease, the advice was simple: "The protection of 'Gardens on Parade' must be based on one main principle, viz. 'SPRAY FOR PREVENTION', spray everything."[33] This advice was not unqualified, however. The sprays, visitors were told, should not be harmful to humans, but in almost the same breath, visitors learned that the entire exposition gardens, to ward off Japanese beetles, had been sprayed by "Japro-cide," a product described in one advertisement as having "oleated coated lead arsenate," a substance ultimately banned as an insecticide in the 1980s.[34]

At all of the fairs, dreams of modernizing America centered somewhere near the American home, the primary engine for consumerism. Indeed, precisely because the fairs of the 1930s sought to reignite consumer fantasies and spending, world's fair planners included modern homes as part of their plan for building America's future. At all the fairs of the 1930s, modern homes, with modern furnishings and appliances, dazzled visitors. The architect Allmon Fordyce captured the mood that the modern kitchen exhibit at the New York World's fair was intended to convey: "The chief function of this kitchen is to lighten the burden of work for the woman who is doing the cooking and housekeeping in her own home, and to provide opportunity for her to share the companionship of her family and friends while she is working." What made this possible, Fordyce exulted, was that the "cooking work space serves, in fact, as an assembly line." "From the stove and work table," he continued, "'Mother' can keep her eye on the children doing their home work at the dining room table, on 'Father' who is reading his evening paper in front of the open fire . . ." No doubt Fordyce made the connection between the model kitchen at the fair and the vision for the American dream house that he and his partner William Hamby had articulated three years before in *Architectural Forum:* "No patent medicine formula. No magic. Fordyce and Hamby have treated the house as a commodity—as merchandise."[35]

As Kristina Wilson explains in her essay that follows, American homes generally and model homes built specifically for the fairs became contested spaces where the battle lines over the meaning of modernity took form in

Robert W. Rydell

everything from where kitchens were supposed to be located to how houses were furnished. George Fred Keck's House of Tomorrow and Crystal House at the Century of Progress Exposition are the clearest examples, with their glass walls and chrome furnishings. However, Wilson demonstrates that even the period revival homes that suggested the strong residual presence of tradition introduced innovations in floor plans, thus complicating any narrative of the 1930s that posits the linear development of modernism.

No less important than the "homes of tomorrow" presented by corporate entities (like those at the Chicago fair) were those put on exhibit by the U.S. government at the 1935 San Diego California-Pacific International Exposition. In his essay about the Federal Housing Administration (FHA) exhibits in San Diego, Matthew Bokovoy explores the promise of the exhibits, despite the inclinations of the progressive architects who designed modern houses for the fair, of abundant financing for homes in the private, not the public, sphere. The overriding message of the FHA hinted broadly that as Americans dreamed about their future, the freestanding, suburban home would be somewhere near the center.

Modernist premillenialist fantasies about the attainability of utopia if only Americans would modernize suffused all of the fairs. As Eric Johannesen explains about Cleveland's Great Lakes International Exposition: "As a demonstration of the modern faith in scientific system and functional design, the lighting and architecture of the Great Lakes Exposition gave ample evidence of Cleveland's position in this movement."[36] But several expositions projected that utopia in space—space that extended far beyond suburbs —as well as time. Promoters of the 1936 Texas Centennial Exposition in Dallas, for instance, imagined their fair as "An Empire on Parade" that would "graphically and dramatically depict the many resources, the glamorous history and the inherent greatness of the vast Southwestern Empire that has been called the 'last economic frontier' in the United States." To make this vision modern, planners sought building designs that would be "expressive of the Southwest." In particular, they sought "simplicity of line and mass" in buildings that would "borrow from the primitive cultures of the Southwestern Indians, who achieved great peaks of artistic expression just prior to the advent of the explorers and colonizers of the Old World." Designers then "introduced a decoration motif gleaned

11

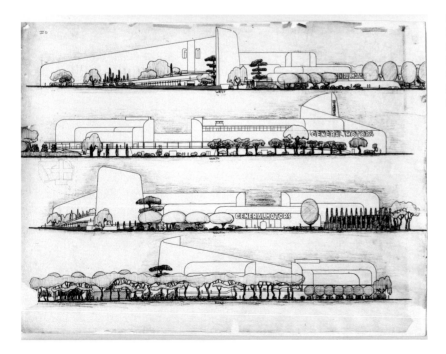

fig. 5 Drawing, General Motors Building, 1938. Garrett Eckbo, landscape architect. New York World's Fair, 1939–1940. Garrett Eckbo Collection (1990-1), Environmental Design Archives, University of California, Berkeley.

from the superimposed cultures of the white races as evidenced in the early missions and other structures which were so typical of the early period of white civilization in the Southwest." The result, one report insisted, was "a happy mergence of these two decors" (see plate 31).[37]

Another world's fair oriented to projecting utopia in space was the 1939–1940 San Francisco Golden Gate International Exposition. Designers of this fair set their sights squarely on the Pacific Rim and on expanding America's economic horizons around the Pacific Basin. To get that message across, exposition planners hit upon a novel design scheme that gave modernist inflections to indigenous, "primitive" art forms. This aesthetic hinted at the vast opportunities that lay within the nation's grasp if only Americans could see the modernization of American society as the first step toward modernizing the rest of the globe. Built on the man-made Treasure Island in the middle of San Francisco Bay, the Golden Gate fair melded Cambodian, Mayan, and Polynesian monumental influences into a fantasyland of harmonious cultural and economic interchanges under the benevolent tutelage of the United States. This design put a "primitivist" twist on the advice of the U.S. commissioners to the 1925 Paris Exposition to develop an American modernism linked to recognizable historical formations. It resulted in a distinctive colonial moderne aesthetic for this fair that resembled nothing so much as the modern "exotic" architectural formulations seen at another Paris exposition—the 1931 Colonial Exposition that had celebrated the civilizing mission of French imperial policies and made French colonialism seem as modern and up to date as any streamlined toaster. Much the same could be said of the visions of American neoimperialism that took visible form on Treasure Island—visions that within two decades would lead Americans first to support and then supplant French efforts to control Vietnam.[38]

Related to the utopia-in-space concept was the idea of Pan Americanism. According to Robert A. González in the essay in this volume, the fairs of the 1930s wedded long-standing interests in promoting economic and political harmony between the United States and Latin America to modernist ideas about design. What the modernists could not free themselves from, however, was the reservoir of racism that underpinned the expositions.

Racialized to the quick, the world's fairs of the 1930s seemed designed to reinforce prevailing racial stereotypes. Nowhere, perhaps, was this more apparent than at the Texas Centennial Exposition in Dallas, where exposition directors, under pressure from the federal government, agreed to a separate Hall of Negro Life but refused to allow African-American architects to design it. The results, in some respects, were predictable. Initially, the building's interior received coats of bright colors because the white contractors thought African Americans liked garish hues. Protests from African Americans and pressure from federal authorities forced exposition managers to order that the interior be repainted. Then, to isolate the building from the public, the directors insisted on planting tall hedges around it. Despite the best efforts of fair planners to degrade and downplay the achievements of blacks, African Americans took the matter of design seriously and, with the help of the African-American artist Aaron Douglas, made clear that they had no intention of leaving the future of modern America to racists.

For the Hall of Negro Life, Douglas composed four modernist murals that inserted African Americans into American history as robust agents of American progress. Drawing on African traditions and modernist techniques, Douglas articulated a counterracist modernist narrative that detailed African-American demands for equality and for inclusion in American dreams for the future. In *Aspiration,* the last of the murals, Douglas positioned silhouettes of three African-American figures looking toward a modern, skyscraper-capped city on a hill. A refracted beacon of light projected the Texas "lone star" on one of the gazers and radiated its glow over the others, as well as over the shackled masses in the foreground. Whether America would ever get to the modernist mountaintop, Douglas made clear, would depend on a radical re-visioning of U.S. history and a careful rethinking of the blueprints for the future to determine who would be included (fig. 6).[39]

Gaining influence over the shape of things to come also animated African-American responses to other Depression-era fairs. In the case of the 1933 Century of Progress Exposition, African Americans protested unfair hiring policies (only a handful of African Americans were employed on the grounds, including a few maids in the model home exhibit) and degrading midway shows, but exposition

fig. 6 Aaron Douglas, *Aspiration*, 1936. Oil on canvas, 60 × 60 in. Mural painted for the Texas Centennial Exposition, Dallas. Fine Arts Museums of San Francisco.

directors took no corrective action until it became clear that, to extend the exposition into 1934, it would be necessary to have the support of the handful of African-American representatives in the Illinois legislature. In exchange for African-American support of this legislation, exposition authorities agreed to a new state law ending racial discrimination on the fairgrounds. The 1939 New York World's Fair also elicited a great deal of protest about overtly racist employment policies, including a mass demonstration at the opening. How widespread was the racism that African Americans had to confront? An internal sales instruction memo to a Milwaukee-based tour company declared in no uncertain terms: "The specific article we are selling is a pre-arranged-tour-for-white-people. We are not offering terms to the 'general public' but to a specific section of the public, just the same as though we had arranged a specific tour for some Fraternal Order and for members of that order only." When New York exposition authorities organized Negro Week celebrations in 1940, African-American leaders were divided over the wisdom of participating in the event. Those who did participate seized the occasion to demand social and political justice not only in the world of tomorrow but in America's present.[40]

The federal government was also concerned with the here and now and the opportunity afforded by world's fairs to show the New Deal in action. As already noted, President Roosevelt took a personal interest in the expositions and traveled to most of them (fig. 7). In a speech at the San Francisco fair, he declared: "I am quite open and unashamed in my liking for expositions." In the case of the Century of Progress Exposition, FDR personally urged the Dawes brothers to reopen the fair in 1934 because of both its positive impact on the midwestern economy and the uplifting effect on people's spirits. As early as 1936, FDR lent his personal support to New York World's Fair backers. "I suggest," he wrote to George McAneny, one of his advisers, "that you and Mr. Davis confer with Representative Sol Bloom. He is greatly experienced in Federal participation in historic celebrations and Expositions. If you and he and I can keep in close contact with the development in regard to the 1939 Exposition, I am confident that the preliminary problems [of securing a federal appropriation] can be successfully met." Later in the planning phase, Edward J. Flynn, the U.S. commissioner for the New York World's Fair, told a group of more than twenty federal officials involved in planning the U.S. Government Building at the fair that "the President is particularly interested in this phase of the exhibit. We talked it over very carefully and he tells me that he does not want these exhibits to play up the individual workings of each department . . . [and] that the different departments must cooperate with each other." Eleanor Roosevelt was no less enthusiastic. When FDR's advisers seemed reluctant to have "the boss" take time to dedicate the theme pavilion at the fair, Eleanor sent a memo to her husband. "Please," she insisted, "don't forget to send the letter" to exposition authorities about the planned dedication. For both Roosevelts, the world's fairs of the 1930s provided a golden opportunity to restore popular confidence in the government's ability to meet the crisis of the Depression and to show American citizens that the government had their best interests at heart in planning for the future. Their concerns reverberated in the minds of U.S. officials who helped plan government exhibits. Theodore Hayes, an assistant U.S. commissioner for the 1939 New York fair, had difficulty containing his emotion: "I saw the people divided by conflicting purposes and new passions, reflecting worse unrest in other nations and standing against our traditional unified strength. I saw in this Fair a precious opportunity to revitalize, to new heights, the fundamental faith in America of millions of Americans by selling and reselling the achievements of government through a building and exhibits which will eloquently declare the high dignity, beauty and potentials of our national solidarity—a chance to paint a picture of the large benefits of our common front that will be worth a billion words." Although they never called it doing the Lord's work, most New Dealers certainly saw world's fairs in this light.[41]

Designing buildings and exhibits that would demonstrate that the government was both modern and a permanent source of stability was the overarching ambition of government planners. As one explained, it was imperative to adapt the design of exhibits to the "tempo of the times."[42] For each of the fairs, Congress passed appropriations for the construction of U.S. government buildings and for exhibits representing government departments and agencies. The Century of Progress Exposition, begun while

14

Robert W. Rydell

Hoover was president, set the tone for what followed.

To appreciate what happened at Chicago, it is important to look at the official U.S. Government Pavilion at the 1931 Paris Colonial Exposition. There, government planners seemed to turn Hoover's antipathy toward modern design into a self-fulfilling prophecy. As if to underscore Hoover's earlier conviction that there was no modernism in the United States, the official U.S. Building at the Paris fair took the form of George Washington's Mount Vernon home. But for all its manifest historicism, the pavilion itself requires a more nuanced reading. Unlike the original Mount Vernon, this structure was not exactly the work of skilled artisans (or slaves). In fact, it was a prefabricated structure rebuilt from the plans and some of the materials that had originally been used to craft the building to house the Virginia exhibition at the 1915 San Francisco fair (fig. 8).[43] Had Hoover read the manifesto his commissioners issued in 1925? Could the government learn as much as industry about the importance of embracing at least some aspects of modernism for promoting its values? At least one commentator, Frederick A. Gutheim, a respected University of Chicago social scientist and high-ranking official at both of the 1939 fairs, thought as much and hinted

that Hoover, as an "alert administrator," had learned something about the importance of applying modern "technique" to "direct and extend the constructive influence of an exposition."[44] The crucial next step would be taken at the 1933 Chicago Century of Progress Exposition, when government planners followed the lead of the Chicago architect Edward Bennett and produced a remarkable modernistic re-vision of how the U.S. government should be represented at a world's fair.

No one ever accused Bennett of being a radical European modernist. Trained at the École des Beaux Arts, and described by one admirer as "Erect, Direct, Confident, Poised, [and] Powerful," he served as one of Daniel Burnham's assistants in the design of the 1909 Chicago Plan. Thoroughly immersed in City Beautiful ideas about city planning and architecture, he was selected as chief architect for the government's Federal Triangle complex of buildings in Washington, D.C.—a position he held at the same time he worked on the federal building and several other pavilions at the Chicago fair. Bennett may have been classically trained, but he was not antediluvian. The design he came up with reflected a careful negotiation between the sleek lines of the modernist movement and the sym-

15

fig. 7 President Franklin Delano Roosevelt greeted by Japanese consul, October 2, 1935. California-Pacific International Exposition, San Diego, 1935–1936. George R. Leighton Collection, Special Collections Library, California State University, Fresno.

metrical balance that characterized neoclassical design. Government and exposition officials were so pleased with Bennett's design that Rufus Dawes, the exposition president, just had to tell the architect that his design "rings the bell."[45]

As the government's final report explained, the entire Federal and State Group at the fair was intended to symbolize "the interdependence of the States and Federal Government." That was only partially true. In fact, the 620–by-300-foot U.S. Government Building, with its three 150-foot-tall fluted towers representing the three branches of government surrounding a 75-feet-in-diameter dome, dwarfed the state structures and hinted at a future in which the federal government would play an increasingly prominent role in the lives of Americans (fig. 9). To highlight the modernness of the government, Bennett worked with Joseph Urban, theater designer and color coordinator for the fair, to integrate the exterior color scheme of the building (white and blue with black trim) with the overall color scheme of the fair (see plate 27).[46]

Once inside, visitors found themselves in a world that was much different from Mount Vernon's. The rotunda blazed with "Chinese red, buff, and terra cotta." The sculptor Raoul Josset, who also designed a statue for the exterior of the building and would go on to create many pieces of public sculpture for the Texas Centennial Exposition, painted a mural "in the modern style" with figures depicting labor, commerce, and the military. No less modern was the building's flooring—Rubbertex with no floor coverings permitted—and the building's modern office furniture that, ideally, would "be similar in design style, and general effect" and be ordered from the Howell Tubular Furniture Catalog, the same firm that provided furniture for Keck's futuristic houses. Martin Jenter, a New York designer hired by the government to coordinate the overall interior design of the building, insisted that exhibit cases themselves be built using modern materials, including laminates like Formica, asbestos, and wood veneer "coated with aluminum stipple paint." All exhibits, Jenter insisted, were to use lettering made from "solid Masonite Tempered Presswood." To outfit its kitchen, Harry New, a former Republican senator and postmaster general in the Harding administration before becoming U.S. commissioner to the fair, prevailed on General Electric to provide "a model kitchen . . . equipped with the most modern appliances available." Inside and out, the building was, according to the government's final report, "treated in the

fig. 8 Postcard, U.S. Government Pavilion (Mount Vernon replica by Sears, Roebuck and Co.). International Colonial Exposition, Paris, 1931. National Building Museum.

opposite
fig. 9 U.S. Government Building. Arthur Brown Jr. and Edward H. Bennett, architects. Century of Progress Exposition, Chicago 1933–1934. Photograph by Kaufmann and Fabry Co. Collection of Jim Sweeny.

16

Robert W. Rydell

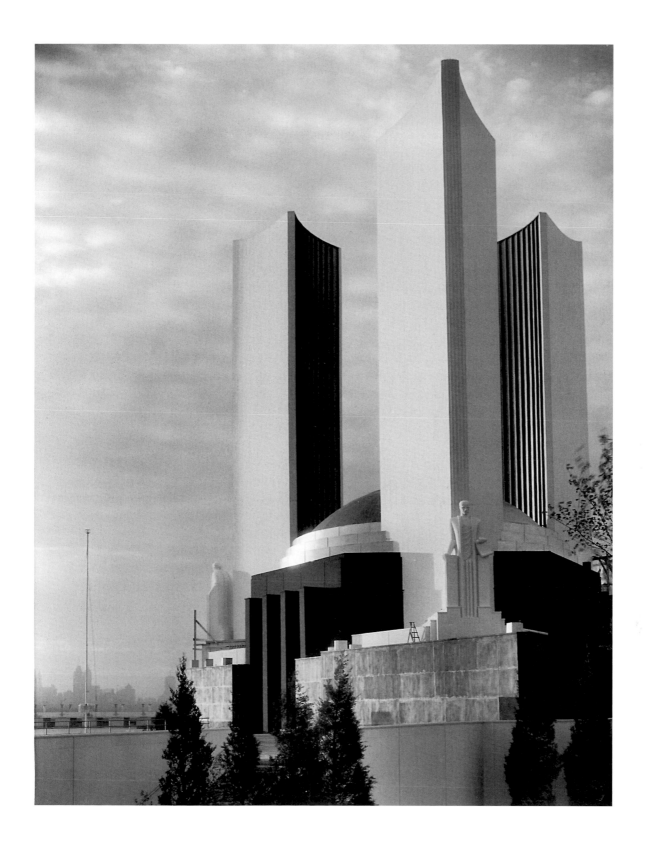

modern style, modified by classic influences. The resultant effect was a harmonious appearance of beauty, dignity, and simplicity." A "modern style modified by classic influence"—this was a summative and formative evaluation. It captured the way government planners—and perhaps American modernists in general—sought to use the exposition medium to nudge the American public toward becoming more modern in the way they saw themselves as both citizens and consumers.[47]

Just how modern were America's world's fairs of the 1930s? To some extent, "modernism" lay in the eye of the beholder. As one irate judge from Pittsburgh asserted in a letter to Rufus Dawes about the sculptor John Storrs's work for the Hall of Science, the piece was not only "ugly but obscene" (see fig. 2). "This nondescript work of supposed art," the judge declared, "depicts a naked man in a wooden-soldierly salute, with a serpent embracing his right leg. The snake has a duck-like bill and a body like a kangaroo's pouch. The meaning of the affectionate clasp of the serpent is not made clear: in fact, there is nothing truly symbolic about the entire exhibit." When asked by Dawes to comment on this antimodernistic screed, Storrs struck a high modernistic note: "I was so afraid that my man might just be accepted and passed by as a silent part of the picture. Naturally I would prefer real appreciation and understanding—but when you cannot have love, hate is better than oblivion." Dawes's sentiments clearly lay with Storrs. He invited the sculptor to join the exclusive club reserved for Century of Progress executives.[48]

There were other perspectives on the modernism of the Chicago fair. America's most famous architect, Frank Lloyd Wright, bitter over the refusal of the Century of Progress architectural review board to include him in the exposition, had this to say: "[The Chicago] fair is just a repetition of the last one. . . . There is not an element in the whole exhibition that can be treated as modern. . . . [It is] just 1893 with the surfaces changed."[49] As if to head off any similar digs from Wright about the 1939 fair, Louis Skidmore, one of the architects who had cut his teeth on the 1933 exposition, said this about the World of Tomorrow show: "We reverse the usual procedure and wrap the building around the exhibits." According to one critic, the designers of the 1939 fair did not think of themselves as "designing" exhibits and buildings. Rather, they used a new term to describe their activities: *packaging.*[50] The results — the RCA Building shaped into a radio tube, the Swift Building into a hot dog, and the Westinghouse Pavilion into a giant magnet—may have pushed the envelope beyond the modern. This is the point of Robert Bennett's contribution to this volume. Where several of the other authors highlight the pull of tradition within these modernist spectacles, Bennett sees the New York World's Fair and the ensuing critique of its version of the modern as containing the seeds of postmodernism. Wright, in other words, may have been right, but for the wrong reasons, in deeming the fairs as anything but modern.

How should we think about the modernism at these fairs? Laura Schiavo's photo essay, appearing in the middle of this volume, proposes some answers and invites readers to come to their own conclusions. And the interview with Richard Guy Wilson in the afterword underscores difficulties of reading the fairs of the 1930s as modernist spectacles when words like *modern, modernity,* and *modernism* (not to mention *postmodernism*) conjure multiple meanings. The point is not whether one of these terms is the best to describe America's world's fairs of the 1930s. The point may be closer to one the art historian Paul Greenhalgh makes in *The Modern Ideal,* namely that embedded in the idea of "the modern" is always an idea of the "next modern."[51] That is what makes these fairs so interesting and important: they helped to make possible the "next modern," our own modern world. This was no mean feat. With global capitalism in crisis, with dictatorships on the march in Europe and Asia, America's world's fairs provided the cultural ballast to steady the American ship of state.

Allow me to close this complicated story with one anecdote. I teach at Montana State University, a university that gained international notice in Robert Pirsig's *Zen and the Art of Motorcycle Maintenance.* Several years ago, I answered the phone in my office and found myself talking with John Newkirk, who was calling from a Bozeman motel and knew of my work on world's fairs. He said he was calling to let me know that he was in town riding a motorcycle with his grandfather, replicating the motorcycle trip his grandfather had made in 1939 between the San Francisco and New York world's wairs.[52] In the early years of this, the twenty-first century, a motorcycle

Robert W. Rydell

ride, tied to memories of world's fairs, linked generations. Perhaps this trip reveals the larger lesson of these fairs: in a time of despair in the 1930s, America's Depression-era world's fairs set imaginations in motion. This was the power of design.

Notes

1. Attendance figures for world's fairs are always debated. Official attendance figures suggest that more than one hundred million people visited America's world's fairs during the 1930s. Of course, these figures did not differentiate between people who went to a fair once and those who went through the turnstiles ten times. So there is no doubt that the figures were inflated. But in another sense, they undercounted the people who took in the fairs through other means, namely the popular press and newsreels. A July report to the New York World's Fair board of directors noted that in the two months following the fair's opening 236 newsreels had been produced about the fair and its exhibits and had been seen by "220 million people." See "Minutes of the Board of Directors," July 20, 1939, New York World's Fair Collection, New York Public Library, box 956. Also bear in mind art historian Paul Greenhalgh's recent observation that "a conservative estimate of attendance would suggest a minimum of one billion people visited the most important 100 exhibitions, in dozens of cities throughout Europe and North America, between 1851 and 1939." See Paul Greenhalgh, *The Modern Ideal: The Rise and Collapse of Idealism in the Visual Arts from the Enlightenment to Postmodernism* (London: Victoria and Albert Museum, 2005), 119.

2. The literature on the world's fairs of the 1930s is relatively small, but growing. For an overview of the fairs, see Robert W. Rydell, *World of Fairs: The Century of Progress Expositions* (Chicago: University of Chicago Press, 1993); Robert W. Rydell, John E. Findling, and Kimberly D. Pelle, *Fair America: World's Fairs in the United States* (Washington, D.C.: Smithsonian Institution Press, 2000). Studies of individual fairs include Cheryl Ganz, *The 1933 Chicago World's Fair: A Century of Progress* (Champaign: University of Illinois Press, 2008); Lisa Schrenk, *Building a Century of Progress* (Minneapolis: University of Minnesota Press, 2007); John E. Findling, *Chicago's Great World's Fairs* (Manchester: Manchester University Press, 1994); Matthew F. Bokovoy, *The San Diego World's Fairs and Southwestern Memory, 1880–1940* (Albuquerque: University of New Mexico Press, 2005); Kenneth Ragsdale, *The Year America Discovered Texas: Centennial 36* (College Station: Texas A&M Press, 1987); Lisa Rubens, "The 1939 San Francisco World's Fair: The New Deal, the New Frontier, and the Pacific Basin," PhD diss., University of California, Berkeley, 2004. Useful starting points for learning about the 1939–1940 New York World's Fair are Helen A. Harrison, ed., *Dawn of a New Day: The New York World's Fair, 1939–40* (New York: Queens Museum/New York University Press, 1980); Warren Susman, *Culture as History: The Transformation of American Society in the Twentieth Century* (New York: Pantheon, 1984), 211–229. Although the literature on the New York fair is growing, no one should think that a definitive treatment of this or of any of these fairs has been written. It would take many months, if not years, to work through the archival records at the University of Illinois, Chicago, for the 1933–1934 Chicago Century of Progress Exposition and the equally daunting archival holdings for the New York World's Fair in the New York Public Library. America's Depression-era world's fairs, of course, were part of a broader panorama of expositions held in Europe and elsewhere. Paul Greenhalgh, *Ephemeral Vistas: The Expositions Universelles, Great Exhibitions and World's Fairs, 1851–1939* (Manchester: University of Manchester Press, 1988); Pieter van Wessemael, *Architecture of Instruction and Delight: A Socio-Historical Analysis of*

19

World Exhibitions as a Didactic Phenomenon (Rotterdam: 010 Publishers, 2001) are good places to begin for insights into expositions beyond the United States. Also important is Allan Pred, *Recognizing European Modernities: A Montage of the Present* (London: Routledge, 1995). For an overview of scholarship on world's fairs more generally, see Robert W. Rydell, "The Literature of International Expositions," in *The Books of the Fairs: Materials About World's Fairs, 1834–1916, in the Smithsonian Institution Libraries* (Chicago: American Library Association, 1992), 1–62; Alexander C. T. Geppert, Jean Coffey, and Tammy Lau, "International Exhibitions, Expositions Universelles, and World's Fairs, 1851–2005: A Bibliography," Henry Madden Library, http://www.csufresno.edu/library/subjectresources/special-collections/worldfairs/ExpoBibliography3ed.pdf.

3. Franklin Roosevelt to Francklyn Paris, telegram, September 17, 1935, Boston Public Library, Rare Book Division, mss. 2767–2768, #412, folder 412–417.

4. Marco Duranti, "Utopia, Nostalgia, and World War at the 1939–40 New York World's Fair," *Journal of Contemporary History* 4 (2006): 663–683.

5. The term *world's fair* is the American idiom for what in the rest of the world were variously called international exhibitions and universal expositions. Today this seemingly trivial matter of nomenclature has led most Americans to believe that world's fairs are no longer held when, in fact, "world expos," as these events are now called, continue to be held and to attract millions of visitors.

6. Robert W. Rydell, *All the World's a Fair: Visions of Empire at American International Expositions, 1876–1916* (Chicago: University of Chicago Press, 1984), 208, 213.

7. Robert T. Small, "Calls Sesqui Last of World's Fairs," *Philadelphia Bulletin,* November 29, 1926, clipping, City Archives of Philadelphia, Sesquicentennial Scrapbooks, vol. 14.

8. Schrenk, *Building a Century of Progress,* 1–28; Findling, *Chicago's Great World's Fairs,* 43–82.

9. Rydell, *World of Fairs,* 92–114. See also John Stephen Sewell, "Paying Civilization's Debt to Industry, Science and Capital," flyer, no date, Art Institute of Chicago, Century of Progress Collection, box 2, folder 6. Through the fair, Sewell hoped, "science, industry and invested capital will secure from the public a more sympathetic understanding than received in the past."

10. On the 1925 Paris Exposition, see W. Francklyn Paris, "The International Exposition of Modern Industrial and Decorative Art in Paris," *Architectural Record* 58 (1925): 265–277, 365–385; Victor Arwas, *Art Deco* (New York: Abrams, 2000); Bevis Hillier and Stephen Escritt, *Art Deco Style* (New York: Phaidon, 1997), 26–55; Judith B. Gura, "Modernism and the 1925 Paris Exposition," *Magazine Antiques* 158 (2000): 194–200.

11. *Report of Commission Appointed by the Secretary of Commerce to Visit and Report upon the International Exposition of Modern Decorative and Industrial Art in Paris, 1925* (Washington, D.C.: U.S. Department of Commerce, n.d.), 18.

12. Ibid., 22, 36–37.

13. Ibid., 22–23.

14. Ibid., 32.

15. See, for instance, Frederick A. Gutheim, "Federal Participation in Two World's Fairs," *Public Opinion Quarterly* 28 (1939): 612. Gutheim served in various advisory capacities to Chicago and New York world's fair planners.

16. Henry Matthews, "The Promotion of Modern Architecture by the Museum of Modern Art in the 1930s," *Journal of Design History* 7 (1994): 43–59; Stewart J. Johnson, *American Modern, 1925–1940: Design for a New Age* (New York: Abrams, 2000).

17. Tim Benton, "Building Utopia," in Christopher Wilk, ed., *Modernism: Designing a New World, 1914–1939* (London: Victoria and Albert Publications, 2008), 154, 164–165.

18. "Interview with Fred L. Black," March 10, 1951, Ford Motor Company Archives, unprocessed collection; Daniel C. Roper, *Fifty Years of Public Life, 1867–1943* (New York: Greenwood, 1968), 296; John Stephen Sewell, "A Century of Progress," June 19, 1931, University of Illinois, Chicago, Department of Special Collections, Records of the Century of Progress Exposition, 15–125; Randi Storch, "Red Squad," Encyclopedia of Chicago, http://www.encyclopedia.chicago-history.org/pages/1049.html.

19. Rydell, *World of Fairs,* passim.

20. For the popularity of the art exhibitions, see, for instance, "Another Great Art Exhibit for World's Fair," *Literary Digest,* August 4, 1934, p. 24.

21. *Report of Commission,* 32.

22. Ibid., 21.

23. Wilson, *Machine Age in America,* 87–88.

24. Norman Bel Geddes, *Horizons* (1932; rpt. New York: Dover, 1977), 5, 289.

25. The best collection of advertising pamphlets generated for America's world's fairs from this era is found in Yale University, Manuscripts Division, Century of Progress Collection.

26. Norman Bel Geddes to Daniel and Hubert Burnham, March 12, 1930, box 19, folder Chicago Adv., University of Texas, Harry Ransom Humanities Research Center, Theater Arts Collection, Norman Bel Geddes Papers.

27. See Susannah Handley, *Nylon: The Story of a Fashion Revolution* (Baltimore: Johns Hopkins University Press, 1999), 31–51.

28. "To-Morrow's Daughter," *Vogue,* February 1, 1939, p. 61; "Radically New Dress System for Future Women, Prophesies Donald Deskey," ibid., 137.

29. "Raymond Loewy, Designer of Locomotives and Lipsticks, Creates a Future Travel Dress," ibid., 141; "To-Morrow's Daughter."

30. Christina Cogdell, *Eugenic Design: Streamlining America in the 1930s* (Philadelphia: University of Pennsylvania Press, 2004).

31. Roland Marchand, "The Designers Go to the Fair," part I, "Walter Dorwin Teague and the Professionalization of Corporate Industrial Exhibits"; Roland Marchand, "The Designers Go the Fair," part II, "Norman Bel Geddes, the General Motors 'Futurama,' and the Visit to the Factory Transformed," both in *Design History: An Anthology* (Cambridge: MIT Press, 1995), 89–121.

32. Garrett Eckbo, "New York World's Fair 1938 General Motors Building," University of California, Berkeley, Environmental Design Archives, folder V203; Marc Treib, *The Donnell and Eckbo Gardens* (San Francisco: William Stout, 2005), 98–187.

33. Gardens on Parade: The Horticultural Exhibition at the World's Fair of 1940 in New York (New York: Hortus Incorporated, 1940), 26, 76.

Robert W. Rydell

34. Francis J. Peryea, "Historical Use of Lead Arsenate Insecticides, Resulting Soil Contamination and Implications for Soil Remediation," Proceedings, 16th World Congress of Soil Science (CD-ROM), Montpellier, France. August 20–26, 1998, http://soils.tfrec.wsu.edu/ leadhistory.htm. Quotation from "Japanese Beetle Insecticides" [advertisement], *Millburn and Short Hills Item,* July 14, 1939, 2.

35. Allmon Fordyce, [no title, 1940], New York Public Library, Manuscripts and Archives Division, New York World's Fair Collection, box 363, f. Fordyce, Allmon; Allmon Fordyce and William L. Hamby, "Small Houses for Civilized Americans," *Architectural Forum* 64 (January 1936): 1, quoted in Hyungmin Pai, *The Portfolio and the Diagram: Architecture, Discourse, and Modernity in America* (Cambridge: MIT Press, 2002), 245.

36. Eric Johannesen, *Cleveland Architecture, 1876–1976* (Cleveland: Western Reserve Historical Society, 1979).

37. "Texas' Centennial of Independence and the Texas Centennial Exposition," no imprint, National Archives, National Youth Administration Collection, record group 119, box 722, Dave Williams File, 1935–1939, folder Dallas.

38. See Rydell, *World of Fairs,* 85–91.

39. Jesse O. Thomas, *Negro Participation in the Texas Centennial Exposition* (Boston: Christopher, 1938); Rydell, *World of Fairs,* 171–182; Renée Ater, "Creating a 'Usable Past' and a 'Future Perfect Society': Aaron Douglas's Murals for the 1936 Texas Centennial Exposition," in *Aaron Douglas: African American Modernist,* ed. Susan Earle (New Haven: Yale University Press, 2007): 95–113.

40. Rydell, *World of Fairs,* 157–192; "Sales Instructions" (mimeograph), March 6, 1939, World's Fair Tours, Inc., Museum of the City of New York, Selling the World of Tomorrow Exhibit, October 17, 1989–August 12, 1990.

41. FDR to Francklyn Paris, telegram, September 17, 1935, Boston Public Library, Rare Books Room, mss. 2767–2768, no. 412, folder 412–417; "Transcript of Conference on N.Y. World's Fair of 1939, Room 1039, South Building, U.S. Department of Agriculture, at 12 noon, August 25, 1937," National Archives, RG 40, Department of Commerce, 84496/12, folder New York World's Fair; Eleanor Roosevelt, "Memo for FDR" (1937), attached to W. H. Stanley to Marvin McIntyre, August 10, 1937; "Address of the President by Radio from Key West, Florida, on the Occasion of the Opening of the San Francisco Golden Gate Exposition, February 18, 1939," Franklin D. Roosevelt Library, OF2147, box 2, folder New York World's Fair, November–December 1938. There is a great deal of correspondence both in this collection and the New York World's Fair Collection in the New York Public Library attesting to FDR's passionate interest in world's fairs. See also Theodore Hayes to Edward J. Flynn, February 3, 1938, National Archives, RG 148, box 3.

42. Theodore Hayes, "Policy of Exhibits," National Archives, RG 148, Box 3.

43. Rydell, *World of Fairs,* 72–82.

44. Gutheim, "Federal Participation."

45. Joan E. Draper, *Edward H. Bennett: Architect and City Planner* (Chicago: Art Institute of Chicago, 1982); Kate Fontaine, "Good City Building Means Good Man Building: An Interview with Edward H. Bennett," *Judicious Advertising,* January 18, 1922, clipping, Chicago Art Institute, Edward H. Bennett Papers, microfilm reel 12; Edward Bennett diary, July 13, 1932, Chicago Art Institute, Bennett Papers, microfilm reel 10.

46. [Description of Federal Building, 1933] in "Final Report," National Archives, record group 43, Records of International Conferences, Commissions, Expositions, Records Relating to the Chicago World's Fair Centennial Celebration, General Correspondence of the Commissions, 1932–1935, entry 1392, box 6, folder Federal and States Group.

47. Ibid.; "General Instructions Regarding Exhibits for Display in the U.S. Government Building at a Century of Progress," Records Relating to the Chicago World's Fair Centennial Celebration, General Correspondence of the Commissions, 1932–1935, entry 1392, box 7, folder Jenter, Martin, 1933–1934.

48. M. Musmanno to Rufus Dawes, June 1, 1933; John Storrs to Dawes (June 1933); both in John Henry Bradley Storrs Papers, Smithsonian Archives of American Art, microfilm reel 1554.

49. "Architects Debate on Fair," *New York Times,* February 27, 1931.

50. "Buildings 'Package' Exhibits," *New York World-Telegram,* February 4, 1939.

51. Paul Greenhalgh, *The Modern Ideal: The Rise and Collapse of Idealism in the Visual Arts from the Enlightenment to Postmodernism* (London: Victoria and Albert Museum, 2005).

52. See the Web page that John Newkirk is building: http://www.theold-manandtheharley.com/.

"Industry Applies"
Corporate Marketing at A Century of Progress

Lisa D. Schrenk

To the business man, to everyone engaged in selling to the public goods or services of whatever character, [the Chicago fair] is a priceless laboratory of object lessons in human nature. It presents a veritable Roman Holiday of salesmanship! Here, in this vast arena of 338 acres, on man-made ground once fathoms deep below Lake Michigan, the merchandising leaders of a hundred different industries have invested millions competing for the public's attention and approval. Meat packers versus motor manufacturers, oil companies versus jewelers, food concerns vying with mail order houses. Scarcely an important phase of American industry that is not adequately represented along this great eighty-four mile battle front of exhibits.

J. Parker Van Zandt and L. Rohe Walter, *Review of Reviews and World's Work,* September 1934

As the long queue slowly inched closer toward the industrial canning machine, excitement intensified among the mesmerized crowd. A spattering of giddy chatter filled the large hall in the General Exhibits Building as the fairgoers patiently waited in line up to an hour and a half to participate in a featured display that was advertised by organizers as both thrilling and modern.[1] With each step forward the din of the contraption grew louder, its mechanical parts repeating an elaborately choreographed dance over and over again with clocklike precision. According to one contemporary account, by the time visitors finally reached the whirling machine, some found witnessing the creation of the small tin-can banks so emotionally overwhelming that they were unable to carry out the simple act of pushing the button to start production of their own colorful souvenirs (fig. 1).[2]

Voted the most popular demonstration at A Century of Progress in 1934, the chrome-plated canning machine, nicknamed the Princess, was the highlight of the American Can Company display. The device fabricated more than a million souvenir banks, each decorated with a bright lithograph of the main exposition pavilions. While the novelty of the canning machine is what drew most fairgoers to the American Can Company exhibit, the display also included informative presentations that illustrated the creation of tin can products in a reverse chronological fashion, from finished consumer goods backward to the raw materials from which the cans were produced. The main objectives of the exhibit were to eliminate misconceptions about packaged foods by educating visitors on the benefits of canning and to make the can a symbol of the positive impact that scientific progress could have on modern man.[3] These goals reflected a larger underlying agenda of the major American businesses exhibiting at the exposition—to counter a growing sense of remoteness felt by consumers toward merchandise that was increasingly being mass produced through the use of complex processes by large national corporations. To develop a sense of familiarity in potential customers, many businesses participating in A Century of Progress created eye-catching exhibits designed to educate the public not only about the company's specific manufactured products but also about its beneficial contribution to modern society.

A Modern Corporate Fair

While the display of consumer goods had played a central role in every world's fair since the Great Exhibition of the Works of Industry of All Nations in London in 1851, what was new in Chicago was the exposition administrators' attempt to connect every exhibit to a common science-centered theme. This encompassing focus, along with process-oriented corporate exhibits like the American Can Company canning machine, helped to make the Century of Progress Exposition a modern fair in the eyes of its organizers.[4] From the start, the planners knew that to be successful their event would have to present a character and structure dramatically different from past fairs. The financial fiasco of the Sesquicentennial International Exposition in Philadelphia in 1926, just as plans for the Chicago event were under way, confirmed for many leading businessmen and politicians that the era of world's fairs was over.[5] Critics believed that the delivery of information to the general public could be accomplished much more efficiently through radio, newsreels, and other modern means of communication. Chicago Mayor William Hale Thompson even dropped plans to host an exposition shortly after he came to office in 1927. But a group of

24

Fig. 1 American Can Company souvenir cans. Century of Progress Exposition, Chicago, 1933–1934. Collection of Lisa D. Schrenk.

Lisa D. Schrenk

prominent citizens, including many current or former heads of major American corporations, quickly convinced the mayor of the potential positive effects that uniting the city's loyal citizens behind a large, visible event could have, and the planning process resumed. On January 5, 1928, a not-for-profit corporation of eighty trustees, chosen from among the city's leading businessmen, was established to hold "a World's Fair in Chicago in the year 1933."[6]

Organizers soon realized that their original idea for the fair, to celebrate the centennial of Chicago, was too provincial in nature. This theme alone could not attract enough international, or even national, interest to guarantee a successful event. They looked to a series of recent European expositions for inspiration and insights into how to design a modern fair.[7] The underlying impetus of many of these European "colonial" expositions, however —to revive support for national imperial policies—was not applicable to A Century of Progress. The Chicago fair needed a theme that was more in keeping with the current political and cultural situation of the United States. After a series of meetings, the planners arrived at a more appropriate focus for their event: the betterment of mankind through advances in scientific technology.

This carefully crafted theme, which provided the necessary forward-looking focus for the exposition, grew out of a deliberate effort by scientists after World War I to sell the public on the important role of science in modern society. Around this time many major corporations, including AT&T, Westinghouse, General Electric, and Kodak, began supporting their own in-house research institutes. The value of these laboratories was reflected upon by a promoter for General Electric who proclaimed, "Pure science of the past, when applied today, is giving us better quality and new products such as the radio, the refrigerator, and, now, the air conditioner."[8]

By the early 1930s, when the nation was in the depths of the Great Depression, many economists promoted the belief that the road to financial recovery would involve scientists and captains of industry working hand in hand with the government.[9] This view reflected a major shift in American society in the early twentieth century as the underlying basis of national economic growth evolved from land acquisition and individual entrepreneurship to a technology-based consumer culture.[10] The main slogan

of the Chicago exposition—"Science Finds—Industry Applies—Man Conforms"—celebrated this contemporary development. The inclusion of "Industry Applies" in the motto reflected the prominent position of manufacturing concerns at the fair and the fact that many of the mass-produced consumer goods exhibited had developed out of recent advances in scientific technology.

With the devastating worldwide economic impact of the Depression, most foreign governments were not in a position to invest the large sums of money required to construct grand national pavilions at A Century of Progress. Heavy tariffs on goods imported into the United States, significantly limiting the commercial benefits of exhibiting foreign manufactured products, only served to magnify an unfavorable situation for the nations of the world.[11] Homegrown industries, however, were quick to fill the resulting void. Even though large American corporations, like foreign governments, were attempting to cope with the financial ramifications of the severe economic downturn, many companies foresaw potential long-term returns in exhibiting at the Chicago fair. As Harvey S. Firestone exclaimed, the event presented "a great opportunity for private enterprise to show its achievements to millions of people."[12] More broadly, the exposition offered an ideal stage from which to launch a massive public relations campaign promoting the important role of industry in reviving the American economy.[13]

Fair organizers heavily courted major corporations to participate in A Century of Progress. This was a logical course of action since, unlike earlier expositions, much of the original financial backing did not come from government sources but was contributed by wealthy business leaders, including Charles and Rufus Dawes of the Pure Oil Company, Julius Rosenwald of Sears, Roebuck and Company, Robert McCormick of the *Chicago Tribune,* and Philip K. Wrigley of chewing gum fame.[14] The planners offered a positive environment for corporations to exhibit by eliminating direct competition between companies for major awards—a common practice at earlier expositions.[15] Instead, they encouraged the creation of cooperative, industry-wide, focal displays that projected a sense of unity among the individual exhibitors.[16] While A Century of Progress was the first international exposition to charge companies for exhibit space, corporations that constructed their own pavilions at the fair were provided building sites free of charge.[17]

Corporate Exhibitors

A shared goal of the corporations participating in A Century of Progress was to educate consumers about their products as a means to increase the overall market for their goods and to promote brand loyalty. To encourage consumption in markets that were already saturated, many manufacturers introduced new features and product styling at the fair. This practice of creating "artificial obsolescence" to generate new sales had become common among businesses during the 1920s, when annual model changes and color choices were introduced to consumer goods ranging from automobiles to kitchen appliances. Some companies presented new technological developments in Chicago to demonstrate that they were leading innovators in their respective fields, while other businesses sponsored venues that, while featuring less direct ties to commercial products, still kept their corporate name in the forefront of fairgoers' minds.

At the time of the exposition many large companies were battling against "continuing public suspicions of the giant manufacturer as soulless corporation."[18] This perception was largely due to a tremendous change that had taken place during the course of the previous generation in the typical relationship between consumer and producer. As average Americans supplanted homemade items with factory-produced goods, they became removed from the production process. At the same time, developments in product design based on advances made in both scientists' laboratories and technicians' shops often led to manufacturing becoming significantly more complex and, as a result, more enigmatic to the average consumer.[19]

One way businessmen attempted to develop closer relationships with potential customers was through advertising, which by the late 1920s more often than not projected a personal, paternal tone. Playing on people's insecurities, corporations would appeal to the emotions of the consumer by presenting themselves in the guise of a caring friend offering guidance in the purchasing of the "right" products. Using carefully chosen words, they seductively suggested that the use of a particular brand of soap, breakfast cereal, or motor oil could not only meet the consumers' immediate needs but also improve their lifestyles and even possibly enhance their status in society. Exhibiting at A Century of Progress gave companies the opportunity to foster relationships with perspective consumers through the creation of arresting educational exhibits that typically allowed for brief, personal interactions between representatives of the company and potential end users.

Businesses exhibited in Chicago in a variety of ways. Large, prominent corporations built their own pavilions, while others sponsored entertainment venues and special events. Hundreds of companies not in the financial position to construct their own structures presented displays in the General Exhibits Building or in one of the other large, fair-owned thematic pavilions. Not only was information on commercial products disseminated through company exhibits, but it also was dispersed through advertising brochures and souvenirs that helped to spread corporate messages across the country as fairgoers returned home and shared their exposition mementos with family and friends.

Corporate Pavilions

The most visible form of advertising for almost two-dozen companies exhibiting at A Century of Progress was the individual corporate-sponsored pavilion.[20] These buildings ranged from small souvenir stands to massive halls that held full-size, fully functional assembly lines producing real consumer products. Various architectural forms were employed to meet the different agendas and goals of the sponsoring businesses. Some companies sought clean modern designs to convey a feeling of progress, while others used representative forms to prominently advertise their commercial goods. A number of businesses, including Owens-Illinois Glass Company and the Masonite Corporation, sponsored buildings constructed out of their own products.

While the first fair pavilions, including the Hall of Science and the Electrical Building, exhibited details recalling the elegant jazz-age forms that were popularized at the 1925 Exposition internationale des arts décoratifs et industriels moderne, by the time construction was under way on the corporate pavilions, the economy had plummeted and architects were beginning to rely on the basic form of the building, along with colored paint and electric

Lisa D. Schrenk

lighting, to create financially sound yet festive modern exhibition halls. The desire of organizers to maintain constant illumination levels in the interior display areas through the use of artificial light led designers to eliminate window openings wherever possible on the major exhibition buildings. This and the use of modern, prefabricated wall materials without prominent decorative elements resulted in large, unbroken spans of exterior surfaces on many of the corporate pavilions.[21] While towers, like those found on the General Motors, the Sears-Roebuck, and the Owens-Illinois Glass Block buildings, formed distinguishable features, many of the pavilions were without clearly identifiable markers. With the architecture devoid of symbolic imagery, signs became crucial in identifying these buildings. Large letters across their facades spelling out the name of the company often served as the dominant design element. The neon lighting of the signs made it possible to identify the individual buildings at night.

Designers of the second group of pavilions relied on representational shapes instead of large scripted labels to distinguish a building's purpose or sponsor. The most literal interpretations included corporate pavilions designed as colossal depictions of commercial products. Three of the most significant examples of these attention-grabbing edifices at the Chicago fair include the Radio Flyer Pavilion, with its colossal boy riding a thirty-five-foot-long, wagon-shaped building; the Havoline Building, topped by a 200-foot-tall thermometer that recorded the current temperature at the fairgrounds; and the Time and Fortune Building, which featured enormous magazine covers in its design (fig. 2). Other pavilions contained elements that offered more symbolic clues to their function. The Ford Pavilion, for example, designed for the 1934 fair season by Albert Kahn, expressed the mechanical side of automobile production through its large, gear-shaped hall; a form that could be read from either the top of one of the towers or one of the rocket cars of the massive Skyride that loomed above the fairgrounds.

During the construction of the exposition, designers in the United States were only beginning to explore the potential of streamlining in architecture to symbolically represent the increasing pace of modern life. Smooth, teardrop-aerodynamic forms and speedlines, made up of groups of three horizontal bands, appeared more commonly in the designs of exhibitor booths than on pavilions in 1933. The most fully streamlined building at the Chicago

27

fig. 2 Postcard, Time and Fortune Building. Century of Progress Exposition, Chicago, 1933–1934. Lake County (Illinois) Discovery Museum, Curt Teich Postcard Archives.

fair that year was a small pavilion sponsored by the Crane Company, which included rounded corners and speedlines serving as guidelines for sans-serif lettering. More prevalent during the fair's second season, the aerodynamic aesthetic was prominently used for new pavilions by several corporations attempting to portray themselves as progressive businesses. The smooth, elongated teardrop form of the Hiram Walker and Sons' Canadian Club Café (affectionately referred to as the Doodlebug), for example, dramatically tapered to a curved end that projected 400 feet into the fairground's central lagoon (see plate 15).

Corporate Exhibits

While individual pavilions offered great visibility for major corporations, other businesses drew attention to themselves through producing visually seductive displays. As with the corporate buildings, the design of all six hundred individual exhibits had to go through a review process by a committee known as the Little Architectural Commission or the "X" Committee, which was made up of the architects Nathaniel Owings, Louis Skidmore, and Otto Teegen. These men were directly involved in designing many of the exhibits, including those for the Westinghouse Electrical Company, Texaco, the Kerr Glass Company, and the National Sugar Refining Company.[22] Much of their work consisted of modernizing displays that arrived with "the concentration in the wrong direction," meaning an excess of ornate details, including "velvet drapes, gold tassels, corded railings and other trappings."[23]

In a 1934 article in *Review of Reviews and World's Work*, J. Parker Van Zandt and L. Rohe Walter discussed the "fundamental principles of successful, shrewd selling" that were illustrated in the corporate exhibits at A Century of Progress. The authors expressed the importance of simplicity in display design, recalling that several of the exhibits in the Hall of Science Building were too complex for most fairgoers to comprehend. Quoting the satirical journalist H. L. Mencken, Van Zandt and Walter claimed that "no one ever lost money under-estimating the intelligence of the American public."[24] Fair organizers early on had expressed a similar view when recommending to exhibitors that displays be not only entertaining but also understandable to the average twelve-year-old.[25] With eighty-four miles of exhibits to choose from, even well-educated fairgoers

were not likely to make the mental effort to study elaborate displays or interpret intricate symbolism when there was so much else of interest to explore. Clear, direct messages that could be absorbed in seconds were preferred.

One of the most popular types of displays at A Century of Progress that projected easy-to-comprehend messages was the diorama. While the miniature, three-dimensional scenes had appeared at earlier European expositions, the Chicago fair was the first time that this kind of informative display was widely used to promote commercial products.[26] The exposition even established its own diorama studio in the Administration Building, where prior to opening day visitors could view the creation of the minute, lifelike settings by teams of painters, sculptors, and architects.[27] Reflecting upon the alluring quality of dioramas, a writer for the exposition's official publication, *World's Fair Weekly*, exclaimed that the models offered a "magic window out upon a beautifully lighted scene of enchanting reality."[28] Corporations saw great value in dioramas both because they attracted fairgoers' attention and because they allowed for the presentation of a large amount of visual information in a relatively small space. While some dioramas at the fair were up to fifty feet in length, most were approximately five feet wide and three feet high. Often several were presented together to illustrate an assembly process, a series of events, or the evolution of a development. For example, in the Sears-Roebuck Building, among a "mammoth merchandising demonstration" that included a 43-by-63-foot map of the United States, ten dioramas portrayed the history of retailing in America, from the Indian trading post to the "highly imaginative conception of the department store of the future."[29]

Corporations also visually pitched their messages through the use of murals. Large, eye-catching works of art decorated walls throughout the fairgrounds, providing backdrops for exhibits in fair-owned pavilions, including the Hall of Science and the Agricultural Building; in various state displays, such as those promoting Michigan, Indiana, and Ohio; and in many of the corporate pavilions. While wall paintings have been produced by artists throughout history, the popularity of the modern mural was reflected in the growing prominence of Diego Rivera and other members of the Mexican "muralista" art movement in the years leading up to the exposition. In some cases, murals played a major role in the design of fair pavilions. The architect Ely Jacques Kahn, for example, envisioned the Johns-Manville Building as a "complete symphonic composition" that fully incorporated Leo Katz's mural *Give Us This Day Our Daily Light* into the pavilion's design. A brochure published by the building materials company explained the meaning of different elements in the powerful composition, which covered 114 panels of Transite Asbestos in the main hall. The executives at Johns-Manville gave the artist free rein in selecting a theme for the work. Instead of focusing on the company's commercial products, Katz expressed a message reflective of the day: modern mankind's need for leadership and light. The artist combined "abstract symbolism and brutal realism" to create a nightmare-inducing image filled with haunting, sinuous monsters that represented cold, heat, sound, and mechanical motion. In the center, a heroic figure on one knee with arms raised upward in desperate prayer represented the universal cry of modern man for enlightenment.[30] Not all murals were so dramatic. Chrysler Motors commissioned wall paintings of iconic works of architecture, including the Presidential Palace in Lima, Peru, and the Shwedagon Pagoda in Rangoon, Burma, to illustrate the various distant and romantic places around the world where their automobiles could be found.[31]

The authors of the *Review of Reviews* article stressed the importance of using exciting forms of dramatization to gain and maintain fairgoers' attention, claiming that one of the strongest, elemental human cravings is to be entertained. Many businesses integrated dramatic performances into their exhibits as a way to attract fairgoers and disseminate corporate messages. The Safety Glass Manufacturers Association, for example, offered people a chance to "satisfy a long suppressed desire to throw a brick-bat at a window" through participation in a hands-on demonstration located in the Great Hall of the Travel and Transport Building.[32] To increase excitement among visitors attending the "most unusual spectacle in the Fair Grounds," the show began with the sound of splintering glass of an imaginary backstage accident.[33] Interested fairgoers were then given the opportunity to attempt to break a piece of safety glass in front of an audience. While volunteers were awarded a "Safety Glass Sharpshooter" pin or "good luck" coin for their fruitless efforts, specta-

tors received a memorable illustration of the beneficial properties of safety glass (fig. 3).[34]

Dramatic entertainment spectacles could be found throughout the fairgrounds. One of the most popular was the Chrysler Motors Track and Sand Pit Show. Chrysler constructed the largest private exhibit at the exposition in 1933 on a seven-acre site near the far south end of the fairgrounds. Their magnificent pavilion, designed by the

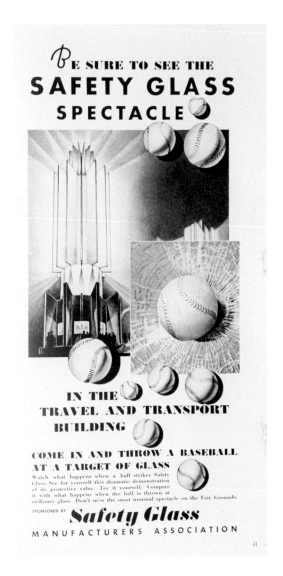

fig. 3 Advertisement, Safety Glass Manufacturers Association. *World's Fair Weekly*, July 1933.

Chicago firm of Holabird and Root, included a glass show-room and four 125-foot-high pylons lit at night by golden-yellow neon fixtures. The interior held the "most complete and amazing automotive engineering displays ever assembled" with more than twenty-five thousand individual elements, including the world's largest display table, covered with every part of a Plymouth Six sedan. The most exciting feature of the Chrysler exhibit, however, was located outside next to the pavilion—a quarter-mile test track, where six times a day the celebrated Barney Oldfield and his crew of "Hell Drivers" demonstrated the capacity of Chrysler automobiles to withstand every kind of road condition, including being driven at fifty miles per hour on a forty-five-degree angled track. The strength of the Plymouth's all-steel body was dramatically illustrated at the end of each performance via a controlled rollover into a sandpit. Between shows, fairgoers could take a demonstration ride around the track with one of the expert drivers at the wheel.[35] Impressed consumers with the necessary resources could then purchase their own Chrysler automobiles right on the spot from a company salesman hovering nearby.[36]

Other corporate-sponsored performances at the fair included the General Electric House of Magic, with black-light demonstrations and a speech-controlled train.[37] The Standard Oil Animal Show, presented several times a day, featured a trainer and thirty-three jungle-born lions and tigers performing death-defying acts in the "Red Crown Cage of Fury."[38] The Atlantic and Pacific Tea Company, meanwhile, presented the A&P Carnival Show in an open-air amphitheater. When Harry Horlick and his Gypsy Orchestra were not presenting their daily concert on the outdoor stage, fairgoers could take in a performance of the A&P Marionettes or visit the nearby A&P Experimental Kitchen.[39]

Visitor participation, as incorporated into the safety-glass demonstration, helped to guarantee a successful corporate exhibit. While the growing popularity of motion pictures was reflected in the presence of films in more than sixty venues across the fairgrounds, the most popular, presented by the Hupp Motor Company, transformed the passive act of watching a film into an interactive extravaganza. For each showing a volunteer was selected to take a "safe-driving test" in a model Hupmobile that was parked behind a glass wall. Other visitors were invited to fill the remaining seats of the vehicle. As the driver started the car, the film began on a screen located in front of the automobile. Both the Hupmobile and movie were visible to other fairgoers gathered outside the large window. Following directions, the driver was required to shift gears and maneuver the vehicle to confront various emergency situations that flashed on the big screen. After completing the "ride," drivers were awarded a "Certificate of Driving Skill" report card that recorded how well they had reacted to the various crisis conditions that had appeared in the film.[40]

The prevalence of movies at A Century of Progress reflected a belief among fair organizers that continuous motion was an important feature of successful modern exhibits. While observing displays at various European expositions in the years leading up to the 1933 fair, Daniel Burnham Jr. and other exposition board members were quick to realize that "still exhibits were dead exhibits."[41] At the Exposition internationale de la grande industrie, sciences et applications, art wallon ancien in Liège in 1930, for example, Allen D. Albert, assistant to the president of the Chicago fair and later secretary to its architectural commission, noted that an expensive, detailed map created out of sugar built to promote Belgium's sugar industry received little attention, while an old-fashioned caramel-wrapping machine drew endless crowds of fascinated onlookers.[42] Incorporating the concept of motion into exhibits, planners believed, was key to attracting and maintaining the interest of modern fairgoers. "People like to see wheels go 'round," according to General Manager Lenox Lohr at the opening of A Century of Progress. "There is motion or the suggestion of movement—progress—in all exhibits."[43]

Many corporations integrated motion into their displays through shows, such as in the Hupmobile driving-test movie, or performances, like the safety-glass demonstration. Several businesses sponsored elaborate action-filled exhibits to attract fairgoers and to promote, either directly or indirectly, the company's products. The Sinclair Oil Company presented an outdoor display of seven life-size plaster dinosaurs that swung their tails and heads and made horrendous sounds. The largest of the menacing-looking dinosaurs, Dino the Brontosaurus, weighed forty

Lisa D. Schrenk

tons and was approximately seventy feet long. According to company executives, the inclusion of the massive prehistoric creatures was intended to portray graphically the corporation's belief that the best oils were "mellowing in the ground during the Mesozoic era when dinosaurs populated the earth."[44] After walking along a path that wound among the moving dinosaurs, visitors passed through a small grotto with product displays and large photographs that illustrated facts about the company and the manufacturing and sale of Sinclair Motor Oils. Accompanying text explained, to those interested enough to stop and read, the connection between the dinosaurs and the crude oil from which the company's motor lubricants were produced.[45] While the dinosaurs were in direct competition with a more elaborate prehistoric midway venue, the World a Million Years Ago, they attracted approximately one million fairgoers a month during the 1933 fair season.[46] Sinclair considered this attendance figure high enough to deem the exhibit a success and resurrected the dinosaur display the following year with only minor improvements to the creatures and surrounding landscaping.[47]

Exposition organizers believed that visitors would find great interest in displays illustrating the development of modern manufactured goods. Corporate executives eager to educate the public about their products made the concept of production the main focus of as many action-filled exhibits as possible. Elaborate industrial presentations that demonstrated the creation of modern products on assembly lines, like the canning machine in the American Can Company display, were located throughout the fairgrounds.[48] Often corporations slowed down the rate of production so that fairgoers could clearly view each individual step of the process.[49] Food exhibits, which drew huge crowds, included a mayonnaise manufacturing machine as part of the Kraft Kitchen located in the Agriculture Building, an operating bottling machine in the Coca-Cola exhibit, and a "certified bacon slicing and packing" demonstration on the first floor of the Wilson and Company Exhibit Building. Four hundred pieces per minute of Wilson's Certified Bacon were prepared with the help of a powerful slicing machine. The continuous wrapping and packaging of the meat was carried out by groups of "lovely girls in trim, natty uniforms" for twelve hours a day, in "the most sanitary manner," under temperature and humidity control (fig. 4).[50] Those fairgoers whose appetites had been whetted could sample Wilson certified products

31

fig. 4 Postcard, Wilson and Co. Sliced Bacon Unit. Century of Progress Exposition, Chicago, 1933–1934. Lake County (Illinois) Discovery Museum, Curt Teich Postcard Archives.

tage of the opportunity and "stole the show" by building the largest and most expensive corporate pavilion at the fair.[64]

Ford spared no expense in his attempt to outdo the other exhibitors. On an eleven-acre site, which had held a United States Army Camp and a village of American Indians during the previous year, he built a spectacular pavilion filled with astonishing exhibits that drew more than 75 percent of all visitors during the 1934 fair season.[65] Albert Kahn's colossal Ford Building, with its 210-foot gear-shaped rotunda, included two projecting wings (fig. 6). To the north, an elongated section 550 feet in length was crowned with large, widely spaced letters spelling out "Ford," and similar letters appeared atop the building's rotunda. Influenced by the rise of streamlining, Kahn designed the signage and building as if attempting to make it easier for people to read the pavilion's modern, machine-age form while rapidly passing it by in a speeding automobile. While the building's color scheme was relatively plain (predominantly white, with accents of dark green, blue, and yellow), the pavilion presented the most lavish use of electric lighting at the exposition in 1934.[66]

The Ford Building included three main exhibition areas: the rotunda contained a focal display, the long hall housed the industrial exhibits, and a shorter wing to the south held historical presentations from the Ford Museum.[67] Henry Ford firmly believed in the "practical educational value" of expositions. His underlying goal in participating in the Chicago fair was to inspire fairgoers to explore new ideas, as he had been motivated to build his first gas engine after viewing the gas-powered water pump motors on display in Chicago at the World's Columbian Exposition in 1893.[68] To ensure a successful exhibit, Ford hired the industrial designer Walter Dorwin Teague to present "the fascinating story of the motor car" through the use of "graphic entertaining forms" of display, while completely avoiding any appearance of direct selling tactics.[69] In order to avoid duplicating General Motors' assembly-line exhibit, the designer developed an abstract dramatization of the assembly process by borrowing many of the more theatrical forms of display from successful exhibits that had appeared at A Century of Progress the previous season, including instructive dioramas, striking murals, full-scale animated working exhibits, motion pictures, and live performances. Teague strove to imbue in all the displays a high level of dramatic presentation as he attempted "to give the public a feeling of intimacy with industry's

34

fig. 6 Ford Building, 1934. Albert Kahn, architect. Century of Progress Exposition, Chicago, 1933–1934. Photo provided courtesy of Albert Kahn Family of Companies.

opposite
fig. 7 Drama of Transportation exhibit, Ford Building, 1934. Century of Progress Exposition, Chicago, 1933–1934. From the Collection of The Henry Ford (85.127.141).

methods."[70] He also introduced a sense of stylistic unity throughout the pavilion by applying a harmonious use of color and graphics to the building and its displays.[71]

Motion was a major factor throughout the Ford exhibits. Fairgoers were drawn to the rotunda's Court of the World by a rotating globe twenty feet in diameter that identified the location of the company's production plants around the world (see plate 51).[72] As with many other pavilions at the fair, Teague covered the interior walls with murals. Wanting to demonstrate the company's commitment to progress, he chose the medium of photography instead of painting. The author of a brochure describing the company's exhibits explained that the massive artwork marked the start of a new epoch of mural making by presenting the "first grand example of what can be done when the camera is substituted for brush and pigment."[73] The twenty-eight twenty-foot-high enlarged photographs created a six-hundred-foot photomontage of the workings at Ford's River Rough plant. Between the photographs were a series of maxims—such as "Progress Comes from Prosperity Built by Work . . . Done in Peace"—expressing the paternal wisdom of Henry Ford.[74] On the floor below sixty-seven vehicles from Ford's personal collection,

beginning with a replica of King Tutankhamen's state chariot and ending with contemporary automobiles, illustrated the evolution of passenger travel in the Drama of Transportation display (fig. 7).[75]

To the right of the rotunda at the entrance to the gigantic Industrial Hall was a second rotating sphere containing a series of dioramas. Reflecting Ford's central theme, "Man must go to the earth for all materials," the miniature scenes illustrated the major resources used in the production of automobiles.[76] Along both sides of the hall numerous additional dioramas, working models, relief maps, photographs, and trained lecturers dramatically traced the progress of raw materials, including iron, aluminum, rubber, asbestos, and, Ford's favorite, soybeans, from their original state to finished parts for a Ford V-8.[77] Motion was also a feature of one of the most popular exhibits in the room, the assembly and testing of speedometers. In a theater located adjacent to the main hall, fairgoers could stop and watch the movie *Rhapsody in Steel*. Produced specifically for the exposition, the twenty-two-minute film featured a puckish hood-ornament imp who, through assorted antics, illustrated the various industries and operations involved in the creation of a Ford car as he orchestrated the various manufactured parts to assemble themselves into a new automobile.[78]

Teague segregated most of Ford's historical exhibits to the Century Room, south of the rotunda. In an area much smaller than the Industrial Hall, displays depicted one hundred years of mechanical progress and included Ford's first workshop and earliest automobile.[79] As in a number of other corporate exhibits at the fair, the historical displays served as a backdrop against which the company's progressive, modern developments could be measured. To the rear of the Century Room was a weathered outbuilding from the Ford family homestead that held exhibits reflecting Henry Ford's keen interest in developing closer ties between agriculture and industry, particularly with regard to soybean production and use.[80]

Ford also employed the past to highlight advances in the transportation industry in a major automotive attraction located just outside the pavilion. Realizing the great popularity of exhibits that incorporated visitor participation, Ford built Roads of the World, an outdoor driving venue designed to compete with the highly successful

35

Chrysler Motors raceway show. Ford's attraction featured a large oval track comprising sections of roadway built to resemble almost two dozen world-famous thoroughfares ranging from the "earliest Roman roads to the smooth paved highways of today."[81] Fairgoers could experience driving on the different pavements by taking a four-minute ride around the loop in a Ford automobile. Near the roadway, an orchestra shell served as the setting for Ford-sponsored daily concerts by the Chicago Women's Symphony and the Detroit Symphony Orchestra.[82] Located along the shore of Lake Michigan and surrounded by the beautifully landscaped Ford Gardens, the outdoor performance hall provided a place for fairgoers to relax and reflect upon all of the wondrous displays they had just experienced in the Ford Building.

Visitors were encouraged to take promotional postcards, brochures, and souvenirs from the Ford Pavilion to share with people back home. One of the most popular mementos was a compartmentalized box that held a dozen small labeled samples of some of the earth's basic materials featured in the Industrial Hall, including iron ore, asbestos, mohair, and soybeans.[83] Less educational Ford souvenirs included tea trays and plates decorated with images of the Ford Building, and round and arrowhead-shaped tokens. An assortment of postcards and free brochures served as reminders of visits to the pavilion for fairgoers and offered snapshots of the building and its exhibits for those who were able to experience the event only vicariously.

Legacy of the Corporate Presentations at A Century of Progress

In their attempt to present a new form of world's fair that clearly reflected the modern era, organizers of A Century of Progress relied upon corporate leaders to provide not only financial backing but also exciting, innovative exhibits that would help draw huge crowds to the event. Despite the economic hardships of the Great Depression, many companies were quick to sign up. At a time when the division between manufacturer and consumer was widening, progressive corporate executives recognized that world's fairs offered ideal opportunities for millions of potential customers to become familiarized with their commercial products. To help guarantee large throngs of fairgoers visiting their exposition exhibits, businesses took ad-

vantage of successful modern display techniques, including the use of dioramas and murals and the presence of moving components and interactive elements, as well as the incorporation of a variety of other innovative and entertaining features.

Having reaped the benefits of exhibiting at the 1933–1934 exposition, many companies went on to construct pavilions and sponsor exhibits at later American world's fairs.[84] Hoping to copy Chicago's success and revive their own local economies, San Diego, Dallas, Cleveland, San Francisco, and New York all held major expositions in the 1930s. Most of the themes and presentation practices that emerged at A Century of Progress reappeared at these later American fairs. A few of the displays from Chicago were unboxed and reassembled without any noted modifications, while others were updated and refined.[85] In order to keep one step ahead of average consumers, who were being exposed to more and more advertising in their daily lives, astute business leaders began employing more sophisticated marketing practices.[86] To counter growing apathy among the general public toward commercial presentations designed primarily to educate, many large companies, most prominently the automobile manufacturers, increasingly favored elaborate exposition exhibits that offered enticing forms of entertainment while less directly promoting their products. For example, General Motors's Futurama, the largest and most popular exhibit at the 1939–1940 New York World's Fair, combined many of the attributes found in successful corporate displays at A Century of Progress with the thrilling elements of popular midway attractions. The result was an exhibit highlighted by a dramatic and memorable amusement ride during which fairgoers experienced a utopian vision of the future predominantly defined by the automobile.

Technology has advanced considerably since the 1930s, allowing corporations to create even more seductive, eye-catching exhibits. But as could be witnessed at Expo 2000 in Hannover, Germany, and Expo 2005 in Aichi, Japan —as well as the eternal world's fair, Disney's EPCOT Center in Orlando, Florida—corporations continue to rely upon the same underlying display techniques that were so prominently and effectively used at A Century of Progress to promote both identity and products to the public.[87]

36

Lisa D. Schrenk

Notes

1. J. Parker Van Zandt, "A Miracle in Cans," *Review of Reviews and World's Work* 90 (1934): 54.

2. According to the reporter, one in nine fair visitors on average had to be prompted, while one in forty "completely lost courage at the critical moment and had to have the machine operated for them." Ibid., 57.

3. Ibid., 56–57.

4. For more information on the Century of Progress International Exposition, see Schrenk, *Building a Century of Progress*.

5. For information on the difficulties of the Sesquicentennial International Exposition, see Rydell, Findling, and Pelle, *Fair America,* 73–76.

6. Trustees included Robert R. McCormick, Julius Rosenwald, and Philip K. Wrigley; Lenox R. Lohr, *Guides Memories: A Century of Progress* (Chicago: A Century of Progress, c. 1935), 1; Paul T. Gilbert, "A Century of Progress Exposition: Herald of a New Age," *Chicago Progress,* n.d., 12.

7. Organizers took note of everything from the best possible materials for pedestrian pathways to basic design concepts for exhibits; Schrenk, *Building a Century of Progress,* 20.

8. Quoted in Robert Buderi, *Engines of Tomorrow: How the World's Best Companies Are Using Their Research Labs to Win the Future* (New York: Simon and Schuster, 2001), 79.

9. Rydell, *World of Fairs,* 93.

10. Olivier Zunz, *Why the American Century?* (Chicago: University of Chicago Press, 1998), xi, 74.

11. Findling, *Chicago's Great World's Fairs,* 54.

12. Firestone press release, June 20, 1932, folder 1-5600, Century of Progress International Exposition Archive, Special Collections, University of Illinois, Chicago [CPIE].

13. At the time many American policy makers believed that widespread consumption of mass-produced goods was the most direct route out of the Depression. Zunz, *Why the American Century?* xii.

14. Daniel H. Burnham Jr., "How Chicago Finances Its Exposition," *Review of Reviews and World's Work* 86 (October 1932): 38; Carl W. Condit, *Chicago, 1930–70: Building, Planning, and Urban Technology* (Chicago: University of Chicago Press, 1974), 5.

15. As reported at the time, there was to be no competition between finished products in order to prevent visitors from being "bored to death looking at miles of completed goods"; Paul Hutchinson, "Progress on Parade," *Forum and Century* 89 (1933): 372.

16. Rydell, *World of Fairs,* 122. For more information on the presentation of industry-wide focus displays at A Century of Progress, see Schrenk, *Building a Century of Progress,* 38.

17. Lenox R. Lohr, *Fair Management* (Chicago: Cuneo, 1952), 34–35.

18. Marchand, *Creating the Corporate Soul,* 265.

19. Inger L. Stole, *Advertising on Trial: Consumer Activism and Corporate Public Relations in the 1930s* (Urbana: University of Illinois Press, 2006), 7.

20. In contrast, only 9 of the 137 buildings at the World's Columbian Exposition, the first Chicago world's fair, in 1893, were corporate pavilions.

21. While a few of the earliest buildings were constructed of plywood or steel panels, gypsum board became the wall material of choice. Large panels of a recently developed form of gypsum board that could withstand exterior use were bolted to steel frames to allow for easy disassembly of the fair pavilions after the close of the event.

22. Chicago World's Fair Centennial Celebration of 1933, Architectural Commission, "Design Section," Report, CPIE.

23. Lohr, *Fair Management,* 114.

24. J. Parker Van Zandt and L. Rohe Walter, "King Customer at A Century of Progress," *Review of Reviews and World's Work* 90 (1934): 22, 24.

25. Eben J. Carey, *Medical Science Exhibits: A Century of Progress* (Chicago: A Century of Progress, 1936), 35. Advertisers at the time inferred that the average consumer had the mental ability of a child between the age of nine and sixteen years old. Stole, *Advertising on Trial,* 17.

26. Lohr, *Fair Management,* 124. Miniature dioramas, with all figures placed in perspective, had previously appeared at the 1924–1925 British Empire Exhibition at Wembley to depict battle scenes and in the replica of Angkor Wat at the 1931 Colonial Exposition in Paris to illustrate the history of French civilizing influences; Nicola Savarese and Richard Fowler, "1931: Antonin Artaud Sees Balinese Theatre at the Paris Colonial Exposition," *TDR* 45, no. 3 (2001), 51–77.

27. A staff of seventeen skilled artists worked at the fairgrounds beginning in 1930 to complete approximately forty dioramas for the event. Edward J. Ashenden, who had perfected the modern diorama for use at the 1924–1925 Wembley exposition, led the group; "Those Mysterious Dioramas," *World's Fair Weekly,* May 20, 1933, 8, 10; Lohr, *Fair Management,* 124.

28. "Those Mysterious Dioramas," 3.

29. "Sears, Roebuck and Co.," 1933, center insert, copy in collection of author. Some of the other corporations that integrated historical presentations into their displays included Merck and Company, the H. J. Heinz Company, the Burroughs Adding Machine Company, and the Stayform Company. The concept of using the past to highlight current and future advances was also incorporated into the exposition's opening-night lighting ceremony, in which energy that had left the star Arcturus approximately forty years earlier—linking the event with the first Chicago international exposition held in 1893—was used to power the dramatic lighting of the fairgrounds. *Wings of a Century,* an outdoor theatrical spectacular, also featured historical developments in transportation beginning with horses and canoes and ending with the latest models of automobiles, locomotives, and airplanes. Even the presence of replicas of past notable buildings, such as Abraham Lincoln's cabin, and of the traditional ethnic villages provided a historic context for the forward-looking, modern fair pavilions that held the corporate and scientific exhibits.

30. "*Give Us This Day Our Daily Light:* A Mural by Leo Katz, On Exhibit in the Johns-Manville Building, A Century of Progress Exposition, Chicago, Illinois, U.S.A., 1933"; copy in collection of author.

31. While artists painted two of the highly colorful murals on pavilion walls in the "conventional manner," three other murals were created using transparent analin dyes stippled onto vertical glass surfaces; "Chrysler Motors at A Century of Progress Presents the Export Murals, A Century of Progress, 1934"; copy in collection of author.

32. Van Zandt, "King Customer," 23.

33. Safety Glass Manufacturers Association advertisement, in *Official Guide Book of the World's Fair of 1934* (Chicago: Cuneo, 1934), 192.

34. Van Zandt, "King Customer," 24.

35. Jim Benjaminson, "Chrysler at the 1934 Chicago World's Fair," http://www.allpar.com/history/plymouth/world-fair-1934.html (accessed September 24, 2008).

36. Chrysler drivers gave between twelve hundred and fourteen hundred rides daily to fairgoers at the exposition; "A Story of Chrysler Heroes," *World's Fair Weekly,* July 15, 1933, 47.

37. Buderi, *Engines of Tomorrow,* 78.

38. *Official Guide Book, 1934,* 144–145.

39. A&P Advertisement in *World's Fair Weekly,* July 8, 1933.

40. Van Zandt, "King Customer," 24.

41. "Report of D. H. Burnham on the Paris International Colonial Exposition," CPIE.

42. Allen D. Albert, "Learning from Other World's Fairs: The Collective Exhibit Marks a New Mode to Replace Older Conceptions," *Chicago Commerce,* November 22, 1930, 14, 22.

43. Sherman R. Duffy, "Motion Key to Fair's Magic, Lohr Says," *Chicago American,* May 27, 1933, 15.

44. "Evolution of the Company Symbol," Sinclair Oil Company, 2006, http://www.sinclairoil.com/history/historys_p1.htm (accessed September 24, 2008). The dinosaurs were assembled by P. G. Alen of Fort Wayne, Indiana, who had carried out similar work for the motion picture industry in Hollywood; "The Sinclair Exhibit at the Century of Progress," press release attached to letter from Sylvester M. Morey to W. H. Raymond, May 2, 1933, folder 1-13608, CPIE.

45. "Evolution of the Company Symbol," "The Sinclair Exhibit."

46. "Most Photographed Exhibit," *Big News, Chicago World's Fair Edition* (New York: Sinclair Refining Company, n.d.), 2. It cost twenty-five cents for adults and ten cents for children to enter the World a Million Years Ago venue, whereas the Sinclair exhibits were free.

47. Sylvester M. Morey, letter to J. Franklin Bell, January 30, 1934, folder 1-13607, CPIE. The Sinclair Corporation went on to sponsor later exhibits of life-size animated dinosaurs, including a major display at the 1964–1965 New York World's Fair. Dino the Brontosaurus went on to serve as the company's mascot.

48. Some of the other commercial products that were produced at A Century of Progress in corporate displays included hosiery, overalls, bread, cigars, pottery, candy, and toothpaste.

49. The Kraft-Phenix Cheese Corporation slowed its mayonnaise production line to one-sixth the normal rate, while the General Motors Chevrolet assembly line produced only one vehicle every twenty minutes instead of operating at the usual rate of one every few seconds; "Modern Mayonnaise Making," *World's Fair Weekly,* November 11, 1933, 9; Malcolm McDowell, "Hold Rehearsal on Building Autos at Fair: General Motors Workers to Test Assembly Line; Design Explained," *Chicago Daily News,* May 17, 1933, 15.

50. "Wilson's Four Major Activities at A Century of Progress, 1934," copy in collection of author; W. G. Shanks, letter to Joseph C. Folsom, January 8, 1934, folder 1-8918, CPIE.

51. *Official Guide Book of the Fair, 1933* (Chicago: Cuneo, 1933), 101.

52. Lohr, *Fair Management,* 137–138.

53. A formal garden featuring the "Singing Color Fountain" and a race car exhibit also helped to draw fairgoers to the Firestone Building; "World's Fair Exhibit to Tell Firestone Story to Millions," *Firestone Non-Skid* 18, no. 7 (1933): 1; "Firestone's World Fair Exhibition Nears Completion," *Firestone Non-Skid* 18, no. 9 (1933): 4.

54. Kahn, architect of many of the modern automotive factories in the Detroit area, designed the building around the production line, stating, "It followed quite logically that, after I had thought out a plan to glorify the assembly line, the rest of the exhibit just naturally fitted into the picture"; "Of News to Us at the World's Fair," *General Motors Magazine,* March 1933, 6, copy in folder 1-6214, CPIE.

55. "See Chevrolets Made," General Motors Advertisement in *World's Fair Weekly,* August 26, 1933. General Motors arranged with fair organizers to be able to drive approximately twenty-five finished automobiles out of the building each day between 6:00 P.M. and 7:00 P.M. in a grand procession through the fairgrounds to the trucking entrance at the North Gate; S. J. Irvine, letter to Mr. Thurman, Chief, Public Protection Division, May 31, 1933, folder 1-6214, CPIE.

56. "Rivera Loses Order for the World Fair; Mural for General Motors Is Canceled as a Result of Rockefeller's Action," *New York Times,* May 12, 1933, 19. Murals did, however, decorate many of the other walls of the 120,000-square-foot pavilion. The craftsman Matt Faussner created inlaid-wood murals for the Entrance Hall, while a series of forty paintings located in the assembly room illustrated each state's contribution of raw materials used in the production of the company's automobiles. These murals were painted by a number of artists, including Axel Linus, Santiago Martínez Delgado, and Miklos Gasper. After the fair closed the "States" murals were donated to Lane Tech High School in Chicago.

57. "What We Saw in the General Motors Exhibit Building at A Century of Progress," 1933, copy in collection of author. The mechanical Native American was created by the New York animatronic firm of Messmore and Damon, which also created other moving figures for A Century of Progress, including prehistoric creatures for the World a Million Years Ago attraction and a talking cow for the International Harvester display; Rydell, *Fair America,* 82.

58. Westinghouse presented a wide range of lively demonstrations of novel lighting in displays housed in the Electrical Building. In 1934 the company offered the first public presentation of the high-pressure mercury-vapor lamp and successfully demonstrated ultraviolet light. Fairgoers flocked to the corporation's "do-it-yourself" hands-on exhibits, which included a self-operating X-ray machine and its own oscilloscope, which turned fairgoers' voices into visible waves. The highlight of the Westinghouse exhibits, however, was its air-conditioned theater, which included five stage sets built upon a rotating platform. This allowed for rapid set changes during a fifteen-minute performance that illustrated the impact of scientific advances on lighting and household appliances; Westinghouse Electric and Manufacturing Company, "Westinghouse Theater with Revolving Stage Will Tell of Home Electrification at Chicago," press release, May 20, 1934; Century of Progress International Exposition Publicity Department, "Westinghouse," press release, May 29, 1934.

59. "A Visit to the General Motors Research Laboratory at A Century of Progress, 1934," copy in collection of author.

60. Dozens of these brochures were collected by the John Crerar Library at the time of the fair and are now housed in the special collections of the University of Chicago.

38

Lisa D. Schrenk

61. The Windy City Postcard Club of Chicago identified hundreds of different postcards printed for the exposition. A majority of the images feature the fair's architecture.

62. Marchand, *Creating the Corporate Soul,* 263.

63. Ibid., 269; David L. Lewis, *The Public Image of Henry Ford: An American Folk Hero and His Company* (Detroit: Wayne State University Press, 1976), 297.

64. Van Zandt, "King Customer," 27.

65. Ford outdrew General Motors (the most popular exhibit at the exposition in 1933) two to one; Marchand, *Creating the Corporate Soul,* 269. The Ford Corporation spent more than $2.5 million on the building and exhibits; ibid., 267.

66. Lohr, *Fair Management,* 80. The building required more than one hundred miles of electrical wire and emitted seven billion candlepower, more than two-thirds of the brightness added to the fair for its second season; A Century of Progress International Exposition Publicity Department, "Lighting 1934," press release, c. 1934.

67. "Ford Exposition Building Century of Progress," *Architectural Forum* 61 (1934): 2.

68. Roland Marchand, "The Designers Go to the Fair: Walter Dorwin Teague and the Professionalization of Corporate Industrial Exhibits, 1933–1940," *Design Issues* 8 (1991): 9; Lewis, *Public Image,* 297.

69. "Ford at the Fair," copy in collection of author. Ford was able to avoid direct selling tactics at the exposition in part by hiring college students instead of relying upon company employees to work in the pavilion; Marchand, "The Designers Go to the Fair," 11.

70. Walter Dorwin Teague, "What Can We Do with an Exhibit to Magnetize the Crowd?" *Sales Management,* January 1, 1937, 63, quoted in Marchand, *Creating the Corporate Soul,* 275.

71. Marchand, "The Designers Go to the Fair," 10.

72. "Ford Exposition: Century of Progress," copy in collection of author.

73. The photographs, taken by George Ebling, a staff photographer for Ford, built upon the machinelike precision of industrial images produced a few years earlier by the painter Charles Sheeler and the photographer Margaret Bourke-White. Ebling's compelling photographs celebrated the power, rhythm, and grandeur of what at the time was the largest industrial plant in the world; "Ford Exposition: Century of Progress"; Henry Ford Museum, "Explore and Learn Pic of the Month," September 2002, http://www.thehenryford.org/exhibits/pic/2002/02.sep.html (accessed November 11, 2009).

74. "Ford Exposition: A Century of Progress."

75. Lohr, *Fair Management,* 137.

76. Ibid.

77. "How to See the Ford Exposition: A Century of Progress, 1934," copy in collection of author; Malcolm McDowell, "Work to Start on Henry Ford Exhibit at Fair in Two Weeks," *Chicago Daily News,* February 14, 1934.

78. "Ford at the Fair"; "Rhapsody in Steel," *Time* 24 (July 9, 1934): http://www.time.com/time/magazine/article/0,9171,769925,00.html (accessed September 25, 2008).

79. *Official Guide Book, 1934,* 137; "Ford at the Fair."

80. One exhibit demonstrated the mechanical procedure for extracting oil from soybeans, while another presented the necessary equipment for producing plastic objects out of the legumes; Lohr, *Fair Management,* 138; "Ford at the Fair."

81. Lohr, *Fair Management,* 137.

82. "How to See the Ford Exposition."

83. Marchand, "The Designers Go to the Fair," 11–12.

84. Henry Ford, in particular, was sold on the value of corporate participation in world's fairs and went on to sponsor some of the largest displays at later American expositions, including at the 1935 California-Pacific International Exposition in San Diego and the Texas Centennial Exposition, held in Dallas the following year. After the close of A Century of Progress, the Ford Motor Company reconstructed the rotunda of its pavilion in Dearborn, Michigan; it stood directly across the street from the company's headquarters until it burned down in November 1962. Many of the exhibits created for the Chicago exposition went on permanent display inside. Those that still projected a "static conventional character" were transformed into compelling presentations by Walter Dorwin Teague, who continued to have a close relationship with Ford and its corporate leaders throughout the decade, designing both buildings and exhibits for the automaker at later fairs; Lewis, *Public Image,* 301; Judith Dressel, "Edsel Ford, Modernist," *The Modern* 14 (2000): http://www.daads.org/modern/1401/ford.htm (accessed November 11, 2009).

85. For example, General Electric revived its "House of Magic" show and General Motors reincarnated Chief Pontiac to once again answer fairgoers' questions about the company's automobiles at the 1936 Texas Centennial Exposition. Firestone, meanwhile, presented a fully functional tire plant similar to the one it built in Chicago at the 1939–1940 New York World's Fair.

86. Corporate executives, needing to justify the large expenditures involved in exhibiting at world's fairs, commissioned detailed analyses to assess the effectiveness of their participation on consumers. They did this by implementing a wide range of appraisal techniques that involved both qualitative and quantitative measures of the public's perception of their displays and the potential impact the exhibits might have on future buying habits; Marchand, *Creating the Corporate Soul,* 278–279.

87. Some of the major corporations that funded the United States Pavilion at Expo 2005, including General Motors, DuPont, and Goodyear, had participated in the American international expositions of the 1930s. A number of companies involved in these earlier fairs also sponsored many of the original Future World pavilions at EPCOT, which opened to the public in 1982. General Electric hosted Horizons, General Motors backed the World of Motion, Eastman Kodak funded Imagination! and Bell Systems (AT&T) sponsored Spaceship Earth.

Old Wine in New Bottles
Masterpieces Come to the Fairs

Neil Harris

During their most popular phase, between 1893 and 1915, American world's fairs celebrated a Beaux-Arts architectural and planning tradition. Grand, classical palaces, aligned on axial avenues, separated by lagoons, cascades, canals, and water courts, emphasized tradition, continuity, and aspiration, linking their sites, and national culture, with favored historical civilizations. Monumental, eclectic, revivalist, and reassuring, the official fairgrounds tended to mask rather than flaunt their considerable technological and bureaucratic modernity. New and temporary as they were, these settings suggested agelessness and permanence, flourishing specially commissioned embellishments, both inside and outside.

Nonetheless, the fairs were, at heart, marketing moments, for manufacturers, nation-states, educators, merchants, entertainers, and entrepreneurs of all kinds. And artists. As a result, despite the patina of age supplied by templed facades and colossal statuary, most of the art actually on display at these fairs was contemporary rather than retrospective. Certainly there were occasional gestures to older art, particularly Anglo-American examples. An interest in origins supported presentation of Gilbert Stuart,

John Stuart Copley, and the great eighteenth-century British landscapists and portraits at some late-nineteenth-century expositions. At the World's Columbian Exposition in Chicago in 1893 hundreds of oil paintings by European artists were lent by American collectors, but they were almost exclusively nineteenth-century, and French.[1] The Philadelphia Sesquicentennial in 1926 offered special displays of tapestries, Islamic art, Rodin sculpture collected by Jules Mastbaum, and French impressionists lent by Durand-Ruel, the celebrated art dealer.[2] But the overwhelming emphasis, here and elsewhere, lay on the present and the recent past. Special juries and national committees of experts guarded the portals to both the international art exhibitions the fairs hosted and the national buildings themselves. These arenas could be extensive in size and elaborate in character. Thousands of art pieces made their way from across the globe to the fair cities. They were attached to official boasts of progress in the visual arts as ambitious as the claims made for the sciences. Contemporary art in historicist settings was the standard method of presentation.

The fairs of the 1930s changed this relationship decisively. They pioneered, or at least notably expanded, what

WHAT CHICAGO LEARNED

The Art Institute Appraises the World's Fair Art Exhibition

fig. 2 Crowds outside the Art Institute of Chicago, 1933. Dudley Crafts Watson, "What Chicago Learned," *American Magazine of Art,* February 1934.

belief then and now.[31] The next day, the final day of the exhibition, the "rear guard" of this "mighty throng" posed for photographs on the grand staircase of the museum, documenting both the crowded final hours and the surprising amiability of the highly compressed audience.[32] At 10 P.M., ten thousand people were still in the building.

The exhibition was accompanied by daily lectures, newspaper descriptions of individual paintings written by Bulliet, columns that would eventually be compiled into a book, and an elaborate illustrated catalogue, which paid careful attention to the provenance of each artwork, emphasizing the significance of the American collectors.[33] Sixty thousand copies were sold. Art Institute officials remarked that the lectures were heavily attended, and that the crowds themselves were respectful of the art on display; a post-exhibition inspection revealed no damage, malicious or accidental (fig. 3).

While the Art Institute collection dominated, standouts from elsewhere were many. They included two extraordinary paintings owned by Stephen Clark of New York, Matisse's *White Plumes* and Cezanne's *Card Players;* a group of eleven El Grecos; Duchamp's *Nude Descending a Staircase,"* the fabled shocker from the 1913 Armory Show

fig. 3 Exhibition visitors, A Century of Progress Exhibition of Paintings and Sculpture, Art Institute of Chicago, 1933. Dudley Crafts Watson, "What Chicago Learned," *American Magazine of Art,* February 1934.

that now belonged to the Arensbergs of California; Miró's *Dog Barking at the Moon,* in the collection of A. E. Gallatin; and a host of others since made familiar by entry into museum collections and extensive reproduction.

All in all, the show's triumph emerged as perhaps the fair's most fondly recalled feature. The "magnificent exhibition of paintings," wrote Albert Franz Cochrane from Boston, "positively dumbfounded the World's Fair officials by its great drawing powers." It was "the greatest, most interesting and memorable single feature of the entire elaborate affair."[34] In the words of the University of Chicago's Robert Morss Lovett, "From the vast confusion of material triumph and vulgar entertainment, to turn to this monument of human endeavor was to find consolation, to become conscious of a principle or order in the chaos of progress, to discern a way of salvation, of making the world a better place for man to live."[35] Here was resistance to the user-friendly, pleasure-seeking, commercially oriented baubles that filled the fairgrounds just to the south, as well as to the all-conquering ethos of business and triumphant science that permeated the corporate and educational pavilions. Contemporary and local artists were not ignored by exposition authorities; there were murals, mosaics, and statuary aplenty to be seen. But the formal art exhibition, even when it touched upon the latest domestic achievements, seemed guided by far more conservative professional principles. Robert Harshe, wrote Albert Franz Cochrane again, "was given entire freedom of action," and Institute organizers were able to insist upon "free choice of exhibits or none at all."[36]

Repercussions were soon felt within the Art Institute itself. Impressed by their success, the curators determined to rehang the entire museum according to chronological principles. Seeking (and obtaining) permission from donor families to dismantle their various memorial rooms and integrate the art they had given within the larger whole, the staff produced, one month after the fair exhibition had closed, what observers agreed was a far more powerful and comprehensible display.[37] The sequential arrangement brought the Art Institute, wrote its director in his annual report for 1933, into the company of places like the Prado, the National Gallery in London, and the Kaiser-Friedrich in Berlin.[38] And it revealed for the first time to some Chicagoans the breadth and strength of the permanent collection.

47

A new season in 1934 required a second act. The organizers attempted to tweak the formula that had been so successful the previous year—it continued to be called a seventy-five-million-dollar show—but with somewhat different emphases. There would still be individual masterpieces of European painting and sculpture, among them several recent purchases from the Hermitage, but they would be pendants to the main thrust—the history of American art—which some argued had been downplayed in 1933.[39] Contemporary work would be featured as well. More than 50 percent of the chosen art was to be American, with an entire room of Whistlers, along with famous paintings by Thomas Eakins, John Singer Sargent, Albert Pinkham Ryder, Mary Cassatt, George Bellows, and others. Buoyed by the 1933 experience, museum and fair officials alike predicted an even larger attendance for 1934.[40] "We consider the exhibit one of the finest collected," Robert Harshe asserted in May 1934, anticipating an opportunity "to equal or surpass the 1,700,000 attendance mark of the 1933 exhibition."[41] One headline proclaimed that the Art Institute was preparing for two million visitors to its Century of Progress Exhibit.[42]

But the second act didn't play. Despite the prophesies and the lavish descriptions, the appeals to nationalism, and a set of publicity stunts, the 1934 event proved enormously disappointing. Attendance was less than one-third that of the year before, not much more than half a million during the five months the special exhibition was on. The largest number of daily visitors came at the very start of the show, fewer than six thousand, just a fraction of the record of forty-four thousand set the year before. Art Institute attendance was less than half of what it had been in 1933. The Art Institute put a good face on matters, listing the total number of visitors during the two Century of Progress Expositions at just under three million, but more than three-quarters of that total had come during the first year.[43]

All sorts of reasons might account for the drop: fatigue with art exhibitions, loss of novelty, fewer conventioneers in Chicago. But at least one critic, C. J. Bulliet, saw the decline as evidence that American art could not compete with European art in any substantial way. Writing in the *Chicago Daily News,* Bulliet observed that Europeans had been quick to accept American ships, guns, submarines,

skyscrapers, automobiles, and movies as world class, and had no trouble elevating them to high status. But art was a different matter. American artists might complain of foreign "propaganda" poisoning the minds of their fellow citizens against the art produced at home, but in fact, with all the propaganda at the disposal of the Century of Progress, it proved impossible to market the American exhibition with any degree of success. And that was because American art was just not up to the international standard. Intelligent taste had spoken, Bulliet insisted, and it was the Europeans who had carried the day.[44]

Whether or not the second art season was a total "flop," as Bulliet insisted, the two exhibitions had benefited the Art Institute considerably. Its refectories and gift shop profited from the large crowds, and its reputation swelled. In 1936, although this was not a quid pro quo, when the fair corporation settled its accounts, the Institute received some thirty-two thousand dollars, representing 20 percent of the exposition profits. For 1933, at least, the fair authorities agreed to allow no competing art exhibition on the fairgrounds, and this undoubtedly strengthened the Art Institute's appeal. Recognizing Daniel Rich's achievement, in December 1933 the trustees generously rewarded him with a handsome 35 percent salary increase.[45] Other honors—medals, honorary degrees, editorial tributes—would flow to Harshe and Rich in subsequent years as the extent of their success became more broadly recognized.

The increased attendance for 1933 did not, however, produce more memberships. As with the blockbuster shows a half-century later, the permanent financial blessings of a temporary show, however popular, were unclear to its museum host. Despite gains to its international reputation, within a couple of years the Art Institute turned to a newly created public relations department, hoping to use the press more effectively in a campaign to earn the goodwill (and philanthropic support) of Chicagoans. And attendance quickly dropped to prefair levels.

Whatever qualifications might surround any assessment of the masterpiece exhibition, there was one immediate rhetorical benefit. At a time when disillusionment with businessmen, business practices, and the wealth-holding class had peaked in America, critics and editorialists sounded an unexpectedly friendly note when commenting on the aesthetics of the robber barons. Writing in

Neil Harris

1933, the year of the Chicago exhibition, on the opening of the Nelson Gallery of Art in Kansas City (today's Nelson-Atkins Museum of Art), the *Art Digest* declared that tycoons like Huntington, Frick, and Morgan had sensed the "cultural need of capitalistic America." Perhaps, it acknowledged, "it was inevitable that old art should appeal to them." Increasing art historical scholarship had "acted on these old capitalists as a hypodermic acts on an invalid." Unsurprisingly, they did not follow the footsteps of the Medici and become patrons of living art, the cause dearest to the *Art Digest*'s heart. Nonetheless, they gave "our nation great collections of art, in spite of the mistakes of which they were often guilty. . . . It is conceivable that some day, in a reconstituted society, they will be regarded as the heroes, the 'vikings' of an old and splendid and romantic era of individualism." Seen from the time of the New Deal, they were the "company of those who, under the 'old deal,' acted as worthy stewards of the wealth created by the Americans of their time."[46]

Coming from a fervent supporter of contemporary American art and the programs of the Franklin Delano Roosevelt administration, this statement was a remarkable concession. The pirates of American industry and finance, pilloried in muckraking texts for decades as rapacious and irresponsible, were now accorded social respectability for their cultural accumulations. The old masters offered a redemptive moment for the frequently demonized millionaires. And the Chicago formula of displaying older art of the highest reputation within expositions emphasizing modernity and progress was carried through in other great fairs of the decade, with some interesting variations.

Both the San Francisco and New York expositions paid homage, each in its own way, to the fabled Chicago success of 1933, by organizing retrospective surveys or selective old masters displays. The old masters retrospective was "the most distinguished success of the whole fair," Forbes Watson harangued the New York organizers just before the World of Tomorrow opened. "It was so successful . . . that the fair mongers were savagely jealous. Its attendance was phenomenal, the sales catalogs record breaking. It was Chicago's greatest achievement."[47] The New York organizers were slower to come to this conclusion, perhaps because so many New York art institutions planned special programs during the two seasons of the fair.[48] And the permanent collections of the Metropolitan (including the Cloisters), the Brooklyn Museum, the Frick, and the Morgan, to say nothing of the Whitney and the Guggenheim, and the ambitious extravaganzas of many local art dealers, offered tourists and resident New Yorkers impressive art coverage from both temporal and spatial angles. But irate letters and invidious comparisons with both Chicago and San Francisco forced fair authorities to act.[49] Angry critics of the early indifference to special fairground exhibitions recalled the Chicago show and pointed nervously to San Francisco's plans. After some prodding a group of volunteers, calling themselves Art Associates, Inc., convened to bring New Yorkers the taste of a great loan exhibition. Deeply involved in old masters planning was the director of the Detroit Institute of Arts, William Valentiner. A legendary figure in the national museum world, Valentiner quickly became disillusioned with the socialites, businessmen, and lawyers in charge of this operation. "Never in my life have I belonged to such a complicated private organization," he confided to his diary, describing the "calamities" he confronted.[50] The staff included some young lions of the American art world— Perry T. Rathbone, who would years later direct the Boston Museum of Fine Arts, and the critic Wolfgang von Eckardt —but the organizing donors, especially Alexander Hamilton Rice, Joseph Widener's brother-in-law, and the Marquis George de Cuevas, married to one of John D. Rockefeller's granddaughters, muddied the waters with their vanity, love lives, and intrigues, according to Valentiner; a spate of legal fights ensued.

Despite the contention and intrigue, a special $300,000 pavilion, the Masterpieces of Art Building, designed by Hood and Fouilhoux, was constructed just before the fair's opening. Far smaller than the forty thousand square feet devoted to more than one thousand artworks in American Art Today, the user-friendly Masterpieces building, with twenty-five rooms and a set of murals by Lyonel Feininger, lacked the intimidation a more monumental structure might have conveyed. Indeed, it set out directly to combat the dreaded "museum fatigue" that afflicted so many gallery visitors. Spanning the five centuries between 1300 and 1800, with insurance values reaching thirty million dollars, the four hundred paintings included eighty-eight shown in the United States for the first time. New York collectors, including Jules Bache (twenty-eight pictures were lent from the Bache collection), Edward Harkness, Samuel Kress, and Stephen Clark, along with Detroit friends of Valentiner (and the Detroit Institute of Arts), were especially generous, but unlike Chicago's, the show included loans from international venues like the National Gallery in London, the Louvre, and the Rijksmuseum in Amsterdam.[51] Pinkerton detectives watched over each room. Calling it a "Little Louvre," a *Time* critic was particularly impressed with the Dutch and Flemish paintings, most notably Van Eyck's *Ince Hall Madonna,* a tiny piece that had come all the way from Australia. Eleanor Clay Ford, the wife of Edsel Ford and a friend of Valentiner's, helped pay for hourly guided tours.[52] New York's Mayor La Guardia, skeptical about modern art, called the exhibit "the most sacred and precious spot at the Fair" when he presided over its opening.[53]

Visitors had many other art options in The World of Tomorrow. In addition to the hundreds of murals, mosaics, and sculptured pieces that were part of the broader landscape, both the British and French pavilions held extensive art displays, an IBM Gallery showed art from the more than seventy countries in which the company did business, and Holger Cahill's American Art Today was on display: an immense assembly of contemporary American art, jury-chosen from more than ten thousand entries.[54] At first glance this might appear to be a repetition of the formulas adopted at the expositions of an earlier generation, but in fact, the high value, established reputation, international origins, and millionaire associations of the old masters made them the fair's most striking and prestigious art display, as at Chicago. And if the impact was less dramatic than at Chicago, and the attendance less impressive, 425,000 visitors still saw the art.

As in Chicago, a second season produced revisions. Exhibitions were reorganized, and some were given different themes. The old masters, now 389 of them and almost all from American owners, were placed in eighteen galleries under the direction of Walter Pach, critic and art historian.[55] Among them were two dozen Kress pictures, some of them promised to the newly created National Gallery of Art. Innovative educational programs and newspaper publicity complemented the effort. The huge American show was pared down. But overall the New York show suf-

fered a bit, not only in comparison with Chicago but also with the publicity coming from San Francisco.[56]

The Golden Gate International Exposition had opened months earlier, in February 1939, taking advantage of California's gentler climate. A smaller fair in a smaller city, it retained strong aesthetic ambitions. As special features, San Francisco presented an impressive grouping of Pacific Basin art, under the direction of Langdon Warner, an array of contemporary American art, collected by Roland McKinney, and an IBM exhibition much like the one in New York.[57] All of this, as well as the masterpieces of art section, was arranged within a modified hangar on Treasure Island, curated by a single Fine Arts Department (fig. 4).[58]

The Masterpieces of Art, directed by Walter Heil, who headed both the De Young and Legion of Honor museums, contained some extraordinary pieces and attracted national attention, for political as well as aesthetic reasons.[59] Heil was able to secure loans from a number of important European institutions, but his most spectacular coup involved Italian paintings. Since the late 1920s the Mussolini government had been exploiting the country's art treasures in the interest of promoting a grandiose vision of Italy.[60] Given the authoritarian character of the Fascist state, the Italian government was able, with or without the acquiescence of curators and museum directors, to lend pictures of extraordinary importance. Thus the Italian exhibition at Burlington House in London in 1930, and a set of loans to a great retrospective in the Petit Palais in Paris in 1935, included masterpieces that no one expected to see outside Italy, works by Raphael, Mantegna, Botticelli, and others. Heil was able to get a group of these paintings, whose insured value stood at some twenty million dollars, for the San Francisco fair—many of which had traveled in the previous decade to London and Paris—most notably Botticelli's *Birth of Venus,* Titian's *Portrait of Pope Paul III,* and Raphael's *Madonna of the Chair.*[61] All in all, the Italian loans included more than twenty paintings and seven works of sculpture, including a Michelangelo Madonna. Heil "apparently helped himself to a couple of great Italian museums which he brought back under his arm."[62] Rumor had it, according to *Time,* that the loan was authorized to San Francisco rather than New York because Mussolini was irritated by Mayor La Guardia's fierce anti-Fascist

fig. 4 Aerial view, Treasure Island.
F. A. Gutheim, "The Buildings and the
Plan," *Magazine of Art*, March 1939.

stance. More likely, the *Time* reporter concluded, having spent "her full fair quota on a pavilion at the New York Fair, Italy had nothing but art to send to San Francisco."[63]

Although the Renaissance masterpieces certainly attracted visitors in San Francisco, they provoked interest throughout the country. Americans were reluctant to let them go. After the first season at San Francisco had ended, the Italian paintings made their way to other cities, including a seven-week stay in Chicago, from November 1939 to January 1940, and then another seven-week stay in New York's Museum of Modern Art, before sailing back to Italy on the SS *Rex* in April 1940.[64] Naturally, the Chicago exhibition brought large crowds of visitors back to the Art Institute, but even New Yorkers, who might have been jaded by the presence of so many great pictures at the Metropolitan and the Frick, were aroused. In its new building at 11 West 53rd Street, MoMA experienced record-breaking crowds. More than 250,000 visitors took advantage of the extended hours, as the museum remained open until 10 P.M. And during the first week the Renaissance masters went on display, MoMA experienced the largest daily attendance in its ten years of existence, 7,206 visitors. San Francisco crowds had been large, but it took some time for the masterworks to outdraw Sally Rand's Nude Ranch.[65] New York rose to the occasion. In the end more than 250,000 viewed the collection, and MoMA invited visitors to vote for their favorite works.[66] By the time the *Rex* sailed, American newspapers had inflated the value of the old masters from twenty million to twenty-six million dollars, as editorialists bid a tearful good-bye to the wandering art.[67] It had been in this country more than fifteen months.

Other parts of the San Francisco old masters group, as well as some of the New York masterpieces, went on their own national tour. Newark and Detroit were among the cities that hosted special exhibitions.[68] The appetite for great loan shows was beginning to influence museum programming significantly.

The true fruition of this trend would come only in the 1960s and 1970s, when entrepreneurial directors, inflationary pressures, innovative promotional techniques, and federal indemnification combined to nurture an extraordinary run of "blockbuster" exhibitions. Like the old masters shows at the fairs, they were aggressively promoted and abundantly attended. Unlike the fair shows, they stim-

ulated extensive controversy, with critics raising questions about commercial tie-ins, expense, distraction from permanent collections, and ambiguous long-term effects on membership. These issues, for various reasons, did not arise in the 1930s. The shows were widely considered redemptive rather than vulgarizing, welcome alternatives to the heavy corporate advertising that was so palpable a presence elsewhere in the expositions.

Timing, particularly in 1939 and 1940, also played its part in strengthening the shows' appeal. With the World of Tomorrow suddenly at war, the old masters suggested a transcendent realm far removed from the violent destruction about to overwhelm humanity.[69] "At a time when reactionary forces in so many parts of the world seem to be turning back the clock of civilization," the *New York Times* observed, commenting on the crowds seeking masterpieces in San Francisco and New York, "these evidences of a great and rapidly growing interest in art in our own country are doubly impressive."[70] The presence of fragile relics that had, in some cases, survived some five hundred years of dangerous history, held out a promise that outdid the boasts of the engineers and technicians. Those Italian masterpieces in particular—"among the noblest the world has produced," a "perfect flowering of that spirit which burst the chrysalis of the Dark Ages"—consoled, inspired, and even hinted at the return, sometime in the future, of a brighter age to succeed the descent into darkness.[71]

Notes

My thanks to Teri J. Edelstein for her indispensable aid in producing this essay.

1. *World's Columbian Exposition, Official Publications: Revised Catalogue, Department of Fine Arts* (Chicago: Conkey, 1893), 147–154. The lenders constituted a who's who of American collectors —John G. Johnson, S. D. Warren, Alfred Corning Clark, Potter Palmer, Henry O. Havemeyer, Charles Yerkes, Martin A. Ryerson, and Henry G. Marquand; only a few works came from institutions. Dominated by Barbizon School painters, the exhibit did include some Impressionists, but not more than a dozen canvases.

2. E. L. Austin and Odell Hauser, *The Sesqui-Centennial International Exposition* (Philadelphia: Current Publications, 1929), 233–234.

3. These exhibitions are discussed, among other places, in Francis Haskell, *The Ephemeral Museum: Old Master Paintings and the Rise of the Art Exhibition* (New Haven: Yale University Press, 2000).

4. This was W. R. Valentiner, "The Importance of Exhibitions of Old Masters," *American Magazine of Art* 20 (March 1929): 127–131. Valentiner, director of the Detroit Institute of Arts, offered a summary of international loan shows in the nineteenth and twentieth centuries, and reviewed Detroit's recent efforts to host major loan shows. He also pointed out that art dealers had been responsible for organizing many recent major retrospectives.

5. For a recent overview of this fair, and extensive annotations, see Schrenk, *Building a Century of Progress*.

6. These data come from annual reports and press articles. See, for example, *American Magazine of Art* 11 (April 1920), reporting that the Art Institute's attendance for 1919 was 1,040,000; the Metropolitan Museum of Art's, according to the same journal (11 [July 1920]: 322–323), was 880,000. In 1928 the Art Institute had a membership of 18,000; the Met, nearly 14,000. See *Chicago Daily News*, November 29, 1928, for a direct comparison of the two institutions.

7. In mid-1930 this was still being presented as the plan by some newspapers. See "Notes On Current Art," *New York Times*, July 13, 1930.

8. Charles Victor Knox, "Mona Lisa May Be Here for 1933 Fair," newspaper source unclear, January 14, 1930, clipping file, Art Institute of Chicago.

9. *Chicago Daily News*, January 19, 1931.

10. See *Art Digest* 6 (January 15, 1932).

11. Malcolm McDowell, "World's Fair Will Use the Art Institute," *Chicago Daily News*, July 8, 1932.

12. *Trustee Minutebooks* 12 (June 23, 1931), archives, Art Institute of Chicago. Director Harshe had suggested this arrangement at a meeting of the Committee on Paintings and Sculpture; *Trustee Minutebooks* 12 (June 2, 1931). There were still high ambitions present among some trustees, for the committee recommended a request of $100,000 to be expended on the "most important exhibition of art ever held in America." But this recommendation was not passed on to the full board.

13. *Trustee Minutebooks* 12 (June 10, 1932), records the contract with the Century of Progress Exposition, committing the trustees to spend no more than fifty thousand dollars to cover expenses in connection with the exhibition. Some of the money was to be spent on special equipment, additional guard services, and improved restrooms, the rest to meet costs incurred in assembling the art.

14. *Trustee Minutebooks* 12 (March 29, 1932). The trustees discussed attendance figures for art exhibits at other world's fairs. The previous week a Century of Progress Committee of the Art Institute had voted to recommend borrowing old masters in Europe and America, and projected that receipts would not be less than fifty thousand dollars. They proposed expending seventy-five thousand dollars to display the art. *Trustee Minutebooks* 12 (March 21, 1932).

15. Charles Fabens Kelley, "Art at the Chicago Exposition," *Christian Science Monitor*, February 20, 1933.

16. The painting hung in the Museum of Modern Art starting in November 1933 and was viewed by more than 100,000 people. This did not diminish its sensational reception in Chicago.

17. See for example, Kelley, "Art at the Chicago Exposition," among many others.

18. "Famous Titian Going to Chicago," *New York Post*, February 28, 1933; "World-Famous Paintings," *Chicago Herald and Examiner*, April 8, 1933; *New York Times*, February 28, 1933.

19. Ernest L. Heitkamp, "33 Fair Art Show to Be Greatest Ever," *Chicago Herald and Examiner*, February 15, 1933.

20. In January 1933, the figure cited was fifty million dollars, but this soon expanded.

21. *Art Digest* 8 (May 15, 1933): 19.

22. "Double Guard for 50 Million Fair Art Show," *Chicago Herald and Examiner*, May 7, 1933.

23. "Institute Exhibition at Fair Surpasses Europe's Galleries," *Chicago Herald and Examiner*, May 17, 1933.

24. "The Art Exhibition," *Chicago Tribune*, June 11, 1933.

25. Quoted in Edward Alden Jewell, "Art of 1893 and 1933: Two World's Fairs," *Parnassus* 5 (October 1933): 8.

26. Carlyle Burrows, "A Brilliant Display of Art in Chicago," *New York Times*, May 18, 1933.

27. C. J. Bulliet, "A Century of Progress in Collecting," *Parnassus* 5 (May 1933): 1 7. Bulliet wrote for many years in the *Chicago Evening Post Magazine of the Art World*, published weekly. After the *Post* collapsed, he wrote for the *Chicago Daily News*.

28. These figures are taken from the Art Institute annual reports.

29. For an example of the statistical frenzy see "World's Biggest Art Lover Crowd Jams Fair Show," *Chicago Tribune*, October 30, 1933.

30. The one millionth visitor received, among other things, a framed reproduction of *Whistler's Mother*; *Art Digest* 7 (September 1, 1933): 20.

31. For some of the statistics see "Art Show Crowd," *Chicago Tribune*, October 31, 1933. The day before, some 40,279 viewed the show.

32. The photograph was reproduced in the *Art Digest* 7 (November 15, 1933): 11.

33. For more on the lectures see Eleanor Jewett, "Illustrated Lectures Explain Paintings," *Chicago Tribune*, August 13, 1933. Bulliet's book, *Art Masterpieces in a Century of Progress: Fine Arts Exhibition at the Art Institute of Chicago*, 2 vols. (Chicago: North Mariano, 1933), was, according to Sue Ann Prince, the best-selling nonfiction book in Chicago during the summer of 1933; Sue Ann Prince, "'Of the Which and the Why of Daub and Smear': Chicago Critics Take On Modernism," in *The Old Guard and the Avant-Garde: Modernism in Chicago, 1910–1940*, ed. Sue Ann Prince (Chicago: University of Chicago Press, 1990), 112.

34. Albert Franz Cochrane, "Chicago Opens Its Second Great Exhibit of

53

Masterpieces," newspaper source obscured, Art Institute of Chicago clipping book.

35. Quoted in Peyton Boswell, "Two Museum Men," *Art Digest* 8 (June 1, 1934): 3.

36. Cochrane, "Chicago Opens Its Second Great Exhibit."

37. "Dead Hand Jarred," *Art Digest* 8 (December 15, 1933): 14. See the discussion of the new hanging in Richard R. Brettell and Sue Ann Prince, "From the Armory Show to the Century of Progress: The Art Institute Assimilates Modernism," in *The Old Guard and the Avant-Garde,* 222–225.

38. *Bulletin of the Art Institute of Chicago for the Year 1933* 28 (March 1934): 33–34.

39. For the art displayed see *Catalogue of a Century of Progress Exhibition of Paintings and Sculpture 1934* (Chicago: Art Institute of Chicago, 1934). The author of the foreword noted that while the previous year's exhibition stressed progress in American picture collecting, "This year native achievement is the theme"; ibid., ix.

40. See, for example, Ernest L. Heitkamp, "More Popular Show for Fair Foreseen," *Chicago Herald and Examiner,* May 27, 1934.

41. Quoted in "$75,000,000 Fair Art Exhibit to Open Next Week," *Chicago Tribune,* May 26, 1934.

42. *Chicago Herald and Examiner,* April 22, 1934; *Chicago Tribune,* April 29, 1934.

43. *Bulletin of the Art Institute of Chicago: Report for the Year 1934* 29 (March 1935): 33.

44. The newspaper editorial was reprinted in *Art Digest* 9 (November 15, 1934): 11, 15. Another critic who found the American display weaker than it should have been, and inferior to the European art of the previous year, was F. A. Gutheim, "Another Year of Progress," *American Magazine of Art* 27 (July 1934): 414–422.

45. The board of trustees of the Art Institute took this action December 5, 1933. See *Trustee Minutebooks* 13 (December 5, 1933), 26.

46. *Art Digest* 8 (February 15, 1934): 3–4. The quotation was reprinted for the opening of the Walters Art Museum in Baltimore; it had been printed originally in December 1933.

47. Forbes Watson, "Realism Today and Tomorrow," *American Magazine of Art* 32 (May 1939): 261. Watson's editorial was an impassioned defense of artistic values and quality against business pandering to consumer tastes and thralldom to salesmanship.

48. The most important among these was undoubtedly the Museum of Modern Art's tenth anniversary show, Art in Our Time, which attracted many fair goers. See, for example, James W. Lane, "Summer Shows in the New York Museums," *Parnassus* 11 (May 1939): 26–28.

49. See some of the letters in a special grouping, "Our Reader's Forum: Art at the Fair," *New York Times,* February 6, 1938. Some of the angriest protests came from those concerned that American artists, particularly contemporary artists, would be omitted. Letter writers included prominent figures, among them the playwright Elmer Rice, the critic George Soule, and the gallery director Edith Halpert. For Grover Whalen's decision to reverse the fair corporation's earlier position and create a building for American art, see "World's Fair Provides a Building for Contemporary American Art," *New York Times,* April 12, 1938.

50. Quoted in Margaret Sterne, *The Passionate Eye: The Life of William*

R. Valentiner (Detroit: Wayne State University Press, 1980), 258. Valentiner's diary entries about the old masters show are recorded on pages 258–265.

51. For an overview of the exhibition just before its opening, and a history of the effort, see Malcolm Vaughan, "Old Masters at the Fair," *Parnassus* 11 (May 1939): 5–13.

52. "Mrs. Edsel Ford Aids Art Show," *New York Times,* July 11, 1939.

53. For an account of the mayor's participation in the opening see "400 Treasures Go on View to Public," *New York Times,* June 5, 1939.

54. The French presentation, planned to include 150 paintings and a series of period rooms, was particularly elaborate. See "Fair Will Exhibit Noted French Art," *New York Times,* March 31, 1939.

55. "New Masterpieces for Fair Art Show," *New York Times,* March 7, 1940.

56. For a detailed comparison between the old masters at New York and at San Francisco (and some reassurance directed to the New Yorkers), see Edward Alden Jewell, "Masters," *New York Times,* June 18, 1939.

57. Like organizers of the other two fairs, San Francisco organizers scheduled a second season of art exhibitions in 1940. Here the most significant feature may have been an Art in Action exhibition, featuring artists, among them Diego Rivera, actually engaged in creating art. See "Artists on Parade," *Time* 56 (June 24, 1940): 69.

58. For a survey of art at the Golden Gate Exposition see the various articles in the *Magazine of Art* 32 (March 1939).

59. See *Masterworks of Five Centuries: Official Catalog, Department of Fine Arts, Division of European Art* (San Francisco: Golden Gate International Exposition, 1939). This catalog is heavily illustrated, and each of the 191 entries indicates where and when the work was previously exhibited, offering information, for example, on which of the Italian paintings had been shown at Burlington House and at the Italian Exhibition. Some of the art had also been seen during one of the two Century of Progress exhibitions in Chicago, in 1934 and 1935.

60. This is described in some detail by Francis Haskell, "Botticelli in the Service of Fascism," in *The Ephemeral Museum,* 107–127.

61. For a recollection of the show's impact see Richard Reinhardt, *Treasure Island: San Francisco's Exposition Years* (San Francisco: Scrimshaw, 1973), 80, 131–132.

62. *American Magazine of Art* 32 (March 1939): 131. This was taken from the Forbes Watson editorial, which also argued that San Franciscans recalled how Chicago's 1933 fair was "literally made by the astounding collection of art" assembled by the Art Institute.

63. *Time* 33 (March 6, 1939): 24.

64. See "Masterpieces of Italian Painting at the Art Institute of Chicago," *Parnassus* 11 (December 1939): 20–21. See also "12,000 Crush to See Italian Art Treasures," *Chicago Tribune,* November 18, 1939.

65. Reinhardt, *Treasure Island,* 132.

66. "Italian Masters Go Back April 13," *New York Times,* April 2, 1940. For the results of the vote, won by Titian's *Portrait of Pope Paul III,* as well as other popular selections, see "Popular Vote-Anomaly," *New York Times,* September 8, 1940.

67. "$26,000,000 in Art Leaves on the Rex," *New York Times,* April 14, 1940.

68. "Detroit to See Fairs' Art," *New York Times,* October 24, 1939.

69. Some of the art displayed in New York in 1939–1940 was retained rather than sent back to Europe. See "Louvre Works Ours for War,"

Neil Harris

New York Times, August 10, 1941. A series of paintings by Fragonard, Chardin, Watteau, and others, lent by the Louvre, was placed in the Metropolitan Museum of Art. The National Gallery of Art took trusteeship of some French and Belgian art and displayed examples in Washington during the war. See the brief description in *The National Gallery of Art: A Twenty-Five Years Report* (Washington, D.C.: National Gallery of Art, 1966), 44.

70. "Art in America," *New York Times,* November 1, 1939.
71. "Art from the Masters," *New York Times,* January 3, 1940.

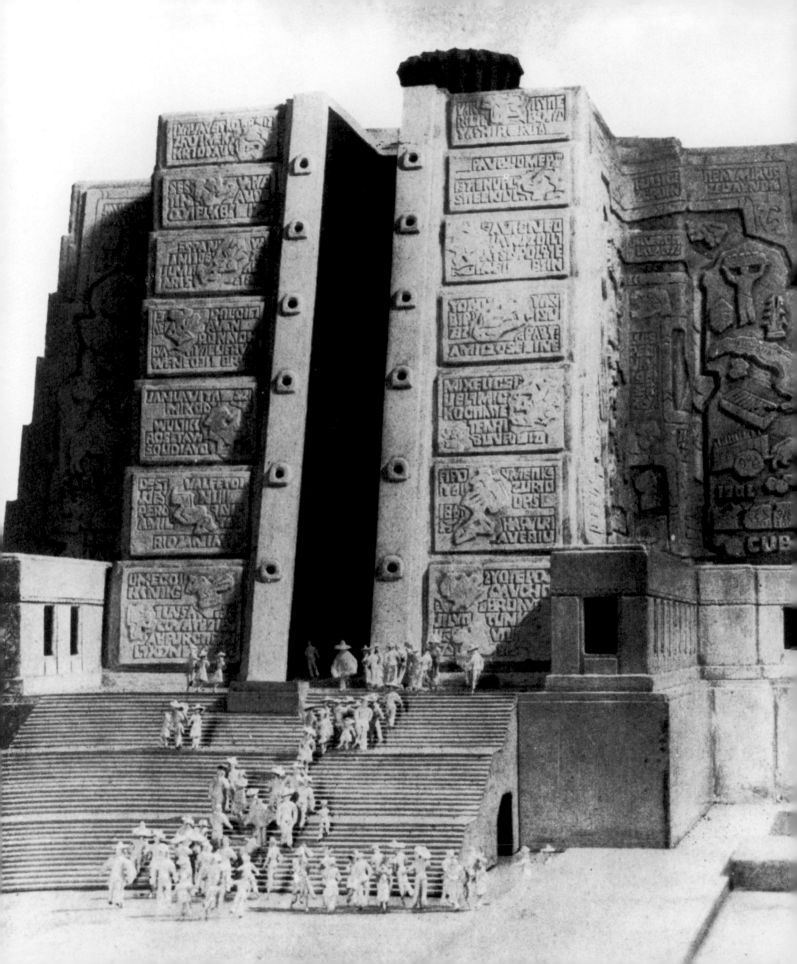

Beyond the Midway
Pan-American Modernity in the 1930s

Robert A. González

The wistfully optimistic world's fairs of the 1930s are today receding from public memory, much like the efforts of Pan-Americanism in that decade, which encouraged a vision of unity and security in the Western Hemisphere. Pan American Airways (Pan Am) also attempted to strengthen these hemispheric ties during the Great Depression, along with the film industry, both promising adventurous tropical excursions as well as potential business ventures for those so inclined. By 1939–1940, at San Francisco's Golden Gate International Exposition, America's economic opportunities with Pacific Rim nations were put on display, prompted in part by Pan Am's exploration of this new international market. The film industry had already captured the swift redirection of Pan Am's "skyward" potential, from Latin America to Asia, in two luring films, *Flying Down to Rio* (1933) and *China Clipper* (1936). The San Francisco fairgrounds, which were to be converted into an airport to host Pan Am's western hub, set the stage with a mesmerizing modern architecture that meshed stylistic motifs, from Southeast Asian to pre-Columbian to Streamline Moderne. This made-to-order American modernism was essentially a transpacific synthesis of recognizable historic forms especially conceived for the San Francisco fair. Its hybridized design strategy resembled what Pan-American enthusiasts had been exploring with their built explorations of the Western Hemisphere. This Pan-American architectural exercise, however, had been taking place since the turn of the century.

The fairs of the 1930s, particularly in the latter half of the decade, began to explore Pan-American architecture with few, if any, historical clichés, largely due to the popularity of the Streamline Moderne of the period. We see a distinct modern language emerge that explores hemisphericism in symbolic terms. By 1930 hundreds of architects had already participated in helping to identify a Pan-American architecture, especially with a competition organized by the Washington, D.C.–based Pan-American Union (PAU) to design a Columbus Memorial Lighthouse. The design entries confirmed that at the start of that new decade there was no consensus on what Pan-American architecture should look like. It was easily expressed in numerous styles, the favored being the Spanish Colonial and the neo-Mayan and neo-Aztec. The world's fairs of the 1930s presented a stage on which a new Pan-American language was briefly explored. Although examples of Pan-American architecture were spotty at these fairs, the movement itself was pervasive in the boosterism that saturated the tabloids and world's fair propaganda—Pan-Americanism was certainly in the air, if not always on the ground.

In examining expressions of Pan-Americanism at these world's fairs, we see the mutually constitutive nature of ideas and buildings, especially relative to the movement's intended message of unity and equality of the American republics. Identifying this is at times difficult, however, given the panoply of cultural representations commonly found in a fair, especially in the zone of cultural entertainment that came to be known as the Midway after Chicago's Columbian Exposition of 1893. Some may confuse Pan-American architecture with the racialized representations of Latin American cultures in these Midway-like sections or the nationalist buildings constructed by and for the Latin American countries in other parts of the fairgrounds. Born out of different design intentions, Pan-American architecture's straightforward premise is more easily detectable when one looks beyond cultural stereotypes. The American modernism of the 1930s, with its emphasis on progress and futurism, gave architects a new way of expressing Pan-Americanism. The question we might ask is to what extent the new Pan-American architecture ushered Latin Americans out of the Midway and the national zones and secured them in a place constructed for all Pan-Americans.

In the United States, the malleable Pan-American concept has been continuously reinterpreted in the built environment since the late nineteenth century to serve national and local aspirations, and it was readily repackaged to address issues of import during the particularly difficult decade of the 1930s. With roots in early-nineteenth-century South America, introduced when Simón Bolívar envisioned a unified front against Spain and the United States, a U.S.-generated Pan-Americanism was later popularized around the time of the Pan-American Conference in Washington, D.C., in 1889–1890.[1] In the decades that followed, various national and local entities throughout the United States began to promote hemispheric unity in the name of commerce, cultural exchange, and later, social and scientific progress. Civic officials and merchant groups were Pan-Americanism's greatest supporters, since they hoped to expand trade with Latin American countries and to

establish their own cities as commercial and cultural hubs. Pan-American boosters also projected hemispheric identities that gained credence and character over time. They fabricated American identities that were typically tied to the Western Hemisphere's distinct cultural, geographic, or political composition. Architecture was frequently enlisted to set the stage for this new Pan-American identity. The historian Arthur P. Whitaker, writing in the 1950s, called this phenomenon the "Western Hemisphere idea." At the core of Pan-Americanism, he wrote, is "the proposition that the peoples of this Hemisphere stand in a special relation to one another which sets them apart from the rest of the world."[2] Hemispherically themed architecture was thus meant to embody this special relationship between the peoples of the Americas, and it was commonly expressed as the union of representative nations. In a Depression-era decade, the concept would eventually play a significant role in reinforcing hemispheric solidarity by pointing to this "logical" partnership.

Pan-America Emerges: From New Orleans to Santo Domingo

Pan-American architectural history extends roughly from the late nineteenth century to the 1970s, with a few later examples. The first half of this period, which takes us to the eve of the decade in question, the 1930s, begins and ends with built projects located in and around the Gulf of Mexico and the Caribbean. It begins with the back-to-back fairs that took place in New Orleans—the World's Cotton Exposition of 1884–1885 and the North, Central and South American Exposition of 1885–1886. At both the original fair and extension, which took place on the same site, two Mexican pavilions that gained immediate notice in the press stood in important locations on the fairgrounds. In the gardens one found a small pavilion, the Mexican Alhambra, and a large structure, the Mexican Barracks, which presented an urban edifice to the Mississippi River. Mexican dignitaries inhabited the second pavilion. In addition to these structures, fair visitors found nearly one-third of the main floor space of the fair's Main Exhibition Hall devoted to Latin American exhibitions. It was logical to see such a prominent Latin American presence at this fair. New Orleans was one of the few U.S. cities with a notable Caribbean influence, and sitting at the mouth of the

Robert A. González

Mississippi, it could serve as the perfect juncture between the United States and Latin America. Ever since the city had produced the nation's first Spanish-language newspaper, *El Misisipi,* in 1808, New Orleans had kept Latin American activity on its radar. It was the instinct to extend the Cotton Exposition and emphasize the city's unique relationship with Latin America that set the stage for the first Pan-American, or hemispheric, fair.

The New Orleans fair is also important because of the manner in which it presented the modern Latin American. The portrayal of a modern lifestyle and erasure of depictions that placed the Latin American low on the development scale was central to promoting the Pan-American message of unity and equality. In future fairs, the indigenous peoples of Latin America would be showcased amidst exotic "others," the pygmies and pinheads exhibited for wonderment's sake. Few world's fairs kept the Latin American out of these zones of freak shows, where "developing" nations and their populace would be displayed in demeaning circumstances. For example, when the Latin American Department was established for Chicago's Columbian Exposition of 1893, the opportunity of exhibiting Latin America was approached with an exploitative slant. Incidentally, this department was headed by William E. Curtis, who was at the time the director of the Bureau of the American Republics (later, the PAU). In anticipation of the fair, the *Chicago Daily Tribune* reported on the "Gorgeous Dress of Savage Tribes," which had already been secured by the Latin American Department for the fair. The enlisted Midway subjects, to be showcased in their costumes made of monkey's teeth and human hair, were indigenous to the Amazon jungles of South America.[3] On another occasion, the *New York Times* reported: "Last of the Caribs for the World's Fair."[4] These "last survivors of the natives discovered by Columbus" were also going to be displayed in the Midway. Such carnivalesque approaches would have been avoided in a fair controlled by organizers who truly sought Latin American business prospects; and some Latin American officials and heads of state began to demand a more humane portrayal.[5]

After the Mexican dignitaries were included in the New Orleans expositions of the mid-1880s, the "modern" Latin American was again showcased in 1901 at Buffalo's Pan-American Exposition, when world's fair organizers pro-

duced the publication *Modern Mexico* for distribution. It may have surprised visitors that at this fair the Latin "breed" was presented in business suits and not loincloths, although a group of Mexicans did appear in traditional costume in a Midway exhibition called The Streets of Mexico. Of the early hemispheric fairs, Buffalo's exposition was the first actually to attempt to explore Pan-American architecture. The hemispheric theme at the New Orleans extension fair was clearly an afterthought; the original fairgrounds had not been designed to explore this concept. In contrast, when the original Pan-American Exposition was planned for Cayuga Island, New York, in 1897 (before it was postponed by the Spanish-American War, then moved to Buffalo), its organizers began with the Pan-American premise. This led to their unprecedented proposal of a single pavilion design dedicated to representing all the republics of the Americas as an integrated structure. For the first time, Latin America would be presented front and center and on equal footing with the United States at a hemispheric fair.

Upon its move to Buffalo, the world's fair was significantly reconceptualized with no regard for the original intentions. A team of architects, led by John M. Carrère, set out to design a fair that instead tried to improve upon and outdo Chicago's World's Columbian Exposition. In the end, a liberally used Spanish-Renaissance style for the fair's architecture was the strongest reference to the "Pan" in the Buffalo fair's title. Carrère and his team considered this style appropriate because it had been the style of the Spanish colonial territories of the New World. Pan-Americanism may have also been considered when the designers conceived the fairgrounds as a colorful rather than a white enterprise, the signature theme that had given the Chicago exposition its popular moniker "The White City." The element of color, however, was more often than not used in the fair's literature to reference the (colorful) urban diversity of the American city. The Latin American nations were not even given a prominent location at the fair; instead, a garden area far from the center of activities was reserved for their modest pavilions. The most prominent fairground space was dominated by the U.S. Pavilion and a grand water feature meant to represent Niagara Falls. This was a fitting ode to North America's grand natural wonder and producer of electrical power. To top it off, the

United States proudly flexed its muscles with a fireworks display titled The American Empire. This imperialist celebration of the newly acquired U.S. possessions of Cuba, the Philippines, and Puerto Rico took the form of an explosive presentation of the outlines of the newly acquired lands against the night sky.

A more thoroughly explored Pan-American architecture was finally introduced with the two Pan-American Union–sponsored competitions that followed. The first, the International Bureau of American Republics Competition for the organization's national headquarters (1907–1910), was limited to practicing architects in the United States. A review of the various design proposals submitted to the Pan-American Union competition shows a preference for Spanish Colonial and Beaux-Arts. The winning design, proposed by Paul Philippe Cret and Albert Kelsey, is memorable, however, not for the submitted plan but for a period of postcompetition redesign that transformed the original submission. The completed building was a notably changed structure that fulfilled the architects' goal—to bring the tropics to Washington, D.C. To do this, Kelsey traveled to Latin America to look for indigenous sources and to explore appropriate tropical styles with which to "complete" the design. His goal was to transform the building with indigenous depictions that represented all of the Americas— what might be called an attempt to represent a pan-native America. This included the introduction of indigenous ornamental alterations, theatrical elaborations that relied on such devices as colorful lights and water features (a design strategy characteristic of world's fairs), as well as tropical plants and live macaws in the building's courtyard.

Upon entering the PAU Building's courtyard, one was exposed to the same type of visual dynamics. The courtyard was staged so as to bring one's attention to an important centerpiece. The sculptor Gertrude Whitney had been commissioned to design an Aztec fountain in the center of this space, a feature that helped bring together unique pan-native expressions, multinationalist representations, and other trappings of diplomacy (fig. 1). The fountain presented Aztec indigenous figures and iconography, and would have been experienced against a backdrop of Incan and Mayan references found on the floor and the vertical surfaces. The fountain's water feature could also be illuminated to reflect the national colors of visiting plenipoten-

tiaries. Working independently of Cret, Kelsey continued this line of theatrics to the exterior of the building. He designed the Aztec Garden, the grounds surrounding a reflecting pool behind the main structure. To complement the pool, Kelsey specified blue-colored finishes in the nearby balustrade and mosaic work that was meant to create the illusion of tropical waters. The pool and gardens were made sacral grounds with the placement of a statue of the Aztec god of flowers, Xochipilli. In an early proposal it was reported that with a flick of a switch the statue was supposed to ascend from within the reflecting pool as the blue lights of the grounds grew in intensity. Countering these extensive pan-native expressions, which had even spilled out to the building's rear spaces, the promise of unity and equality was visually hijacked when it came to the building's main facade. The binary display on the building's Beaux-Arts main elevation—the classically featured oppositional North and South American statue—is most clearly translated as the United States versus Latin America. The depiction of the hemisphere in this oppositional relationship did not live up to the mission of unity. Given the numerous ways that the Western Hemisphere was depicted throughout the building, with the repeated logo depicting the Western Hemisphere's silhouette, with a map of the American continents in the Columbus Library on the ground floor, and with the flags of the American republics in the Gallery of Patriots and National Flags on the second floor, the architects could have sustained an antihistoricist strategy for depicting the Americas. The interest in playing up stereotypes with the tropical, indigenous, and colonial references could not be resisted.

A few years later, when Albert Kelsey was asked to design a building for the organization of the Brotherhood of North American Indians (BNAI), he addressed the pan-native aesthetic more directly. While this project was never built, Kelsey commented on the opportunity he felt he now faced. He remarked that he could now produce what he and Cret were not able to fully achieve with the Pan-American Union project. With this, he acknowledged that the PAU Building had been transformed to meet a challenge that he felt was still unresolved. His solution is not entirely convincing. Kelsey designed the new BNAI structure as a mirror replica of the PAU Building, but in a Spanish Mission style. His intention was to fully explore a pan-

Robert A. González

fig. 1 Courtyard, Pan-American Union Building, Washington, D.C., May 1943. Behind Gertrude Whitney's Aztec Fountain, one can see the indigenous ornament at the base of the wall, and, at the cornice, the national crests of the American Republics. Photograph by John Collier. Farm Security Administration, Office of War Information Collection, Prints and Photographs Division, Library of Congress, LC-DIG-fsac-1a34530.

native theme throughout the building's interior and not just in the main public spaces, as with the PAU's courtyard and garden. In future Pan-American architectural explorations, as we shall see with the San Diego and Dallas world's fairs, architects continued to explore different ways of incorporating pre-Columbian and Native American representations to express a unifying picture of the Western Hemisphere. These citations were often used as no more than representative "cultural" common denominators of the Americas.

It took the second competition, open to the citizens of the world, to finally inspire a more thorough exploration of the full meaning of Pan-Americanism in built form. Given his experience with the first Pan-American Building, Kelsey was hired by the PAU to serve as technical director for the second competition. As he had done before, he embarked on another trip to Latin America to gain inspiration for the competition directive he was about to write. Kelsey's and the PAU's promotional efforts paid off, and the Columbus Memorial Lighthouse Competition yielded 455 entries from forty-nine countries. This surpassed in scope and in the number of contributors other notable U.S. competitions, including the recent Chicago Tribune Competition. The architects of the world were asked to consider a monument in the Dominican Republic's capital city of Santo Domingo—the so-called birthplace of the Americas. The monument was supposed to combine an airfield, a lighthouse, a crypt where Christopher Columbus's bodily remains would be kept, and a museum. The competition actively pursued entries from many countries and delivered the largest number from Latin America ever seen in an international competition. An overview of the Columbus Memorial Lighthouse competition entries reveals four categories that dominated the design schemes. Three had already been explored with the hemispheric fairs and the Pan-American Union building: homage to Christopher Columbus and/or Spanish heritage; the presence of an indigenous hemispheric subject; and the opposition of North and South America (not necessarily presented in U.S.–Latin American terms in the entries). These themes were explored in any number of styles, and the choices ran the gamut, from Beaux-Arts to Mayan revival to Streamline Moderne.

In the first round, judges Raymond Hood, Eliel Saarinen, and Horacio Acosta y Lara selected a group of projects that reflected their own interests in revivalist architecture. It is at this point in the process that we see a rejection by the jurors of a fourth thematic category that had not yet surfaced. In the second round, when Frank Lloyd Wright replaced Hood, the jurors' assessment shifted to one that favored the neo-Mayan earth forms that Wright himself was exploring. The winning entry belonged to a British architecture student, Joseph Lea Gleave. His scheme was a cruciform structure that seemingly emerged from the ground, but in combining the aerodynamic form of an airfield with a lighthouse and a pan-native form, the scheme brought together historical and modern elements. Gleave represented the continents' indigenous heritages in pan-native fashion, with abstract surface articulations and stepped dynamic forms that eluded known typological categories. The structure's signature feature was a giant cruciform-shaped light that was supposed to brighten the night sky on special occasions. Gleave's design entry falls into this fourth design strategy because it managed to present an abstraction of the Western Hemisphere expressed in terms of technological progress and in a modern language. This category also included projects from prominent figures like Alvar Aalto, Tony Garnier, and Konstantin Melnikov, surprisingly overlooked by the jury. Aalto and Garnier, for example, explored this concept in two spiral-oriented designs, both in concrete, that were devoid of historical symbolism. While the original model that Gleave presented to the jury in 1930 was undoubtedly neo-Mayan, he later transformed his design when he was asked to present it at Chicago's Century of Progress Exposition in 1933 (figs. 2, 3). The scale model built in Chicago was unmistakably Streamline Moderne. It is very likely that Gleave was influenced by what he saw on the grounds when he arrived in Chicago to build his model. In its new form, the lighthouse model resembled Holabird and Root's Chrysler Motors Building (fig. 4). Gleave's design illustrates how the pan-native representation was easily incorporated into the Streamline Moderne language, resulting in an architecture that could simultaneously reflect the indigenous and the technological, in this case, with its massive light beams. While the neo-Mayan style weighed down the original design entry with historicist baggage, the abstracted Chicago model presented a successful stage in the movement beyond stylistic clichés.

Robert A. González

above

fig. 2 Competition model, Columbus Memorial Lighthouse, 1930. Joseph Lea Gleave, architect. Note the indigenous ornamentation on the walls, and the circular indentations along the central entrance, which are noticeably missing in the Chicago scaled model. Photo courtesy of the Joseph Lea Gleave estate, from the collection of the Patronato Faro a Colon, Santo Domingo, Dominican Republic.

right

fig. 3 A model of the Columbus Memorial Lighthouse to be erected on the Island of Dominica by the Dominican Republic, just west of the Hall of Social Sciences between building and lagoon, June 20, 1933. Century of Progress Exposition, Chicago, 1933–1934. Keystone-Mast Collection, UCR/California Museum of Photography, University of California, Riverside.

fig. 5 Hollywood Motion Picture Hall of Fame. California-Pacific International Exposition, San Diego, 1935–1936. © San Diego Historical Society.

Picture Hall of Fame (fig. 5). Opposite this, the neo-Mayan-styled Federal Building completed the composition (see plate 28). Here the common denominators of the Americas came together—the northern and southern indigenous cultures. Not entirely forgotten, this once "unifying" space is today a parking lot called the Pan-American Plaza. It is not unlike the hundreds of similarly named plazas, streets, and avenues across the Americas that make reference to Pan-Americanism. Clearly, the organizers of San Diego's second fair had no intention of making it an homage to the Western Hemisphere, which is confirmed by the fair's popular, U.S.-referencing moniker: "America's Exposition." Whitaker's writings on the Western Hemisphere Idea emphasized the common experiences shared by North and South America, and the colonial experience resonated with this conception. Colonization presented a level of homogeneity of another, albeit problematic, dimension. Although indigenous experiences are by nature not homogenous and are regionally specific, indigenous representations were more often than not inaccurately used to broadly refer to "anyplace" America. The Spanish colonial past was actually a shared heritage that materialized with some consistency across the Americas and that pointed to inter-hemispheric experiences that surpassed modern borders. In many instances, we see either reference, colonial or indigenous, used randomly as a cultural signifier to represent the Pan-American sentiment.

Competing Gateways: Miami and Dallas Streamline the Pan-American

In Florida and Texas, planners more explicitly explored a Pan-American agenda beyond the realm of architecture and world's fairs. It is arguable that a faster-growing Hispanic population in Florida and Texas, with strong cultural ties to Cuba and Mexico, respectively, resulted in a more ambitious appropriation of the Pan-American rhetoric in both states. In Texas the prevalence of a Spanish Colonial aesthetic as part of the cultural landscape was partly due to the presence of the Catholic missions, and the popularization of one in particular, the Alamo. This is not to say that California's cultural landscape was not influenced by the same structures and the noted *Ramona*-inspired mission designs.[9] In Florida, the colonial legacy was largely attributed to importations of styles, such as Henry Flagler's

neo-Colonial-, Spanish-, and Mediterranean-inspired hotels, and to actual heritage sites, namely Saint Augustine, the nation's oldest city.

Throughout the 1930s the term *Pan-American* regularly appeared in the national press and was often associated with Miami's activities. The city's Pan-American Day events received generous coverage in the *New York Times,* as did reports of Pan Am's expanding operations. The effects of the economic downturn were mitigated somewhat by the New Deal, especially the Public Works Administration (PWA), which sponsored numerous federal projects in the state. The original proposal for a Pan-American fair in Miami was, in fact, conceptualized to win PWA support, and the site, an island in Biscayne Bay near the city's downtown, was envisioned as a hemispheric hub that could easily link to Pan Am's growing markets (fig. 6). Roosevelt's Good Neighbor Policy of 1933, however, was to have the strongest influence on the Pan-Americanism of this Miami fair. While the concept of "Good Neighbor" directed national attention to Latin America, it also emphasized the United States' progressivism, encouraging a view of two separate entities that contradicted the very notion of Pan-Americanism. The fairground's designs actually bifurcated the Western Hemisphere with a main pavilion tacitly fore-grounding the United States as the host nation and an array of modestly sized and marginally located Latin American pavilions. Despite the obvious hierarchy, in the minds of its creators the simple inclusion of Latin America was enough to make this fair Pan-American. As the project developed, however, other hemispheric themes emerged, positing the Americas as a cohesive whole.

The design for the Pan-American Exposition Building and Convention Hall was introduced in 1935. It exhibited strong basilical references of a Spanish Colonial aesthetic, but it was depicted in a Streamline Moderne style. The proposed Miami fair was the design of Phineas E. Paist, August Geiger, Richard Kiehnel, Russell Thorn Pancoast, George L. Pfeiffer, Edwin L. Robertson, and Robert Law Weed.[10] Given Paist's involvement, it is not surprising that the scheme resembled Paist and Steward's later design of the Florida Building for the New York World's Fair of 1939–1940 (fig. 7) and might therefore be considered a precursor to the New York Building. A revised scheme called the Pan-American Trade Mart was published in 1940.

PROPOSED PAN-AMERICAN TRADE MART
FOR THE CITY OF MIAMI, FLORIDA

CITY COMMISSIONERS
E. G. SEWELL, Mayor
FRED W. HOSEA
ALEXANDER ORR, JR.
R. C. GARDNER   L. L. LEE
C. D. VAN ORSDEL   City Manager

ASSOCIATED ARCHITECTS
AUGUST GEIGER
KIEHNEL & ELLIOTT   E. L. ROBERTSON
PAIST & STEWARD   WEED & REEDER
RUSSELL T. PANCOAST   V. E. VIRRICK
RICHARD KIEHNEL, F.A.I.A., Chairman

fig. 6 Proposed Pan-American Trade Mart. Pan-American Trade Mart: An Institution to Fully Reveal and Develop the Resources of the Americas (Perspective of the Initial Buildings) by the City of Miami (Miami, ca. 1940). Fred P. Cone Collection (1937–1941), State Archives of Florida.

Located on the entire city-owned Causeway Island, the inward-facing exposition pavilions formed an intimate setting for cultural exchange. But as the strong vertical of the U.S. Building, clearly seen in the bird's-eye view, confronted the passive crescent layout of the adjacent pavilions housing Latin American consular offices, hemispherical status was unmistakable.[11]

The main building featured a prominent tower, referred to as the Pan-American beacon, which was supposed to represent hemispheric unification. In numerous studies, this feature was expressed as a unifying symbol with a torchlike element at its top. In one depiction it is spewing smoke, and in another it exhibits lights shining in all directions. It is later referred to as the Tower of Eternal Peace. The beacon was supposed to connect the fairgrounds to Miami's nearby downtown and symbolically connect greater Miami to the faraway lands featured in this tropical fair. The dominance of the imposing main building, however, reflected a New Deal understanding of U.S.– Latin American relations, since its implied diplomatic hierarchy reflected the Good Neighbor policy of President Roosevelt, who had publicly endorsed the project in 1939. And since the fair's organizers were attempting to pro-

cure PWA funds, they may have wisely avoided a design that would have represented the Americas as a single, unified architectural body.

The renaming of the fair as the Pan-American Exposition and Industrial Merchandising Mart reinforced the commercial goals at the core of the project.[12] This objective was evident, too, when Pan Am began aggressively promoting the fair as an adjunct to its expanding passenger and mail service. Apparently, the company was determined to involve itself in expositions on both U.S. coasts that year, given the planned conversion of the San Francisco's Golden Gate International Exposition fairgrounds into an airport hub when that fair closed. Declaring the exposition "a practical way" of demonstrating "a 'Good Neighbor' policy," Pan Am hailed it as "an Institution to Fully Reveal and Develop the Resources of the Americas" and one that deserved the full support of the federal government.[13] But when the government denied the PWA application for this grand commercial vision, the project experienced its first impasse of many to come. By the time the United States entered World War II, Miami officials had offered the city up to the national cause of war. The changed city, with hotels, golf courses, and beaches ded-

69

Florida Building

New York World's Fair 1939   A-17

fig. 7 Postcard, Florida Building. Paist and Steward, architects. New York World's Fair, 1939–1940. The resemblance in form is evident between this pavilion and the main structure of the Pan-American Trade Mart. National Building Museum.

Beyond the Midway

icated to military service, would have not been favorable to any fair's grand opening.

The Pan-American theme was explored again when Miami's City Planning Board revived the project near the end of the war. At that point, board member Frank F. Stearns promoted the idea of a Pan-American city, in which Causeway Island became the *Centro de Pan Americano*. From the island, a network of hemispherically themed byways and highways would radiate in all directions, including a Pan-American Concourse, a *Paseo de las Americas,* and a Pan-American Highway.[14] The various destinations included a new Pan-American Building, an International House and Club, the Villa Viscayne, the Pan Am Airport and Pan Am Airways offices, the Inter-American Affairs offices, the Pan-American League headquarters, and even the University of Miami's International House. The ease with which institutions were renamed and conceived within this hypothetical Pan-American city is a testament to the viability, and likewise, superficiality, of the proposed fair and its architectural expression.

A revised design, the last in this almost decadelong phase, was published in 1944 in the *Miami Daily News,* promising a place "Where the Americas Shake Hands." It represented Latin America with twenty-three modestly sized pavilions surrounding the previously designed principal building.[15] Once again, the United States was positioned metaphorically as the adult at the head of the table.[16] In this scheme, a pedagogical flower garden at the opposite end of the island was offered as a model of hemispheric completeness. All the lands spanning the continents—from Alaska to Chile—were to be represented in floral form in a large map of the Western Hemisphere. The very nature of the garden suggested an organic framework within which Pan-Americanism might evolve over time. One could imagine the natural tapestry growing freely, with geopolitical borders blurred as the plants proliferated. Pan-Americanism's logical outcome would have been presented to the world and cultivated. This proposed world's fair, later called Interama, was revived numerous times in the 1950s and 1960s but was never realized. Conceptualized as it was as a full-blown Pan-American themed fairground, this last design iteration took on a challenge that had not been attempted since the Cayuga Island design that preceded the Buffalo fair.

Right around the same time, a complete regression to the old Pan-American clichés revealed itself in an extension fair proposed in Dallas. The Greater Texas and Pan-American Exposition of 1937 was planned to follow the Texas Centennial of 1936, a fair coordinated by the architect George Leighton Dahl. These fairgrounds consisted of twenty-six buildings designed under Dahl's directorship in a style described as Art Deco in the exposition literature, but referred to by Dahl as "Texanic." Unlike organizers of the New Orleans extension fair, the planners of the Dallas extension fair sought to totally repackage the original fairgrounds, a necessary step given that the grounds were distinctly southwestern. Perhaps in an effort to overcome this trait, the theme of Pan-Americanism was treated in theatrical terms. The entire fairgrounds, it was reported, were going to be repainted in green, yellow, and purple. Minor ephemeral structures were constructed and fairground rituals were invented to play up the theme. One of the brochures for the fair reported: "In a subtropical setting, replete with the luxuriant foliage of the *tierra caliente,* rise the magnificent buildings of the Pan American Exposition. Designed after the glorious edifices of Chichen Itza, Cuzco and Tenochtitlan, that are now one with Ninevah and Tyre, these structures house the commercial and governmental exhibits."[17] The brochure continued to describe other key locations, such as a Plaza de las Americas, a Patio de Honor, a Pan American Casino, a Pan American Village, and the arena for the Pan American Games. The Ford exhibit building was going to be neo-Mayanized and called the Palacio Pan-Americano, or the Pan-American Exhibit Hall (fig. 8). There is no record that this ever occurred, and the building was later torn down.

As the Miami City Planning Board member Stearns had imagined a Miami-turned-Pan-American City, the reconceptualized Dallas fairgrounds were portrayed as a complete cityscape—the ideal backdrop for the fictitious Pan-American subject. It was complete with renamed civic buildings, avenues, housing, and recreational and sports facilities, all created to serve the city. But the fair officials went too far. Perhaps to downplay cultural contrasts (Anglo versus Mexican), they sought a fairgrounds staff that matched the fair's "Latin flavor." They announced that only "Latin type" brunettes, or "Texanitas," were going to be hired as official hostesses.[18] This was not the first time

Robert A. González

that women's bodies had been used to signify larger concepts of national and ethnic identity. In promotional material for Buffalo's fair, the continents had been illustrated as two embracing females, a blond and a brunette. The revised Dallas fair, with its commingling of Aztec, rodeo, and Americana, indicated that the complicated, invented hemispheric subject it projected had not been resolved in the sociopolitical reality of Dallas, Texas. This was the first world's fair to be held in the Southwest, which explains the exaggerated depictions of regional distinction. The repackaged Texas Centennial Exposition, however, seemed to have backfired. In northern U.S. cities, the concept of Pan-Americanism had been treated as a foreign idea (blonde versus brunette), but in Texas this raised critical, unresolved issues concerning local histories; Texas, after all, had been Mexico before 1848. It would have made greater sense for this type of fair to occur in a city with a larger Mexican-American population, where a Pan-American populace was already present. The flag chosen to fly over the Texas Centennial Exposition, which was based on the banner that was carried by Cortez during the conquest of Mexico, would have resonated with a Laredo or a San Antonio population quite differently,

given their larger Mexican-American populations. In Dallas, Cortez's flag was no more than a stage prop. HemisFair '68, the cleverly named exposition, which took place in San Antonio in 1968, finally presented an exploration of Pan-Americanism that resonated with the local population.

Inter-America House of Tomorrow

World's fair design took a new turn with New York's unforgettable fair of 1939–1940, specifically with its Theme Center and the evocative presentation of the Trylon and Perisphere. The theme structures raised important questions about U.S. cities, most notably with the model city, Democracity, located within the Perisphere. The ascending curve of the Helicline and visions of fairgoers entering to listen to a voice-over present the future of "our" cities, all occurring within the awesome spherical shell, created one of the most memorable and iconic symbols of the decade. A subconscious disquietude that perhaps prompted this model city presentation was found in the zone devoted to foreign nations. With its flapping flags and national anthems, this area of the fair imparted the sense of impending conflict in the air. International anxiety was, in fact, overtly addressed by the Good Neighbor policy, which was

E-104   PAN AMERICAN EXHIBIT HALL, GREATER TEXAS AND PAN AMERICAN EXPOSITION, DALLAS, 1937

PALACIO PAN AMERICANO   7A-H1107

fig. 8 Postcard, Palacio Pan-Americano. Pan American Exposition, Dallas, 1937. From the collections of the Texas/Dallas History and Archives Division, Dallas Public Library.

delivered through numerous staged events featuring Latin American diplomats and statesmen; and the security guarantees Pan-Americanism offered were enthusiastically embraced. The New York fair reported the largest representation of Latin American national pavilions and exhibitions ever seen on U.S. territory to that time. Latin American representation was found in the independent structures of Argentina, Brazil, Chile, Cuba, the Dominican Republic, Ecuador, Mexico, Peru, and Venezuela. The other nations were featured in the Hall of Nations or in a section of the fairgrounds called the Pan-American Wing.[19]

This presence was further heightened with the added feature of the Pan-American Union Building, a significant gesture given that the League of Nations also had a pavilion at the fair (fig. 9). The *Bulletin of the Pan-American Union* reported that another model of the Columbus Memorial Lighthouse was presented within an atrium space inside. With this single institutional building, Pan-Americanism was at last notably presented as antihistoricist— all regional associations were introduced with symbols, flags, crests, and maps, and there was not a single sign of the pan-native aesthetic. This temporary structure was worlds apart from the PAU's headquarters building in Washing-

ton, D.C. This fully modern-style structure imparted a minimalist air that not only consciously avoided preconceived depictions of Latin America but also presented a blank slate that served as a formidable backdrop for numerous staged events.[20] Looking to Latin America in the fair's foreign section meant looking to the future. The *New York Times* made note of the PAU Building's austere form, a stark white box with a commanding and welcoming bay of columns. The newspaper reported: "On a steel arch over the entrance fly in colorful unison the flags of the twenty-one republics, members of the union."[21] The flags were also hung on the interior walls, and a principal feature was "a large animated relief map of the American Continent" that illustrated the dynamic interrelationships of the hemisphere with a complex system of lights. Technologically savvy presentations of Latin America were noted in the press. The world would also take note of modern Latin American architecture, which had arrived with this fair— most notably with Lucio Costa and Oscar Niemeyer's design of the Brazilian Pavilion. This building later gained international attention as a case study in tropical architecture. Latin America's involvement was impressive, as was the building representing the Pan-American Union

fig. 9 Pan-American Union Building, New York World's Fair, 1939–1940. Digital file © Eric K. Longo/Collection of Eric K. Longo.

Robert A. González

in Washington, D.C., but participation soon became a problem. By mid-September, fair management was trying to strengthen Latin American interest in the fair's second season, which would open again on May 11, 1940. A number of countries had already reported they would not participate. After Argentina abandoned its pavilion, which had been designed by the Argentine architect Armando d'Ans and the U.S. architect Aymar Embury II, the building was converted to an Inter-America House, and the director general of the Pan-American Union, Leo S. Rowe, spoke at its reinauguration on June 22, 1940. His speech emphasized the increasing need to consider American unity in a war-torn world.

Others shared the Argentine Pavilion, like the CBS radio facilities and the World Trade Center, but it was mostly known as the central node of exchange and hospitality for visiting Latin Americans. Despite the pavilion's distinct modern look, in the spirit of goodwill it was referred to as a "house." Like the PAU's fairgrounds building, with its unassuming architectural expression, the domestication of this high-style pavilion is worth noting. This reference may have also pointed to the PAU's own headquarters in Washington, D.C. The Cret and Kelsey design was often referred to as the House of the Americas, and the original competition directive had also suggested a domestic theme. Nevertheless, the Inter-America House indicated that this was the eve of a new public image for the PAU. We see this occur when the concept of the Inter-America House was later transported to New York City itself, where a private dwelling across from the Museum of Modern Art was renovated to house a new "system of hospitality for visitors from Latin America." Adopting the same name and mission, a new organization began planning such events as the Inter-American Music Festival held in Carnegie Hall in October 1941. A similar "home" also appeared in San Francisco around the same time. Also called the Inter-America House, it remained in operation through 1946. Universities like Mills College in Oakland, California, and the University of Texas at Austin also launched similar "houses" or "Casas Inter-Americanas."

The Pan-American movement was ever-present in the 1930s, making an appearance at almost every U.S. fair in that decade. While the Golden Gate International Exposition in San Francisco, the last fair of the decade, turned

its attention to the Pacific Rim, Pan-Americanism was not entirely left out of the picture. As part of the "Art in Action" project, the Mexican artist Diego Rivera was invited to paint a mural for the fairgrounds. He did not finish his mural until three months after the exposition closed, but the aim of the "Art in Action" section was to let visitors see art being produced before their eyes. Nevertheless, Rivera's contribution brings this decade of Pan-American activity at the world's fairs to an interesting conclusion. His mural's long title describes his hemispheric conception: *Pan-American Unity, or the Marriage of the Artistic Expression of the North and South of this Continent: Materialization of the Gifts for the Creative Mechanical Expression of the North, by way of Union with the Plastic Tradition of the South* (fig. 10). With his mural, Rivera called for the merging of the (Latin American) artistic and (U.S.) technological expressions of the New World. The historian Jeffrey Belnap has noted that "Rivera developed a cultural model in which he argued that the world-historical destiny of the Americas lay in the dialectical fusion of these two systems, a fusion that would sublate the technological modernity of the machine within Greater America's resilient indigenous tradition."[22] Rivera symbolized this concept of the best of both worlds with an invented figure, an indigenous technoid that he painted at the center of his mural. This technoid was actually the transformed Aztec goddess Coatlicue, depicted as a "half-stone, half-machine" figure.[23] Technically a cyborg, which is an organism with enhanced abilities due to technology, Rivera's creation represented Pan-American unity in an entirely new way. The stark juxtaposition and fusion of Indian culture and North American technology made sense to Rivera; he did not see the Pan-American project as a compilation of separate elements. In his hemispheric model, the indigenous being could be visibly strengthened by North American technological forces, and vice versa, and transformation and fusion were requirements. Rivera was no stranger to the concept of fusing the technological and the native. After all, he was living in a Le Corbusier–inspired "machine for living in," a house that had been painted in bright Mexican colors and fenced in with tall cacti.

Rivera's Pan-Americanism greatly informs this examination of hemispheric architecture in the late 1930s. The mural reminds us that hemispheric representations by

Latin Americans also challenged the way Anglo-Americans depicted the New World. It did not take long, in fact, for the United States to take note. In 1943 the Museum of Modern Art's exhibition Brazil Builds demonstrated that Latin America had approached the modern project on its own terms, and, at times, even surpassed U.S. modernist expectations with unique visionary designs for the future that were unimaginable in the North. Oscar Niemeyer's Brasilia and the two university cities in Mexico and Venezuela come to mind. While Latin American architects did not offer equivalent modern expressions of Pan-Americanism, knowledge of Latin American architectural developments, like those seen at the New York World's Fair, must have advanced perceptions of the Pan-American project as a whole. This is not to suggest, however, that damaging stereotypes did not endure. Even the Spanish word for tomorrow—the oft-used pejorative *mañana*—clashed with futuristic images. The utterance of mañanaland would have conveyed not movement or progress but putting off any movement until a time that would never arrive.

If only for brief moments, the 1930s witnessed a new language of architectural modernism that helped assert Pan-Americanism as a project of unification. The PAU's world's fair structure, with its solid columns, served as a symbol of strength for the numerous diplomatic engagements that took place within and in front of this structure. The building helped elevate the Latin American diplomats without preconceptions, allowing them to stage their offerings of economic opportunities at this important world's fair. The relative closeness in time of the New York and Dallas fairs, however, reminds us that while modern architecture had fully entered the picture, the Pan-American subject was not guaranteed a set path of expression. The Midway days of racism and romanticism were certainly over, and hemispheric architecture expressed in modern form certainly invited new and positive expressions. However, the two design proposals that presented the concept in its most modern form—Miami's unbuilt Pan-American Exposition and the New York fair's temporary PAU Pavilion—also remind us that visionary proposals and ephemeral structures do not lead to permanence. A new formula for expressing Pan-Americanism in the decades to come was not set in motion, and projects were not free of images of Bolívar, Columbus, and pan-native expressions after the 1930s. Contemporary Pan-American architectural explorations still make occasional appearances today, and the concept continues to invite explorations, with these iconic images remaining as the favored expressions.

74

fig. 10 Diego Rivera, *Pan-American Unity . . .* (panel 3), 1940. Mural painted for the Golden Gate International Exposition. All rights reserved. Unauthorized public performance, broadcasting, transmission, or copying, mechanical or electronic, is a violation of applicable laws. © City College of San Francisco. www.riveramural.com.

Robert A. González

Notes

1. For an extensive overview of this conference and the succeeding Pan-American conferences that were organized by the PAU, see Samuel Guy Inman, *Inter-American Conferences, 1824–1954: History and Problems* (Washington, D.C.: University Press of Washington, D.C., and the Community College Press, 1965); G. Pope Atkin, *Latin America in the International Political System* (San Francisco: Westview, 1989).

2. Arthur Preston Whitaker, *The Western Hemisphere Idea: Its Rise and Decline* (Ithaca, N.Y.: Cornell University Press, 1954), 1–2.

3. *Chicago Daily Tribune,* July 28, 1891.

4. *New York Times,* July 14, 1892, 6.

5. See Mauricio Tenorio Trillo's account of how President Porfirio Díaz insisted on fair and accurate depictions of Mexicans at the world's fairs in *Mexico at the World's Fairs: Crafting a Modern Nation* (Berkeley: University of California Press, 1966).

6. Valerie Fraser, *Building the New World: Studies in the Modern Architecture of Latin America, 1930–1960* (London: Verso, 2000).

7. As Robert Rydell has noted, "Cole organized an exhibition of five living groups of Native Americans, put them under the direct charge of a local real estate speculator, and placed the resulting Indian Village adjacent to an exact replica of a Mayan Temple, between the concession avenue and the automobile manufacturing exhibits. The Indians were supposed to 'live primitive existences as their ancestors did before them'"; Robert W. Rydell, "The Fan Dance of Science: American World's Fairs in the Great Depression," *Isis* 76 (1985): 534.

8. Requa states, "One of the surprising and impressive facts I learned from this study is that the principal elements or fundamental features of our so-called Modern styles of architecture had all been admirably employed in the creation of the prehistoric buildings of America. There is striking similarity in the arrangement of masses and the use of horizontal lines; in the employment of geometrical design in the ornamentation, and in its application in a few well selected spots, particularly for doorways, friezes and parapets"; Richard S. Requa, *Inside Lights on the Building of San Diego's Exposition, 1935* (San Diego: Parker H. Jackson, 1977), 52. This is a reissue of a title originally published in 1937.

9. While some of California's cities, with their proximity to Mexico and increasing Hispanic demographics, were perfect candidates for the title of "Gateway to the Americas," they did not pursue it with the same intensity.

10. The architects served as the actual editorial staff of the professional magazine *Florida Architecture and Allied Arts,* which Kiehnel inaugurated in 1935. Additional architects later joined the team. Mayor E. G. Sewell enlisted the team, and consequently the idea of creating a Pan-American-themed trade mart or exposition building has been attributed to Sewell or his successor, Mayor C. H. Reeder. The fair's date of origin has also been dated at 1915 or 1919, when the city first acquired Causeway Island. See "Pan-American Center Bill Opposed," *Miami Tribune,* January 4, 1947. An earlier fair proposed by the architect H. Hastings Mundy appeared in Port Greater Miami in February 1932.

11. In a revised scheme, there is mention of the firms Kiehnel and Elliot, Paist and Steward, and Weed and Reeder.

12. Later, in 1943, the architect Gordon Eugene Mayer also proposed the "Pan-American Trade Mart and Social Center."

13. Governor Frederick Preston Cone correspondence, 1937–1941, Florida State Archives.

14. Frank F. Stearns, "Pan-American or International Center or World Exposition (Permanent) at Miami," report, April 1944. Stearns based his findings on his book *City Planning in Miami: 1941–42.*

15. The plan shows a larger number of pavilions, many dedicated to other functions and support services.

16. This scheme appeared in the *Miami Daily News,* December 5, 1944.

17. "Greater Texas and Pan-American Exposition, Dallas 1937," postcard packet; private collection.

18. *Dallas Times Herald,* February 16, 1937.

19. *Bulletin of the Pan-American Union,* July 1939, pp. 387–412.

20. Another exposition occurred in Tampa, Florida, the Pan-American Hernando de Soto Exposition in 1939. This exposition was planned to celebrate the four hundredth anniversary of the explorer's landing.

21. *New York Times,* September 3, 1939.

22. Jeffrey Grant Belnap, "Diego Rivera's Greater America: Pan-American Patronage, Indigenism, and H.P.," *Cultural Critique* 63 (2006): 64.

23. Ibid., 91.

Modern Design Goes Public
A Photo Essay

Laura Burd Schiavo

On the eve of Chicago's 1933 Century of Progress Exposition, Alfred Granger, president of the local American Institute of Architects chapter, reflected on the undertaking of the architectural commissioners chosen to design the fair. They had, he wrote, "come home from [the 1931 Paris Exposition Coloniale Internationale] inspired by the effects achieved through the use of new materials, new form and the possibilities of electric lighting and wished the forthcoming exposition in '33 to be wholly 'modern' in every respect."[1] As Granger predicted, the design for that fair, and that of the five that followed over the next seven years, deviated substantially from the historically inspired, heavily ornamented designs of previous American expositions.

In 1937, anticipating the world's fairs being planned for New York and San Francisco two years later, the industrial designer Walter Dorwin Teague described the benefit of the multiplicity of fairs during the 1930s. A member of the New York World's Fair Board of Design, Teague explained: "Heretofore world's fairs have been spaced so far apart that each has been planned out of a vacuum. . . . But we have had a series of fairs in the past five years; we have been able to observe the reactions of the public,

the effect of exhibits on the spectators and the degree of interest they aroused."[2]

These two quotations, one from an architect, the other from an industrial designer, suggest the fruitfulness of the moment for their respective professions. Emboldened by developments abroad and at home to create "modern" fairs, they engaged in a prolific and productive exchange about the nature of contemporary expositions during an energetic decade of world's fair activity. After all, expositions dating back to 1851 and the first such endeavor, London's Great Exhibition of the World of Industry of All Nations, had featured architectural innovation and showcased invention. How, the architects and designers debated, would these look different? The designed elements of the expositions—the fairgrounds, the pavilions, and the exhibits—can be viewed as their reply, expressions of modernism in the hands of (largely) American practitioners. Although there was no coordination from fair to fair, the architects and designers collaborated on multiple projects for multiple fairs in various combinations. Beyond their roles for the expositions, they were each other's teachers, students, and partners.

But this was not a discussion that happened exclusively behind closed doors or on the pages of architectural magazines. The world's fairs were decidedly public. They introduced modern design to the tens of millions who visited the fairs and those exposed to them through extensive coverage in popular periodicals, on the radio, and in newsreels (plates 1–3). What might have been an aesthetic experiment or marketing ploy before 1929 soon became an urgent response to crisis. During the Great Depression, the spectacular demonstrations aligned modern design with a vision of a better future that celebrated consumer progress and trumpeted mass production and corporate leadership. The world's fairs were popular interpretations of what it meant to be modern in the 1930s, lessons that could be taken home and applied to everyday lives.

Laura Burd Schiavo

opposite
Plate 1
A teacher in Mileston, Mississippi, explains the Trylon and Perisphere, symbols of the New York World's Fair, to her students in 1939. Marion Post Wolcott. Gelatin silver print. Farm Security Administration Collection. Photographs and Prints Division, Schomburg Center for Research in Black Culture, New York Public Library, Astor, Lenox and Tilden Foundations.

above
Plate 2
For its February 1939 issue, *Harper's Bazaar* commissioned Stuart Davis to depict his impressions of the New York World's Fair two months before its opening. Davis's modernist vocabulary of collage, distorted form, exuberant color, and flattened shapes depicts fair structures including the Trylon and Perisphere and Ford's Road of Tomorrow. Stuart Davis, *Impressions of the New York World's Fair*, 1938. Gouache on paperboard. 13 3/4 × 22 1/8 in. Smithsonian American Art Museum. Transfer from the United States Information Agency through the General Services Administration.

Modern Design Goes Public

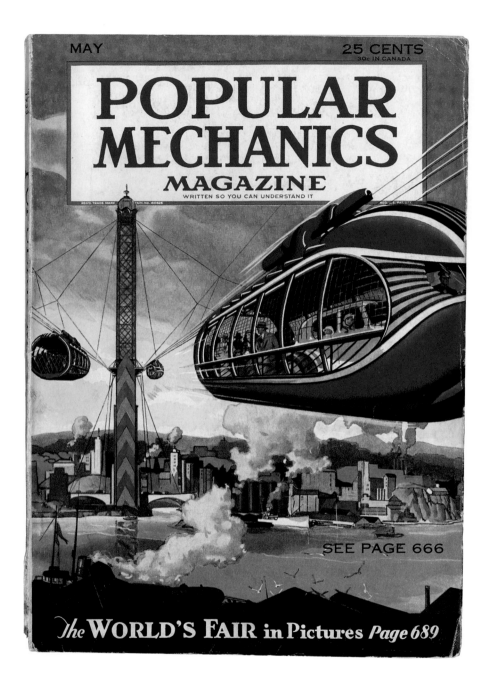

Plate 3
This issue of *Popular Mechanics* magazine (1933) included an illustrated, sixteen-page spread focused on new building materials and new applications of old materials at the Century of Progress Exposition. The cover featured the Sky Ride. National Building Museum.

Laura Burd Schiavo

Fairgrounds

The architects who selected the plans for the exposition fairgrounds—especially those created specifically for the 1930s world's fairs in Chicago, New York, and San Francisco—held different opinions about how to create intelligible landscapes. While all agreed that the plans had to facilitate visitors' sense of orientation in plots ranging from four hundred to twelve hundred acres, some were wedded to their Beaux-Arts training and the persistent neoclassical attitude that associated geometry with logic and clarity of design. They preferred axial plans and broad boulevards. Others, more willing to break from custom, argued that less symmetrical plans would open the possibilities for transporting visitors to places like no other.

The Century of Progress Exposition veered the farthest from tradition in plan, an innovation due largely to the architect Raymond Hood. Eight architects, including Hood, made up the commission that determined the elements to be included in proposals for the grounds and ultimately selected the plan for the Chicago fair (plate 4). The required elements included a dominant building in the center celebrating scientific achievement, an airport projecting into Lake Michigan, and major water features "comparable with the . . . Columbian Exposition of 1893." Hood argued that symmetrical plans were "monotonous" and proposed a design that broke from axial symmetry (plate 5). An informal layout, he believed, allowed more creative expression by the architects of individual pavilions, best assisted the flow of people, and most easily accommodated inevitable changes in the number and design of structures. The eventual serpentine plan bore closest resemblance to Hood's proposal. It wound along two main areas, the long, narrow man-made Northerly Island and a mainland site across a lagoon (plate 6).

Despite a variety of earlier proposals for New York and San Francisco, the design committees for both fairs settled on plans dominated by axial hubs (plate 7). At the Golden Gate International Exposition unequal axes broke to some degree with the symmetry of a traditional approach, but the plan's basis in a series of courts reflected the legacy of the classically trained architects (plate 8). Ironically, the New York World's Fair, deemed the most modern by later critics, was the most traditional in plan. The largely conservative board of design rejected a plan for a serpentine path presented by a member of the more progressive "Fair of the Future Committee."[3] The fair's "Theme Center" (the Trylon tower and spherical Perisphere) formed the core, with thematic zones radiating in fanlike segments around it (plate 9). In neither San Francisco nor New York did the organizing scheme extend to the entertainment zone, and the failure of the plans to take into account multiple entrance points prevented uniformity in the vistas encountered by fairgoers. Critics of the New York fair maintained that the absolute order was at odds with an avowed spirit of change and that insufficient elevations prevented views of the most important vistas.

A number of design inspirations set the grounds apart from previous expositions. The planners shared an enthusiasm for air travel and attended to the question of how the grounds would appear from above. The inclusion of Chicago's Sky Ride and the offering of blimp rides over the grounds of many of the fairs attest to this awareness. In addition to their interest in how the grounds would look from the air, planners in Chicago, New York, and San Francisco devised innovative color schemes that coordinated the buildings and flora to help orient visitors on the ground. Although eventually deemed ineffective for navigation, the ideas expressed a modern engagement with the innovative use of color.

81

82

"Just how the crowds pouring into this circle from so many directions are to know which way to turn and *how* to get where is still an interesting question."

Talbot Hamlin, *Pencil Points,* November 1938

Laura Burd Schiavo

Modern Design Goes Public

AQUARIUM   PLANETARIUM   U.S GOVT BLDG.   ELECTRICAL GROUP   HORTICULTURAL BLDG.   PABST BLUE RIBBON CASINO
AVENUE OF FLAGS   HALL OF SCIENCE   DAIRY EXHIBIT   GERMAN BLDG.   AGRIC. EXHIB.   HALL OF STATES   SOCIAL SCIENCE   ENCHANTED ISLAND
SHOW BOAT   MULLER-PABST CAFE   BYRDS ANTARCTIC SHIP
GENERAL EXHIBITS GROUP   HALL OF RELIGION

84

Laura Burd Schiavo

Labels visible on panorama: HOLLYWOOD, STREETS OF PARIS, 23RD ST. ENTRANCE, A. & P. CARNIVAL, BELGIAN VILLAGE, PANTHEON, THE MIDWAY, GETTYSBURG, GENERAL MOTORS BLDG., CHRYSLER MOTOR BLDG., TRAVEL & TRANSPORT

PANORAMA OF THE CENTURY OF PROGRESS EXPOSITION
CHICAGO ILL. 1933

Plate 6

The serpentine nature of the plan is detectable in this panorama of the Century of Progress Exposition, which also depicts two dirigibles overhead. The Hall of Science (in the middle ground below the left tower of the Sky Ride) satisfied the requirement of a dominant building celebrating scientific achievement. At only 176 feet, it lacked the considerable height of the skyscraper in Hood's plan. Prints and Photographs Division, Library of Congress, digital ID pan6a28300.

Plate 7
Bernard Maybeck, whose career in California was mainly devoted to residential, Arts and Crafts architecture, acted as associate architect for the San Francisco fair. This early schematic for the fairgrounds shows a semicircular plan featuring a large arena. The exposition buildings surround a lagoon punctuated by skyscraper-inspired viewing towers. Bernard Maybeck Collection (1956-1), Environmental Design Archives, University of California, Berkeley.

Laura Burd Schiavo

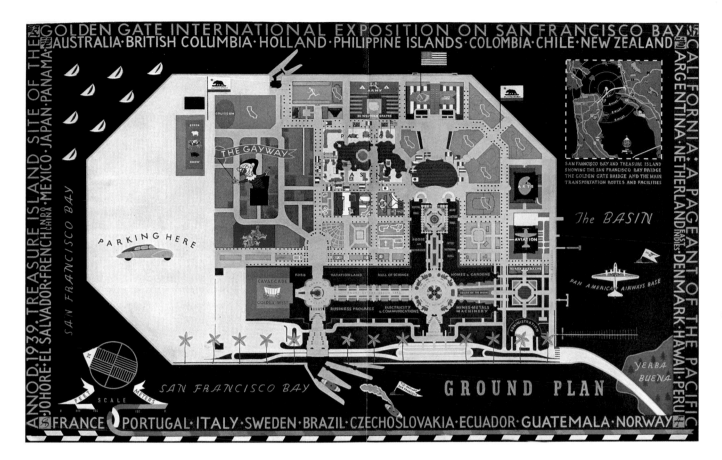

The map contains the following text:

GOLDEN GATE INTERNATIONAL EXPOSITION ON SAN FRANCISCO BAY

AUSTRALIA·BRITISH COLUMBIA·HOLLAND·PHILIPPINE ISLANDS·COLOMBIA·CHILE·NEW ZEALAND

ANNO D. 1939 TREASURE ISLAND SITE OF THE
JOHORE·EL SALVADOR·FRENCH INDIA·MEXICO·JAPAN·PANAMA

CALIFORNIA·A PAGEANT OF THE PACIFIC
ARGENTINA·NETHERLAND EAST INDIES·DENMARK·HAWAII·PERU

THE GAYWAY

PARKING HERE

SAN FRANCISCO BAY

SAN FRANCISCO BAY AND TREASURE ISLAND
SHOWING THE SAN FRANCISCO BAY BRIDGE
THE GOLDEN GATE BRIDGE AND THE MAIN
TRANSPORTATION ROUTES AND FACILITIES

The BASIN

PAN AMERICAN AIRWAYS BASE

YERBA BUENA

SAN FRANCISCO BAY   GROUND PLAN

SCALE   FEET   METERS

FRANCE·PORTUGAL·ITALY·SWEDEN·BRAZIL·CZECHOSLOVAKIA·ECUADOR·GUATEMALA·NORWAY

87

Plate 8
Four forty-foot-wide directional maps featuring a design by Ernest Born greeted visitors just inside the entrance gates at the San Francisco fair. This graphic representation makes clear the unequal axes and courts developed by the architects Lewis Hobart, William Merchant, Timothy Pflueger, Ernest Weihe, George Kelham, and Arthur Brown Jr. It also illuminates the dominance of the parking lot and its proximity to the Gayway entertainment zone. *Architectural Forum*, June 1939.

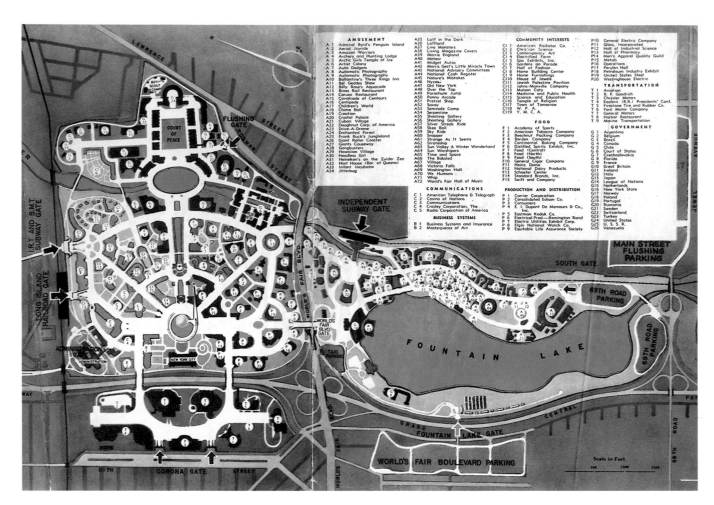

Plate 9

This map illustrates the axial design of the New York World's Fair, with the Trylon and Perisphere at the base and thematic zones emanating outward, a spokelike plan preferred by the more conservative members of the designers committee, including chairman Stephen F. Voorhees. Julian E. Garnsey's color scheme was less traditional. Each zone was assigned a color reflected in the plantings and flags whose tone intensified as one moved farther from the base, a scheme meant to assist with orientation. *Official Guidebook of the New York World's Fair 1939* (New York: Exposition Publications, 1939). Digital file © Eric K. Longo/Collection of Eric K. Longo.

Laura Burd Schiavo

Fair Moderne

In her account of the design of the groundbreaking Century of Progress Exposition, Lisa Schrenk argues that the deliberations of the architectural commission reflected a contemporary debate in American architecture over the direction of progressive building design.[4] Was modernism a style, a new set of principles governing the relationship between a building's function and its design, or the incorporation of new materials and the embrace of new construction methods? The question had not been resolved when the gates opened in May 1933, nor would a definitive answer emerge during more than a decade of world's fair design and construction. The resolution, rather, was that American modernism would incorporate all three. At the world's fairs this meant a style that favored flat surfaces and simple forms and geometries, buildings that accommodated large exhibition halls, and innovation in materials and construction.

"The Fair shows in a way nothing else could—albeit often falsely—new uses of materials, construction, and design to millions of people who would never see architectural magazines or good foreign buildings."

Lincoln Kerstein, *The Nation*, June 20, 1934

Although there were few outright modernists among the architects who designed for the fairs, their work deviated substantially from the historically inspired and heavily ornamented work associated with the Beaux-Arts tradition (plate 10). While the pavilions were by no means uniform, architects responded enthusiastically to their clients' desires for buildings innovative enough to intrigue the public. (It was a fair, after all, that had given the world the Eiffel Tower.) And they eagerly embraced the opportunity to experiment provided by the temporary nature of the expositions. The chance to design was particularly attractive during the Great Depression, when building activity had plummeted. In part, decisions favoring unadorned facades were born out of necessity, as many of the buildings were constructed on a tight budget due to the cost-cutting necessitated by the Depression. Flat, windowless facades were as much a matter of thrift—made possible by air conditioning and artificial lighting—as they were homage to the flat surfaces favored by Walter Gropius, Le Corbusier, and Ludwig Mies van der Rohe.

Although many embraced a simplification of form, most fair buildings were not in strict accordance with the orthodoxies associated with the European avant-garde that would come to be known as International Style (plates 11, 12). One of the most typical styles was a stripped classicism that created contemporary expressions of known forms by simplifying a classical repertory to its bare essentials (plates 13, 14). Departing from the more angular classicism were the smooth lines and surfaces of streamlined architecture (introduced sparingly in Chicago and most predominantly in New York) that produced the illusion of sleek, aerodynamic form evoking movement and progress (plates 15–18). The most playful structures at the fairs were those that took literally the modern notion that a building should "speak" its purpose, where exterior shapes plainly and cleverly indicated content (plates 19–22). The critic Frederick Gutheim disparaged these corporate-sponsored pavilions as Corporation Style—"a bastard dialect of architectural larceny and advertising."[5]

Architects working on the West Coast expositions were inclined to reference indigenous, (vaguely) regional cultures for aesthetic inspiration. The alleged affinity between building practices dating back hundreds of years and contemporary stylistic preferences gave modernism a gloss of authenticity. Richard Requa described the buildings he created for the California-Pacific International Exposition in San Diego, which alluded to the ancient architecture of the Americas rather than to the colonial past, as evoking the "simple and unpretentious type of building which was, perhaps, more completely expressive of the masses and their civilization."[6] The rich brown stone and triangular entrance portal of his Federal Building paid homage to the Mayan Palace of the Governor in Uxmal, Yucatan, Mexico (plate 23). In San Francisco, this sampling of motifs stretched across the Pacific, borrowing from the details and massing of "Oriental, Cambodian, and Mayan styles" to create "an effect of basic beauty, refinement and richness . . . interwoven with a mystical touch of yesterday."[7] The exposition's particular brand of "Pacifica" modern complemented the rhetoric of the fair, which encouraged expanded exchange along what has since become known as the Pacific Rim (plates 24, 25).

Not all of the buildings at the fairs employed overtly modern design. Some, like the classicist Arthur Brown Jr.'s Tower of the Sun, expressed a preference for more traditional forms. The nearly four hundred–foot centerpiece of the Golden Gate International Exposition alluded to a medieval tower. It rose in stages, including immense open arcades with allegorical figures of Industry, Agriculture, Science, and the Arts, carillon bells, and a spire topped by a wrought iron phoenix (plate 26). Gutheim called it "the same old stuff all over again."[8]

The absence of a definitive style at American world's fairs of the 1930s is illustrated by the buildings sponsored by the U.S. government in Chicago, San Diego, and San Francisco. Even when function was shared (as with these pavilions that housed exhibits about government programs), form varied widely. In Edward Bennett's Federal Building for Chicago, the traditional dome and towers representing the three branches of government were offset by the use of color and a simplification of form (plate 27). The San Diego example by Richard Requa imparted an indigenous cast to the federal program (see plate 23). Timothy L. Pflueger's light, airy structure for San Francisco looked to neither classical nor indigenous tradition. The building incorporated exhibition space within two colonnaded wings joined by an open loggia of forty-eight columns, abstract representations of the states (plate 28). Pflueger's use of natural light and delicate, temporary materials earned the building praise as "monumentally modern."[9]

The plain facades of many of the pavilions left room for, and indeed made necessary, decorative elaboration in color and light. The stage designer Joseph Urban developed a palette of twenty-five colors for the Chicago fair. Urban specified distinct and striking combinations of three or five colors for buildings' individual surface planes, echoing the use of color by progressive European modernists in the 1920s (plates 29, 30). The effect—often masked by the predominance of black-and-white photography in

the era—offered a striking and conscious departure from the white, neoclassical buildings of the 1893 Columbian Exposition. The largely stucco surfaces of the San Francisco pavilions, painted in nineteen colors favoring shades of ivory, gold, brown and blue, were treated with flakes of micarta that rendered them reflective. In contrast to the range of color at these fairs, the muralist Julian Garnsey developed a yellowish-brown color scheme for the Texas Centennial to reduce the sun's glare (plate 31).

The most significant accomplishment in decoration at the fairs was the multicolored nighttime illumination of pavilions, pylons, fountains, and sculptures. Chicago's 1933 Century of Progress Exposition pioneered the large-scale use of colored gas-tube lighting to outline towers and pylons. The core of the lighting scheme, however, was a system of nearly three thousand floodlights focused on the already colorful structures. By decade's end, the lighting designer for the New York World's Fair restricted the use of floodlights, calling them "archaic." Lighting designers in New York and San Francisco took advantage of the versatility and effectiveness of new low-intensity fluorescent lights, often concealing the light sources to make it appear that the buildings glowed from within (plates 32, 33). In San Francisco, ultraviolet light sources were first used in a major outdoor installation. Comparing the 1939 fair to the Columbian Exposition, New York World's Fair President Grover Whalen expounded that while the "White City" had promoted neoclassical purity, the New York fair would "make people demand color in their cities just as they now demand color in their kitchens and bathrooms and clothes"[10] (plate 34).

The most lasting design legacies of the 1930s world's fairs are not the buildings themselves, most of which were torn down at the end of a season or two (plate 35). Rather it was the continued use of building materials pioneered or marketed at the expositions (gypsum board [drywall], Masonite, aluminum, plywood) and the idea of prefabrication whose legacy most endures in the built environment of the late twentieth and early twenty-first century (plates 36–41). Given the need for vast exhibition spaces, the fairs were also important settings for experimentation in creating engineered structures that freed architectural space from the constraints of masonry-based forms (plate 42).

Laura Burd Schiavo

Plate 10
The architects who designed for
the fairs of the 1930s were reacting
against a tradition as much as they
were embracing a definable innovation. The clearest reference for their
departure was the neoclassicism of
the White City of the World's Columbian Exposition (1893), seen in this
image of the Palace of the Mechanic
Arts and lagoon. Photograph by
Frances Benjamin Johnston, 1892.
Frances Benjamin Johnston Collection, Prints and Photographs Division,
Library of Congress, LC-USZ62-16999.

Plate 11
William Lescaze designed the Magnolia Petroleum Company Building and Café at the 1936 Texas Centennial, one of the closest adherents to International Style at the fairs. The Swiss-born architect, whose work had appeared in the Museum of Modern Art's Modern Architecture: International Exhibition (1932), helped introduce European modernism to Texas with the floating planes, cantilevered decks, and slender metal piers of this structure. Courtesy Dallas Historical Society. Used by permission.

Laura Burd Schiavo

Plate 12
Some of the most celebrated buildings at the fairs were foreign pavilions.
The art historian Eugen Neuhaus
championed Gardner Dailey's Brazil
Pavilion at the Golden Gate International Exposition as being "in the
modern idiom." Rather than symbol-
izing the state with a historicist edifice
"burdened with bombastic ornament,"
Neuhaus argued, Dailey designed an
elegant structure, "effective in the
honest use of contemporary materials."
Gardner Dailey Collection (1998–1),
Environmental Design Archives,
University of California, Berkeley.

94

Plate 13
The Hall of State for the Texas
Centennial, designed by a team of
architects under the direction of
chief architect George Dahl, consists
of a central pavilion flanked by symmetrical, porticoed wings. The flattened columns, decorated with
the Texas Lone Star, are a stripped
version of the classical form. From
the collections of the Texas/Dallas
History and Archives Division,
Dallas Public Library.

Laura Burd Schiavo

Plate 14

The architects Nimmons, Carr, and Wright selected a classical scheme for the Sears, Roebuck and Company Building in Chicago, but enhanced it with color (a red tower and red columns) and "streamlines" emanating from the central tower. [COP_17_0004_00169_001], Century of Progress Records, 1927–1952, University of Illinois, Chicago, Library.

Plate 15
The rounded forms popularized by
the era's industrial design lent a
streamlined air to the Hiram Walker
and Sons' Canadian Club Café.
Photograph by Kaufmann and Fabry
Co. Collection of Jim Sweeny.

Laura Burd Schiavo

97

Plate 16
Streamlining was inspired by the field of aerodynamics associated with vehicular design. William Lescaze and J. Gordon Carr's hangar-shaped Aviation Building at the New York World's Fair capitalized on this association, a concept clearly realized in this rendering. Mark Freeman, *World's Fair Aviation Building,* 1939. Graphite and water color on paper, $7^5/_8 \times 10^3/_8$ in. The Wolfsonian–Florida International University, XX1990.3531.

Plate 17
The three sections of William Lescaze and J. Gordon Carr's Aviation Building, which fit together to provide a look of frictionless efficiency, were also functional units. The entrance lobby and restaurant, most visible in this photograph, were backed by hangar-shaped and half-dome sections which housed exhibition halls. Digital file © Eric K. Longo/Collection of Eric K. Longo.

Laura Burd Schiavo

Plate 18
The automobile companies commissioned some of the largest and boldest pavilions at the fairs, preeminent among them the architect Albert Kahn and the designer Norman Bel Geddes's General Motors Building, with its mammoth, sweeping walls and curving ramp. Photo provided courtesy of Albert Kahn Family of Companies.

Plate 19
Walter Dorwin Teague, who had designed the actual cash register for National Cash Register, magnified his design for the world's fairs in Dallas and New York, and San Francisco's Golden Gate International Exposition, seen here. Trained in engineering as well as design, Teague engineered the gargantuan symbol to calculate daily attendance at the fairs. Courtesy of Bancroft Library, University of California, Berkeley.

Laura Burd Schiavo

Plate 20
The quintessence of architecture as advertising, Louis Skidmore and Nathaniel Owings's Continental Baking Company Building at the New York World's Fair mimicked the iconic Wonder Bread packaging. The two architects had served on the design and development staffs for the Chicago fair and formed a partnership in 1936. Skidmore and Owings designed more buildings for the New York World's Fair than any other architects. Digital file © Eric K. Longo/Collection of Eric K. Longo.

Modern Design Goes Public

San Diego Historical Society

Plate 21
Shell Oil Building and Information
Booth. California-Pacific International
Exposition, San Diego, 1935–1936.
Photograph by Harry T. Bishop.
© San Diego Historical Society.

Laura Burd Schiavo

103

Plate 22
Not all the clever architecture at the fairs was sponsored by corporations looking to advertise their brands. The fair-sponsored Marine Transportation Building, brightly painted in ultramarine blue, signified its purpose with simple forms resembling gigantic twin ocean liner prows. Designed by Ely Jacques Kahn and Muschenheim and Brounn, the building was enhanced by a mural of ship motifs by Lyonel Feininger. Digital file © Eric K. Longo/ Collection of Eric K. Longo.

Plate 23
Richard Requa called the Federal
Building, part of the "prehistoric
group" he designed for San Diego's
California-Pacific International Exposition, a "free interpretation" of
the Mayan Palace of the Governor
in Uxmal, Yucatan. © San Diego
Historical Society.

Laura Burd Schiavo

PORTALS OF THE PACIFIC
1939 World's Fair on San Francisco Bay

Plate 24

The ramparts of the main portals of the Golden Gate International Exposition, designed by Ernest Weihe and featuring elephant sculpture by Donald Macky, were spread in a heavy massing reminiscent of pyramids of the Far East. Artist unknown, *Portals of the Pacific*, 1939. Lithograph, 33 1/4 × 46 1/4 in. Wolfsonian–Florida International University, XX1993.4500.

Plate 25
The square pilasters of the exhibition halls lining the periphery of Treasure Island provided a practical solution to the site's prevailing trade winds. The inner courts of the Towers of the East, embellished with stylized allusions to Angkor Wat in Cambodia, created the effect of an ancient walled city. The towers sat across the lagoon from the modern glass Federal Building (see plate 28). Towers of the East. *Magic in the Night: Official Souvenir, Golden Gate International Exposition* (San Francisco: Crocker, 1939). Color plate produced by American Engraving and Color Plate Company from photograph by Gabriel Moulin. National Building Museum.

Laura Burd Schiavo

Plate 26
Arthur Brown Jr., *Tower of the Sun,*
n.d. Gouache on paper (mounted
on board), 17 × 10 ½ in. Courtesy
of Bancroft Library, University of
California, Berkeley.

Laura Burd Schiavo

Plate 28
Federal Building. Timothy Pflueger,
architect. Golden Gate International
Exposition, San Francisco, 1939–
1940. Courtesy of Bennett Hall. Digital
file © Business Image Group.

Modern Design Goes Public

Plate 29

Joseph Urban specified distinct and striking color combinations for the individual surface planes, including the blue, orange, yellow and white of the main court of Paul Philippe Cret's Hall of Science with its jagged setback tower. Hall of Science (detail). *Progress in Industrial Color and Protection at "A Century of Progress"* ([Chicago:] American Asphalt Paint, 1933). Special Collections Research Center, University of Chicago Library.

Laura Burd Schiavo

"It was marvelous — swipes of color 40 feet high and 400 feet long. They [the architects] messed up the plan with a small exhibit building—but your color will bring back the form. It is going to save the show."

Raymond Hood to Joseph Urban, May 7, 1933

112

"Emotions are excited toward gaiety, liveliness, beauty and the joy of living by shades of red, rose, orange and yellow . . . while greens, blue greens and blues are used as tranquilizers."

A. F. Dickerson, lighting designer, Golden Gate International Exposition, Architectural Record, 1939

Plate 32
Tower of the South. *Magic in the Night: Official Souvenir, Golden Gate International Exposition* (San Francisco: Crocker Company, 1939). Color plate produced by American Engraving and Color Plate Company from photograph by Gabriel Moulin. National Building Museum.

Laura Burd Schiavo

Plate 33
The triangular Petroleum Industries
Pavilion, designed by Gilbert Rohde
in collaboration with the architects
Walker, Foley and Smith, included fins
of corrugated steel ascending its outer
surface in four concave strips. Behind
each strip was a channel with fluorescent tubes that bathed the building in blue light. Digital file © Eric K.
Longo/Collection of Eric K. Longo

Laura Burd Schiavo

opposite

Plate 34

The New York World's Fair Theme Center, with its spherical Perisphere, triangular Trylon tower, and spiral Helicline ramp, was a study in geometric forms. Visitors ascended by escalator to the Perisphere, where they viewed the exposition's theme exhibit, Democracity, and then retuned to ground level via the Helicline. The steel-framed structures were clad with gypsum board and painted white to emphasize the purity of form. Digital file © Eric K. Longo/Collection of Eric K. Longo.

Plate 35

Many of the Texas Centennial buildings still stand today in Dallas's Fair Park, one of the only remaining collections of intact exposition structures in the United States and one the best examples of a suite of modern architecture of the period. The fairgrounds are seen here in a 1936 view of the Esplanade at night. Courtesy Dallas Historical Society. Used by permission.

Plate 38

The Trylon and the Perisphere were framed in steel and supported by a foundation ring of concrete. The Trylon rose directly from the base. The Perisphere was raised seventeen feet on tubular steel columns, as clearly shown in this rendering by Hugh Ferriss. The ribs and joints of the steel framework seen here were detectable beneath the gypsum board surface in the finished structure (see plate 34). Hugh Ferriss, *Construction of Trylon and Perisphere,* ca. 1938. Lithograph, 19 3/4 × 26 3/4 in. The Wolfsonian–Florida International University TD 1993.12.1.

Laura Burd Schiavo

THE HOME OF THE NEW ERA

Good Housekeeping-Stran-Steel House

A Steel House You Would Want to Live In

A Century of Progress presents among its many wonders the Good Housekeeping-Stran-Steel House. Its simplicity of design and good proportions kindle the age-old love of home, but the difference between this house and many another is its Stran-Steel frame construction, its modern insulation and its fire resisting exterior of Macotta Panels. The house has six rooms with attached garage and with a roof garden over the two wings. It can be built at a cost of from $8,000 to $9,000.

Steel framing is the keynote of this modern house.

This is not a house which comes as a unit like a ready-cut house, nor is it pre-fabricated. It must be built just as any house is built, from specifications drawn up by an architect and carried out by a builder, but steel framing is used in place of wood framing. This construction may be appl to houses of quite different design, as well as

Stran-Steel will be sold by lumb building material dealers in centers of the United

Stran-Steel m and wooden b types of archi tect's plans.

Just as peg b

however, is the nail. The steel has continuous nailing grooves into which the nails are driven.

1. **STEEL CONSTRUCTED**—Can be erected by any carpenter from the usual set of plans for any style house.

2. **FIRE PROOF AND SANITARY**—This fire-resisting construction provides owners with lower insurance rates and offers proof against vermin, termites, fungus and musty odors.

3. **GREATER PERMANENCE**—No major repairs are necessary on a Stran-Steel house for many, many years.

4. **GREATER RESALE VALUE**—Houses built with Stran-Steel frames have greater mortgage and resale value, because they will settle, plaster does not crack and doors and windows fit hung.

p that the living is done on one dining alcove at one end. At o bedrooms with a bathroom directly in back of the din-'s room are at the an upstairs r sleeping. Director th effi-blend-

ned the

Plate 39

At multiple fairs the steel industry sought to advocate new uses for an established material. The Stran-Steel House at Chicago's world's fair modeled the use of steel, which had rarely been applied to residential exteriors. The Soule-Steel "Unibilt" House at San Francisco's exposition, on the other hand, promoted the use of steel in prefabricated houses, but clad the steel frame with stucco. Pamphlet, Good Housekeeping Stran-Steel House. Courtesy of Dr. Monica Garcia Brooks. Collection of Dr. Kathy Seelinger, Ensign-Seelinger Home, Huntington, West Virginia.

119

Plate 40

Putting its product explicitly on display, the U.S. Steel Pavilion, seen here on the right in the Production and Distribution Zone at the New York World's Fair, captured the beauty of steel and thus promoted its use as more than an industrial material. The metallic finish was enhanced with the application of blue paint to the external structural ribs. At night, fluorescent lights caused the glowing ribs to reflect in the shiny steel dome. Digital file © Eric K. Longo/Collection of Eric K. Longo.

Plate 41
The California architect William Wurster, known for his innovative uses of local materials suitable to the climate and ranch-style houses, designed the Yerba Buena Club, which was enclosed in glass surrounded by a wood trellis. *Architectural Forum* named the building, which served as a women's club, one of the most "distinguished" at the Golden Gate International Exposition. William W. Wurster/ WBE Collection (1955-2), Environmental Design Archives, University of California, Berkeley.

Laura Burd Schiavo

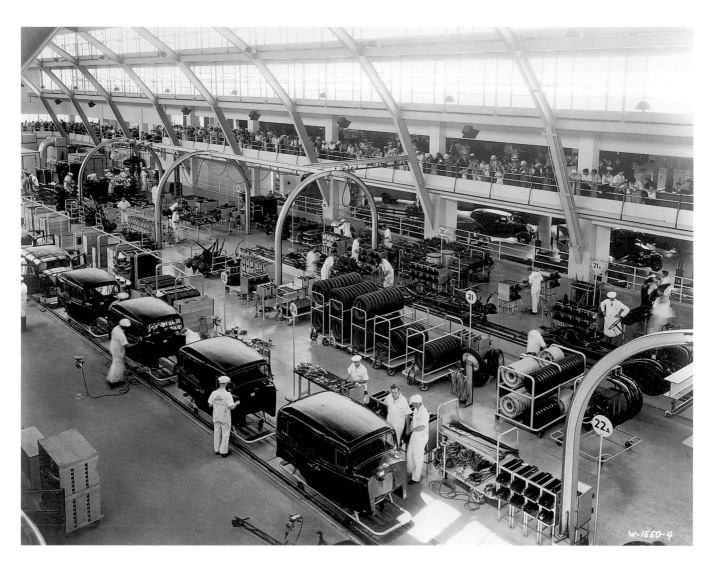

121

Plate 42
The architect Albert Kahn applied his experience designing the massive, uninterrupted interiors of automobile plants to the creation of large, open exhibition halls in Chicago, Dallas, San Francisco, and New York. The ceiling of steel and glass supported by ninety-foot steel arches in the exhibition hall of the General Motors Building in Chicago sheltered a working assembly line and an observation deck. Photo provided courtesy of Albert Kahn Family of Companies.

Innovation in Exhibition

From their start, expositions were meant to incite consumer desire. In pavilions dedicated to the display of goods, exhibits showcased row upon row of clocks, glassware, and, as industrial production heated up, pyramids of ketchup bottles and other mass-produced goods, as well as the machines that made them possible (plate 43). By the late nineteenth and early twentieth century, displays had become more sophisticated, advancing from show-casing product to demonstrating production. The ultimate expression of this trend came at the Panama Pacific International Exposition in 1915, where Henry Ford installed an assembly line that churned out as many as twenty-five Model Ts a day.[11] The world's fairs of the 1930s continued the engagement with exhibiting processes of manufacture. As Lisa Schrenk explores in her essay in this volume, pavilions across the fairgrounds exhibited the production of cars, the bottling of mayonnaise, and the manufacture of tires.

> **"A fair is essentially a meeting place for buyers and sellers."**
>
> Walter Dorwin Teague, *American Architect and Architecture*, September 1937

Following the trend of innovation in display, the fairs of the 1930s transformed the modes, methods, and even the mission of exhibits yet again. During the 1920s and 1930s corporations were involved in the development of an increasingly sophisticated public relations strategy. In the face of a broad distrust of mass production and the Depression's challenge to capitalism, industry stakeholders sought to convince the public of the trustworthiness of the corporation and the benevolent future that industrial capitalism promised—to hail the role of industry and technology in the crafting of a brighter future. World's fairs became prime venues for designers to experiment with how design innovation could visually and viscerally dramatize the promise of industrial capitalism.

Corporations hired industrial designers (Raymond Loewy, Walter Dorwin Teague, Gilbert Rohde, Henry Dreyfuss, and Norman Bel Geddes, among others) to help them put their best, and most modern, foot forward. Designers advised against creating magnified sales booths at the expositions, and as the technologies of production became more complicated, they forswore the goal of technical "consumer education." Rather, they sought to provide innovative and engaging exhibits that shared a vision of the future, a sense of the power and promise of industry, and an image of the place of consumers in that world (plate 44). But it was not only on behalf of corporations that designers labored to produce innovative displays. Fair-sponsored, state, and international pavilions also employed these innovators to craft their images in a modern exhibition format (plates 45, 46). As a result of the work of the industrial designers, "educational" exhibits in many instances outshone popular shows in the amusement zones.

The designers created showstoppers that dazzled, informed, and invited visitors into fantasies of consumption. As Schrenk recounts, they created immersive environments that included photographic murals and hailed the use of motion to heighten engagement. In many cases their design was influenced by the aesthetics of streamlining, a style particularly suited to presenting production and consumption as a seamless process, devoid of interruption or friction. An attention to "flow lines" was meant to facilitate fairgoers' progress through exhibitions.[12] The environmental design, which included circular forms and pathways, sweeping railways, revolving installation elements, ramps, and moving sidewalks, not only kept visitors moving and interested but also contributed to a sense of smoothness and ease (plates 47–50).

The new format of the diorama helped teach simple messages about the relationship of natural resources to manufactured goods. Other exhibits placed those goods in context, and helped visitors perceive themselves as active participants in the world of consumption (plates 51–53). The best examples of such spaces were the model homes described in Kristina Wilson's essay in this volume, often the most popular exhibits at the fairs (plate 54). At the same time that forward-looking museums began turning away from the systematic ordering of artifacts

Laura Burd Schiavo

> "The modern technique of sightseeing is this: you sit in a chair (wired for sound) or stand on a platform (movable, glass-embowered) and while sitting, standing, you are brought mysteriously and reverently into easy view of what you want to see. There is no shoving in the exhibit hall of Tomorrow. There is no loitering and there is usually no smoking."
>
> E. B. White, *New Yorker*, May 1939

toward the display of their collections in context, so too did world's fairs, far more popular venues, make similar strides.[13]

The ultimate in the design of continuous, controlled, immersive visitor experiences came as encounters with the speed and efficiency of the new automobiles. Ford sponsored driving experiences in San Diego, Dallas, and New York. At the Road of Tomorrow at the New York World's Fair, visitors test-drove cars along a spiral ramp built into the pavilion (plate 55). Fairgoers queued on long lines winding around the streamlined General Motors Building to experience the Futurama exhibit designed by Norman Bel Geddes (see plate 18). Once inside, they circled down a ramp along which were displayed maps projecting the expanded need for highways in the coming decades. After arriving at a 35,000-square-foot diorama of the landscape of the future, visitors sat in 552 "soundchairs" on a moving conveyor and listened to a recorded narration explaining that growth and productivity would require an expanded and improved highway system (plate 56). Their vision focused by blinders, they peered down on the model in which speedy cars smoothly merged from access road to expressway. After viewing a downtown intersection in the model, visitors stepped out of the pavilion into a life-size version of the same space (plate 57). They had, quite literally, entered the "world of tomorrow."

123

124

above
Plate 43
Typical of nineteenth-century world's fair exhibits, the Wilson Sewing Machine Company display at the 1876 International Centennial Exhibition in Philadelphia presented decontextualized rows of the company's product. (The addition of the mannequins begins to suggest use.) The detailing of the gazebo structure and the railing contrasts sharply with the display aesthetic of the 1930s fairs. Print and Picture Collection, Free Library of Philadelphia.

opposite
Plate 44
Henry Ford hired Walter Dorwin Teague to design the exhibits in the enormous Ford Building featured during the second season of Chicago's Century of Progress Exposition. In the center of the rotunda a gigantic globe illustrated the reach of Ford's operations, indicating manufacturing plants and other holdings in Europe, Asia, and Central and South America. Installations like this, dramatically rendered in Hugh Ferriss's drawing, highlighted industry's role in shaping the future of the United States and the world. The Ford V-8 engine insignia embellished the railing. Hugh Ferriss, Ford Globe, 1934. Gelatin silver photoprint of artist's drawing, $8\frac{1}{4} \times 10\frac{1}{4}$ in. Century of Progress Exposition, 1933–1934. Permission granted by The Henry Ford (P.833.59921).

130

above
Plate 49
Walter Dorwin Teague created this installation for the U.S. Steel exhibit in San Francisco. The sweeping lines, the smooth surfaces, and the incorporation of a stylized map are typical of Teague's exhibits at the fairs. Photograph by Esther Born. Ernest and Esther Born Collection (2001-15), Environmental Design Archives, University of California, Berkeley.

opposite
Plate 50
The smooth, flowing shape of the relief map of South America in Ernest Born's design for the Brazil Pavilion contrasts with the far more angular lines of Gardner Dailey's architecture. Handmade modern furnishings of Brazilian hardwoods decorated the pavilion. Murals (here by Jane Berlandina) and raised lettering were common to many exhibits at the fairs. Gardner Dailey Collection (1998-1), Environmental Design Archives, University of California, Berkeley.

Modern Design Goes Public

Plate 51
This domed structure featured in the industry section of the Ford Building at the Chicago fair dramatically imparted Henry Ford's message about the relationship between the natural world and industry. Graphic arrows link the components of the Ford V-8 with their respective "basic elements," each represented by a diorama. The horizontal lines on the base of the structure and the railings and the rounded form imply an allegedly frictionless relationship between natural resources and industrial production. Photo provided courtesy of Albert Kahn Family of Companies.

Laura Burd Schiavo

133

"People must *flow* in an exhibit. Audiences follow the line of least resistance just as water does, and it is much easier to take them around a slow curve than to make them turn an abrupt corner."

Walter Dorwin Teague, *American Architect and Architecture*, September 1937

Plate 52

Walter Dorwin Teague's design for the Ford Cycle of Production in New York was a stylized interpretation of the assembly line Ford had first introduced to expositions in 1915. The rotating platform of concentric steps rose thirty feet above a circular base one hundred feet in diameter. Like Teague's 1934 installation for Ford in Chicago (see plate 51), the exhibit illustrated the evolution from raw materials to finished cars, here adding animated, racialized, cartoonish figures in more than eighty vignettes of automobile manufacture, from cotton picking and asbestos mining to the production of molded plastic. From the Collection of The Henry Ford (P.O. 4845).

THERE IS MORE ROMANCE IN MO

GENERAL ELECTRIC AIR CONDITIONING SUMMER AND WINTER

W-1760-2

Plate 53
This exhibit, part of the elaborate General Electric display at the Century of Progress Exposition, helped visitors visualize GE's products as part of their daily lives. The clever cutaway installation signified that a modern home was one outfitted with GE appliances. The lettering above reads, "There is more romance in modern industry than in all history." [COP_17_0001_ 00014_023], Century of Progress Records, 1927–1952, University of Illinois, Chicago, Library.

Laura Burd Schiavo

Plate 54

Millions of visitors walked through the Design for Living House at the Chicago world's fair with its modern furnishings and layout. Gilbert Rohde designed furnishings that could help separate the functions of the large, multipurpose living room. Chicago History Museum.

Plate 55

At Ford's Road of Tomorrow visitors test-drove cars along a spiral ramp built into the pavilion, circling for more than half a mile around a garden court and through a tunnel lined with murals depicting modern highway construction. Concealed lighting strips along the guard rails created a spectacular vision at night. The curved walls and rounded parapets of the General Motors Building are visible in the background of this photograph. Albert Kahn was the architect for both buildings. From the Collection of The Henry Ford (P.O. 19796).

Laura Burd Schiavo

Plate 56
Futurama exhibit spectators,
General Motors Building. Photograph
by Margaret Bourke-White. Harry
Ransom Humanities Research
Center, University of Texas, Austin.

Laura Burd Schiavo

Plate 57
Intersection of the Future installation, General Motors Building. Harry Ransom Humanities Research Center, University of Texas, Austin, courtesy the Estate of Edith Lutyens Bel Geddes.

Notes

This essay, and the National Building Museum exhibition on which it is based, would have been impossible without Lisa Schrenk's seminal work on the architecture of the Century of Progress Exposition. I wish to thank Robert Rydell, Chrysanthe Broikos, Sarah Leavitt, and Martin Moeller for reviewing early drafts of this essay. Thanks also to the curatorial team for *Designing Tomorrow:* Deborah Sorensen, Brigid Laurie, Stephanie Anderson, Amy Barr, Andrew Costanzo, and Diane Riley.

1. Alfred Granger, *Chicago Welcomes You* (Chicago: A. Kroch, 1933), 235, quoted in Lisa D. Schrenk, *Building a Century of Progress: The Architecture of Chicago's 1933–34 World's Fair* (Minneapolis: University of Minnesota Press), 58.
2. Walter Dorwin Teague, "Exhibition Techniques," *American Architect and Architecture,* September 1937, p. 33.
3. Eugene A. Santomasso, "The Design of Reason: Architecture and Planning at the 1939/40 New York World's Fair," in *Dawn of a New Day: The New York World's Fair, 1939/40* (New York: New York University Press, Queens Museum, 1980), 32.
4. Schrenk, *Building a Century of Progress,* esp. chapter 2.
5. Frederick A. Gutheim, "Buildings at the Fair," *Magazine of Art* 32 (1939): 286.
6. Richard S. Requa, *Inside Lights on the Building of San Diego's Exposition, 1935* (San Diego: Parker H. Jackson, 1977), 59. This is a reissue of a title originally published in 1937.
7. *Official Guide Book: Golden Gate International Exposition on San Francisco Bay* (San Francisco Bay Exposition, 1939), 108.
8. Frederick A. Gutheim, "The Buildings and the Plan," *Magazine of Art* 32 (1939): 136.
9. Alfred Frankenstein, "Pageant of the Pacific," *Magazine of Art* 32 (1939): 134.
10. Quoted in "Dream of Fair Colors," *Movie Makers,* June 1939, p. 276. See Helen A. Harrison, "The Fair Perceived: Color and Light as Elements in Design and Planning," in *Dawn of a New Day,* 45–46.
11. Roland Marchand, *Creating the Corporate Soul: The Rise of Public Relations and Corporate Imagery in American Big Business* (Berkeley: University of California Press, 1998), 264.
12. Douglas Haskell, "Tomorrow at the World's Fair," *Architectural Record,* August 1940, p. 66; Teague, "Exhibition Techniques," 31. See also Marchand, *Creating the Corporate Soul,* 281.
13. For a discussion of this movement in museums see Steven Conn, *Museums and American Intellectual Life, 1876–1926* (Chicago: University of Chicago Press, 1998), chapter 7.

Designing the Modern Family at the Fairs

Kristina Wilson

As scholars in this volume and elsewhere have argued, the U.S. world's fairs of the 1930s were driven by two dominant forces: the public's fascination with science and the engines of corporate wealth.[1] Perhaps nowhere were these twin forces so compellingly aligned than in the model home exhibits included in each fair. In the collections of model homes—which began as a phenomenally popular cluster of eleven houses in Chicago, continued in smaller groups in San Diego, Dallas, and Cleveland, and concluded with a parade of fifteen houses in New York's Town of Tomorrow and a staggering twenty five houses in San Francisco—the public could see, on an intimate, domestic scale, how science could improve daily living. Fair houses inevitably featured the most up-to-date appliances in the kitchen and demonstrated new household systems such as air conditioning (especially effective since the fairs were all open in the summer months). Some fair houses ventured further than mere demonstrations of present-day science by presenting technology that was blatantly futuristic, such as Chicago's House of Tomorrow, which featured doors that opened and closed with the wave of a hand and a garage to house the family car and hydroplane.[2]

In the model homes of the fairs, visitors encountered science, physically and immediately, through the gleaming products of countless corporations. Indeed, visitors' appreciation of scientific progress became inseparable from their ability to identify the corporations that had applied science to the domestic sphere.

While the model homes in the 1930s fairs can be seen as veritable jewel boxes in which fascination with scientific progress merged eloquently with an ethos of consumerism, in this essay I want to examine them from a different perspective. As highly public displays of that most private of spaces—the single-family home—the model houses of the world's fairs literally provided shelter to a standardized, model American family. An analysis of the trends that circulated through the various houses reveals how the American middle-class family was idealized during the decade of the Great Depression. While some aspects of domestic life seemed poised to change dramatically in these model homes, other elements remained firmly attached to domestic precedents established in the later nineteenth century. Ultimately, the model homes of the 1930s fairs were sites of contestation, where modernizing forces repeatedly intersected with traditional idioms, and where the definition of the modern American family was thus continually negotiated and redrawn.[3]

The changes found in these houses did not progress uniformly over the course of the Depression years; that is, the houses did not become emphatically more radical by the end of the decade. Rather, patterns of living and standards of furnishings varied, with some more "modern" elements stronger in the early fairs and others more prominent in the later fairs. In the first part of this essay I examine the proliferation of styles in the model homes, both in their furnishings and in their exterior design. There were, oddly enough, many more modernist interiors and exteriors earlier in the decade; by 1939, furnishings and architectural style had become more reliant on period-derived models. In the second part of the essay I focus on the floor plans of the houses. I propose that the earlier houses, despite their aesthetic modernity, held fast to nineteenth-century practices in organizing domestic space, while the houses from the 1939 fairs, more conservative in style, offered several innovations in the allocation of domestic space—innovations that would become standard in the post–World War II modern ranch house. The historian Lawrence Levine has described the decade of the 1930s as "a complex world of conflicting urges: a world that looked to the past even as it began to assume the contours of the future."[4] It is this world of conflicted ideals that is captured in the world's fairs' model homes when they are examined from the various perspectives of interior furnishings, exterior design, and floor plan: in some ways they became more modern as the decade progressed, and in other ways more attached to precedent. As we turn to a closer analysis of individual houses, this complexity will persist, revealing a society where the struggle to balance tradition and the new were constantly being recalibrated.

A Cacophony of Styles

One of the most surprising elements in the model homes is their stylistic plurality, both in architectural form and interior furnishings. In Chicago, more than at any other fair, the architectural style of the houses was almost uniformly modern (loosely defined as blocky masses, planar facades, little ornament, and broad expanses of windows); in every other fair for which photographs survive, the houses

were a mix of modern and various period revival styles, ranging from Spanish Colonial in the California fairs to traditional center-entrance Colonial designs in New York. Moreover, the percentage of modern houses in each fair decreased as the decade wore on, with the consequence that the earlier fairs seem to be, in general, more aesthetically radical than the later ones. In San Diego in 1935, fully half of the homes were modern; in Dallas in 1936, one of four homes was explicitly modern; the few images that survive from Cleveland in 1937 suggest there were no modern homes. In New York in 1939, four out of fifteen homes were emphatically modern, while in San Francisco, one critic claimed that only three of the twenty-five were modern (but my somewhat more generous assessment puts it at seven).[5]

Likewise, the furnishings with which these houses were outfitted varied dramatically, and there were greater numbers of modernist interiors earlier in the decade than later. Some houses displayed an austere, German-inspired modernism, predicated on tubular steel and an overall effect of efficient minimalism, while others featured a blockier, somewhat heavier modernism that used more wood and upholstery. (I have called this mode of modernism in the United States, which catered to consumer desires for bodily comfort and familiarity, livable modernism.)[6] Yet other houses contained sets of turned-wood chairs and trestle tables, commonly marketed as Early American, and some had suites of floral upholstery and carved wood chairs that might have been labeled Queen Anne or Chippendale by manufacturers and retailers. In short, the furnishings ran the gamut of styles available to the consumer of the 1930s.

Such stylistic variety may seem to be at odds with the fairs' focus on technology and the future. However, when viewed through the lens of the corporate interests that shaped the fairs, the proliferation of styles evident in these model homes was to be expected. Throughout the 1930s, furniture manufacturers delved into the modernist market with varying degrees of commitment and enthusiasm, and usually offered a line of modernist designs alongside a wide range of period lines. While modernist designers may have been committed to the utopian ideals that underlay modernism in Europe—including a belief that smaller modern homes would benefit from multifunc-

Kristina Wilson

tional, smaller furniture and that a lack of ornament liberated the mind from the confines of history—their beliefs must be distinguished from those guiding furniture manufacturers and retailers. The latter group was remarkably open in its tastes: manufacturers and retailers alike were willing to offer anything that might sell in these years. Thus the cacophony of furnishing styles on view at the various world's fairs of the 1930s must be seen as a consequence of the catholic approach to styles found in the commercial sector.

Nonetheless, within the marketplace of the 1930s, modernism possessed a level of distinction that set it apart from period styles en masse. First, it was often the most unusual-looking style on the furniture floor to a casual browser: few curves, little ornament, often a sense of bluntness. Second, modern designs were promoted by elite institutions such as museums, which elevated any object classified as modern to a status somewhere near art. And third, advertisements routinely associated modern styles with ideas about change, improvement, and youthful optimism. Because modernism had this distinction, where it appears in the model homes of the world's fairs may be significant: its appearance might signal a willingness to try different patterns of living, or at least a willingness to promote different domestic standards. I use *may* and *might* because it is also possible that the appearance of modernism signaled nothing more than a marketer's desire to vary the merchandise. In short, I do not want to attribute too much significance to the appearance of modern design in these model homes, but I do want to interrogate the lifestyles that they prescribe.

The most avant-garde interiors of the 1930s world's fairs were to be found in Chicago.[7] It is this fair, therefore, that gives us the best purchase on the significance of modernism as a domestic style. The collection of eleven model homes was among the biggest successes of the Chicago fair. In the summer of 1933, more than 1.5 million visitors traipsed through the homes, and because of the wear exacted on their interiors, each house was refurnished for the 1934 season. Many of the homes embraced a fully modernist aesthetic, none more famously than George Fred Keck's House of Tomorrow. As several scholars have discussed, Keck's twelve-sided, glass-walled house offered an optimistically futuristic vision of the American home.[8]

None of the glass walls opened to the outdoors (although there were a few glass doors onto the various terraces), and the air inside was instead ventilated through heating or cooling systems; the kitchen was entirely electric. The various rooms of the house were arranged on the main floor like pie pieces around the central stairway core, with the two bedrooms and a bathroom to one side and the open living room–dining room and the kitchen on the other. In both the 1933 and 1934 decoration schemes, the living room was anchored by a collection of wide, deep, upholstered armchairs with blunt lines (the 1934 furniture was designed by Gilbert Rohde for the Herman Miller Furniture Company) (figs. 1, 2). The room felt open because it contained relatively few pieces of furniture, which were placed to maximize the sense of spaciousness. The 1934 version had a geometrically patterned deep pile rug, which added texture and irregularity to the room. Its tufted, rounded armchairs, with their extraordinarily deep seats, offered to envelop the sitter's body, and such unusual elements as the asymmetrical cabinet or three-legged side table offered passages of surprise and visual delight to the inhabitant. It was an interior that catered to the comfort of the physical body and the joy of the psyche. In contrast, the 1933 living room was dominated by a large, angular macassar ebony pier table with two broad, conical lamps; these objects introduced a sense of spareness and geometric clarity to the room. Thus, while the two versions of the living room shared several features, the 1934 iteration moved toward a greater blurring of contours and a general sense of blended textures and warmth.

The Chicago homes also displayed period revival styles. The living room of the Stran-Steel House in 1934 was furnished largely with a selection of objects indebted to the slender, neoclassical impulses of early-nineteenth-century Federal furniture (fig. 3). A curved, fringe-skirted sofa (certainly not Federal) was grouped with a pedestal table, a scrolled armchair, and an upholstered chair on cabriole legs. Around the mirrored fireplace, a pair of upholstered easy chairs and tapered-legged side tables created an inviting place to sit. Fireplaces had been a symbolic heart of American family living spaces since the nineteenth century, when a fascination with the colonial-era open hearth and the sentimental idea of a family gathered around it came into vogue. Despite its status as an unnecessary accessory

143

fig. 1 Living room, House of Tomorrow, 1933. George Fred Keck, architect. Century of Progress Exposition, Chicago, 1933–1934. Chicago History Museum.

fig. 2 Living room, House of Tomorrow, 1934. George Fred Keck, architect. Gilbert Rohde, furniture design for Herman Miller Furniture Company. Dorothy Raley, *Homes and Furnishings at the Chicago Century of Progress Exposition* (Chicago: M. A. Ring, 1934).

opposite
fig. 3 Living room, Good House-keeping Stran-Steel House, 1934. O'Dell and Rowland, architects. Dorothy Raley, *Homes and Furnishings at the Chicago Century of Progress Exposition* (Chicago: M. A. Ring, 1934).

in an age of central heat, throughout the first decades of the twentieth century the fireplace continued to have a strong psychological appeal, and architects and designers of all stylistic orientations willingly incorporated it into their plans.[9]

While the Stran-Steel House living room unquestionably embraced a historicized aesthetic, it ultimately provided a setting for domestic life that was remarkably similar to the modernism of the 1934 House of Tomorrow. Throughout these homes one finds an emphasis on enveloping, bodily comfort in the proliferation of deep-seated, thick-cushioned upholstered pieces. These interiors also catered to the mental ease of the inhabitant, providing cozy furniture for conversation or interesting objects to gaze upon. The major difference lies in the question of quantity: the modernist interiors simply had fewer objects in them, giving primacy to a sense of openness and spaciousness, while the period-styled interiors had more pieces of furniture and a greater sense of congestion. The modernism of the Chicago houses indicates that designers did not wish to challenge the capitalist ideal of the individual private home as a place of retreat and rejuvenation, but they did want to address the experience of confined spaces that charac-

terized so many homes in the years of the Great Depression. These designers wanted the public to reevaluate its penchant for accumulation and to sacrifice the practice of conspicuous display for a greater sense of openness and the ease that comes with having fewer pieces to navigate (and clean) in a given room.[10]

Of the four model homes in the Dallas fair of 1936, one was emphatically modern. The living room of this house was furnished almost entirely with pieces designed by Rohde for Herman Miller, and their arrangement indicates the persistence of several ideals embodied in the Chicago houses (fig. 4).[11] The pair of armchairs by the fireplace provide a place for individuals to literally take warmth from the family hearth; both the pair of armchairs in the photograph's foreground and the L-shaped sectional sofa against the window provide amenable settings for conversation, tea, or cocktails; and the card table group next to the radio is an arena in which the family, or its guests, can gather to play games. In short, the entire room was designed to foster welcoming retreat and social engagement. And despite the large number of objects in the room (more than in any modernist room in the Chicago homes), the emphatic open space in the center of the photograph and the predominance of blunt, angled contours give it an air of clarity and spaciousness.

In the model homes of the 1939–1940 New York fair (making up the group The Town of Tomorrow), there were far fewer examples of modernist interiors, and the remaining houses pursued a stricter adherence to period styles than the period-"inspired" interiors in Chicago. Critics were, in general, less enthusiastic about the furnishings in New York than in Chicago, as is evidenced by tepid reviews and the lack of coverage in major shelter magazines (*House Beautiful,* for example, devoted only two pages to the New York homes in 1939, while in 1933 it ran a three-page article on a single house at the Chicago fair).[12] In the architectural journal *Pencil Points,* the critic Talbot F. Hamlin complained,

One thing, alas, is to be found in both sets of houses [in New York and San Francisco]—terrible furnishing and decoration. Not one of those which I saw in either Fair showed any but the vaguest sense of that quality of repose and quiet comfort which comes from the fitness of the means to the end. Everything seems to have been

fig. 4 Living room, Contemporary Home. DeWitt and Washburn, architects. Gilbert Rohde, furniture design for Herman Miller Furniture Company. Texas Centennial Exposition, Dallas, 1936. Courtesy Dallas Historical Society. Used by permission.

done in the most complicated, most stunty, most vulgarly ostentatious manner, and this goes for the houses which were theoretically modern as much as for those in the "styles." . . . All the interiors seemed more like the over-full show windows of a not too high-toned shop rather than the environment for human living.[13]

Hamlin's final turn of phrase may have been an allusion to the Swiss architect Le Corbusier's famous description of the house as a "machine for living," and as such reveals his bias.[14] Hamlin, in accord with European modernist architects, believed that homes should facilitate ease and comfort of living through simplified design. He criticized the furnishings in the fairs' model homes for their excessiveness: there were too many objects that were too ornate, and the homes became, in effect, models of excessive display rather than models of modern living. However, Emily Genauer, an arts editor for the *New York World-Telegram*, found qualities to celebrate in the modernism of the New York fair. Describing the mode of modernism put forth in Chicago as "straight simple lines and chunky forms," she argued that the influence of the 1937 Paris World's Fair had contributed to a broader sense of modernism in 1939. She described the new trend as one of "graciousness"

and "elegance," "whether it is straight, softly tapering, or flowing in wide but disciplined curves," designed to appeal to "our emotions rather than our intellect."[15] Whereas Hamlin believed that the fairs offered inadequate (or nonexistent) modernism, Genauer interpreted the modernism at the New York fair as a style that more willingly engaged with popular ideas about the home.

The most emphatically modern house in the New York fair was the House of Glass, designed by Landefeld and Hatch and decorated by Modernage Furniture Company. (Modernage furnished two of the fair's four modernist interiors.) Modernage was a manufacturer and retailer of modern furnishings based in New York City; it was founded in 1926 and advertised itself throughout the 1930s as an affordable source for modernist furnishings.[16] Over the years the retail arm sold objects by many modernist designers (and the architect Frederick Kiesler designed its showroom in 1933), but its manufacturing arm, the source of the most affordable objects, was never associated with any specific artist. Instead, it offered pieces that were often clearly derived from designs created by known figures such as Rohde or Donald Deskey.[17] That Modernage, a manufacturer known more for its knock-offs than for its original

147

fig. 5 House of Glass. Landefeld and Hatch, architects. New York World's Fair, 1939–1940. "Modern Houses Top N.Y. Fair," *Architectural Forum*, July 1939.

designs, was the primary supplier of modernist furnishings for the fair is revealing. Its popularizing mission made it an appropriate choice for the fair, where some visitors would be seeing modernist furnishings in person for the first time. Yet its designs, often derivative or poorly conceived, were lower in quality than the modernist objects from the earlier fairs. The choice of Modernage thus meant that visitors to the fair did not see the best modern design available, and suggests that organizers for the Town of Tomorrow were either less knowledgeable about modern design than earlier fair organizers, or less invested in it overall.

The House of Glass was one of the largest and most expensive homes in the fair, and was architecturally indebted to the international style: it had a flat roof, ample terraces to front, back, and side, and continuous ribbons of window (sometimes alternating with glass brick) around its surface (fig. 5). Modernage furnished the living room with a built-in sofa before the fireplace (attached to a series of built-in bookshelves); it also featured a pair of barrel-form armchairs with sloping arms (somewhat less radical, perhaps, than the purely cylindrical forms of Rohde's chairs in the Dallas house).

In a poll conducted by *Architectural Forum* of visitors to the Town of Tomorrow, the favorite house was the modest building known as the Bride's House, also designed by Landefeld and Hatch and furnished by Gimbel Brothers department store.[18] The Bride's House was superficially more conservative than the House of Glass, with its pitched roof and red brick chimney; however, critics described it as modern because of the use of glass brick to partition the dining alcove, and the recreation room which opened directly onto a side terrace. In the living room, the furnishings were less explicitly modern than the Chicago or Dallas interiors, and even less so than in the House of Glass (fig. 6). A pair of upholstered settees in a broad floral pattern, with diminutive, tapered legs, were arranged around the fireplace. Together with the slender, tapered legs of a side table and coffee table, these objects created an effect of sinuous, curvy elegance that echoed Emily Genauer's description of modernism at the fair. Yet the living room also included at least two more upholstered armchairs, a built-in bookshelf, and a heavy wooden desk, creating an interior space far too crowded to be graceful. If the House of Glass maintained some of the spare openness of the Chicago modernist interiors, the Bride's House

left
fig. 6 Living room, Bride's House. Landefeld and Hatch, architects. New York World's Fair, 1939–1940. "Modern Houses Top N.Y. Fair," *Architectural Forum*, July 1939.

148

seemed to fit Hamlin's complaint: its many pieces of furniture made the room seem cramped, more invested in showing off the wealth of its owners than in catering to their ease of living.

The modernist interiors in New York were far outnumbered by historically based interiors. Many houses had living rooms in which the central focus of the fireplace was framed with a pair of upholstered, skirted armchairs with rolled arms (taken from the eighteenth-century wing chair form) and floral patterns.[19] The New England House, designed by the architect Cameron Clark, was a representative example. Its early American–flavored living room (also furnished by Gimbel Brothers) included the requisite pair of skirted wing chairs and turned-leg side tables (fig. 7). Its mantelpiece featured classicizing ornament, akin to that found in early-nineteenth-century New England homes; above this, a square mirror had a carved, rococo frame.

As in Chicago, the modernist interiors in New York ultimately seemed designed to enable a similar manner of domestic living as the period-revival-influenced interiors. All recognized the symbolic importance of the fireplace and placed it at the center of living room organization; all fostered social interactions and provided bodily comfort.

Moreover, the modernist interiors in New York inclined toward overpopulation—every chair had a side table, and perhaps also a coffee table before it, and the sheer number of objects made clear passage through spaces difficult. The modernist interior no longer challenged middle-class acquisitiveness; it, like the period interiors, promoted accumulation and enabled the display of material wealth.

Although no interior images of the San Francisco houses have yet been discovered, Hamlin's disparaging comment indicates that he felt the West Coast interiors, like those in New York, suffered from too many objects and too heavy a reliance on period styles. The exterior architectural design of the homes, too, indicates a level of stylistic variegation similar to the New York fair's homes. Among the more avant-garde designs was Gardner Dailey's Woodside Hills and William Wilson Wuster's Kent Woodlands.[20] Both featured living rooms that projected from the back of the house and had windows on three sides. Dailey's design was particularly avant-garde, with its flat roof and expanses of floor-to-ceiling windows. More affordable was Birge M. Clark and David B. Clark's Leland Manor, designed in a so-called "modernized craftsman" style (fig. 8).[21] The slightly sloping roof, with a two-and-a-half-foot overhang, gave the **149**

opposite right
fig. 7 Living room, New England House. Cameron Clark, architect. New York World's Fair, 1939–1940. "Modern Houses Top N.Y. Fair," *Architectural Forum*, July 1939.

fig. 8 Exterior, Leland Manor. Birge M. Clark and David B. Clark, architects. Golden Gate International Exposition, San Francisco, 1939–1940. "Exposition Model Homes," *Pencil Points*, May 1939.

effect of the single-story house gently hugging the horizon, similar to the effect Frank Lloyd Wright had achieved in his Prairie Houses but with an even greater simplicity (owing in part to the smaller size of the house). Leland Manor also featured an open living room that extended the full depth of the house's central section, with windows to the front and two doors opening directly to the back terrace (fig. 9). The more traditional houses in San Francisco featured steeply pitched roofs, such as Oak Grove Manor (designed by Leo J. Sharps) and Oak Knoll Manor (by Charles F. Maury).[22] In both of these houses, the living room was positioned to the right of a center entrance, more akin to the center-entrance floor plan of a typical eighteenth-century Colonial house.

Despite the proliferation of styles in the homes of the world's fairs of the 1930s, it is clear that some kind of modernism was more prominent in the earlier fairs, while the later fairs returned to more conservative period styles. Any explanations for this must be speculative at best. The Chicago fair was held at the grimmest point of the Great Depression; during the New York and San Francisco fairs, although the country was undoubtedly still feeling the effects of the economic crisis, the most bitter years had passed and a level of stability had been recovered for many families. The darkest moment in the national crisis may have bred the most emphatic attempt to deal with it. In the years when consumers felt least empowered, Chicago's modernism tried to address the loss of ability to accumulate: it advocated fewer objects and a greater sense of openness, qualities which were intended not to alienate inhabitants but rather to make them feel less confined and more the lords and ladies of a spacious interior. Moreover, the simple forms were supposed to be easier to clean, alleviating housework for the wife, who might be working outside the home to help support the family. By 1939, when the brutal reality of the early 1930s had begun to fade, designers offered interiors that once more flattered the American family's ability to acquire, with their busy arrangements of numerous objects. In a promotional movie produced by Westinghouse for the New York fair, a passing comment about modernist furnishings reveals some intangible attitudes toward the style. A grandmother and her granddaughter pause before a display of modernist furniture, and the elder woman urges the younger to bring her socialist boyfriend to see it; after all, she concludes, even he must be interested in domesticity. By the end of

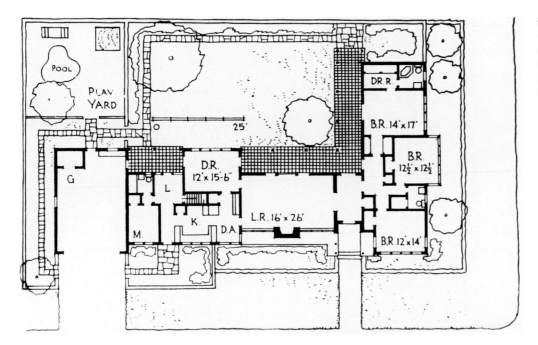

fig. 9 Floor plan, Leland Manor. Clark and Clark, architects. Golden Gate International Exposition, San Francisco, 1939–1940. "Exposition Model Homes," *Pencil Points*, May 1939.

the movie, however, the socialist has been exposed as an intolerant cad, and the modernist furniture, in retrospect, is tinged with his association (the granddaughter chooses the midwestern capitalist boy instead). Modernism, in this logic, promoted minimal materialism, which threatened the American ideals of capitalism and free competition. In such a context, it is little wonder that New York's modernism was both smaller in quantity and changed in quality to more closely reflect the principles of period-styled American families.

Modern Floor Plans

If the aesthetics of architectural styles and furnishings of world's fair homes appeared to become increasingly conservative over the course of the 1930s, the floor plans reveal a different, though equally complicated, story. These changes indicate a significant, if gradual, shift in family living patterns toward a postwar lifestyle of increased efficiency and informality. The changes in orientation of the living room and kitchen, described below, were to become standard elements in the 1950s suburban ranch (exemplified by developers such as William J. Levitt on the East Coast and Joseph L. Eichler on the West), making the 1939 model homes true early-stage examples of this influential type. At the same time, certain forms based on nineteenth-century precedent, such as the strict division of social and private spaces and the maintenance of a dining room, remained tenacious throughout the decade. In short, the change in floor plans among the model fair homes can be seen as a gradual, if incomplete, process of modernization, which appears to contradict the growing conservativeness of architectural and furnishing aesthetics.

The suburban Victorian single family home, developed in the latter half of the nineteenth century, was characterized by its many rooms: as historians have argued, the increasing professionalization of middle-class life seems to have insinuated itself into the domestic sphere, and each separate task in the family realm was assigned its own unique space.[23] Thus a house often contained a formal front parlor and a more casual back parlor; a separate dining room devoted to meals; a study in which the man of the house could retreat from domestic chaos; the kitchen and maid's quarters, which usually demanded their own

distinct architectural space; and bedrooms for children and adults, often accommodating no more than two people. Emerging from this maze of rooms were three fairly distinct zones: a public or socializing zone on the main floor (with degrees of intimacy, as the front and back parlor indicated); a service zone comprising the kitchen, laundry, and servant rooms; and the family's private zone of bedrooms, almost always on the second floor. Although house design was drastically simplified in the early decades of the twentieth century—in the bungalows of the 1900s and even the suburban period-styled houses of the 1920s, multiple social and study spaces were condensed into a single living room, servant's rooms were eliminated, and kitchens were streamlined—one element of the Victorian ideal remained intact: the separation of social and private zones.[24] Accordingly, in the model homes of the 1930s fairs, bedrooms and bathrooms were, without fail, segregated to one side, wing, or floor of a house. Bathrooms intended for use by guests were incorporated somewhere near the vicinity of the kitchen and were readily accessible from the living room; if no such separate guest bathroom existed, almost every house provided a short hallway or foyer space around the bathroom, making it possible for guests to reach it without treading on the sacred privacy of bedrooms. And what happened in these bedrooms? They were not merely places for sleeping or dressing, as is evidenced by the fairly generous size of the rooms and the tendency to furnish them with desks or comfortable armchairs. Children played with friends or studied in their rooms, and mothers talked to their children, or perhaps a particularly close friend, in their rooms. Bedrooms were not simply a separate space designed to meet the function of sleeping, but rather were a zone where a different order of intimacy and informality dominated.

If the fairs' homes revealed a stubborn Victorian-ness in their rigorous zoning between public and private, the status of dining rooms in these homes reveals a more confused relationship to precedent. The Victorian-era separate dining room had been under attack by designers, architects, and home economists throughout the first decades of the twentieth century; most believed that a dining room was a flagrant waste of space in an era of smaller homes and increased informality. The alternative to a dining room was either an alcove adjacent to the main space of the

151

living room, or simply a corner of the living room itself, perhaps furnished with a table that could be converted, by inserting leaves, into a dining table when needed. With the onset of the Great Depression, when fewer people had the resources for entertaining and perhaps lived in even smaller spaces than before, the argument against the separate dining room seemed to speak to the logic of the times.[25] Accordingly, in the model homes in the Chicago and San Diego fairs, about one-third had a separate dining room altogether, while most had either a modest alcove or a small corner of a living room designated for dining; in a few, no space appeared to have been planned for dining at all. Yet in 1939, the majority of houses shown in both New York and San Diego had designated dining spaces, usually an entirely separate room or else a well-defined alcove off of the living room. The rooms indicate an apparent move back to the Victorian standard, and perhaps a lingering attachment to the ideal of having a distinguished dining space where guests could be impressed and the family gathered together for special occasions. Indeed, a survey conducted by *Architectural Record* in that year found that a majority of respondents preferred a separate dining room in their houses (and most of them desired the formal ideal of a coordinated dining room suite to furnish the room).[26] This change—away from a more informal and less traditional style of domestic living—suggests some of the complicated forces at play during the decade of the 1930s. While the brutality of the early years of the Depression may have made designers and architects more willing to assert ideas of modernized living in the fairs in Chicago and San Diego, by the end of the decade those same players seemed to understand that the public had held fast to an ideal of grand hospitality from an entirely different era. The appeal of this vision of dining and entertaining may have been made stronger, in fact, by the adversity of the decade; as Lawrence Levine has suggested, the economic crisis inspired surprisingly little revolutionary thought and action, and many citizens seemed instead to cling to stable images of a more prosperous status quo.[27]

Thus far, my analysis of the floor plans of the model houses suggests a move *away* from modernization over the course of the 1930s. This trend is contradicted, or at least complicated, by changes to the position of both living

rooms and kitchens. At the beginning of the twentieth century, as the space where guests were entertained, the living room typically faced the front or more public side of the house. The industrial designer Norman Bel Geddes had argued as early as 1931, however, that living rooms should be positioned at the back of the house to allow for "seclusion" and access to the outdoors of the backyard.[28] His rationale—that the back of the house has greater privacy—indicated a shift in ideas about what the living room was used for, and more broadly what the home was to be used for. By privileging the family's privacy over its public face, he implied that houses should be for the comfort of its inhabitants foremost and that guests were not only less important but also perhaps less present. In short, he presumed that the American home was less a place for entertaining than it may have been previously, and his vision implied a suburban sea of isolated families, a society atomized within its architectural skin.

Bel Geddes, as was often his lot, proved to be far ahead of society's desires when he urged the backyard-facing living room. In the model homes in Chicago, despite the modernity of the exteriors, only one-third of the houses had a living room that faced the back of the house. In San

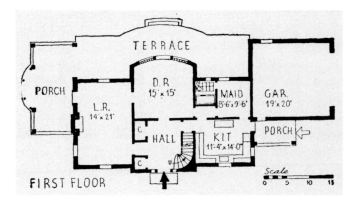

fig. 10 Floor plan, Electric Home. James W. O'Connor, architect. New York World's Fair, 1939–1940. "Modern Houses Top N.Y. Fair," *Architectural Forum,* July 1939.

Diego most of the houses had living rooms that spanned one full side or else opened exclusively to the back. In New York, many of the houses adhered to a center-entrance floor plan and placed the living room to one side of the central hallway; these living rooms spanned the entire depth of the house, and often had doorways opening to terraces on the back or side. Thus, despite the conservative template, alterations were made that oriented the life of the family toward the more private sides of the house and away from its public face.[29] Finally, in San Francisco, a new style of floor plan began to emerge that changed the concept of the living room altogether. In the majority of these houses, one entered through a small alcove or foyer directly into a living room that spanned the full depth of the house. This living room was positioned in the central block of the house (with service and private zones often relegated to wings). While the living room, as in the New York houses, had a front face, its orientation was clearly to the back, where, via glass walls or doors, it engaged a backyard patio (fig. 10).[30] This living room was literally the core of the house; in most designs, one had to traverse its length in order to walk from bedroom to kitchen, and guests entering the front door were thrust almost immediately into its space. These living rooms were inescapable, and because of that, had a more dynamic, less formal quality than even the living rooms in New York: they were spaces for sitting still and for walking through, for welcoming guests and (in the absence of a library or study) for repose and relaxation. While these houses enabled a greater level of privacy for the family with their backyard orientation, they also proposed a new calibration of public and private, one where the household itself was less fastidious about hiding outsiders from its daily goings-on. This new style of living, both more nuclear-family-focused and more casual, represents a significant level of modernization within the model homes of the fairs.

The changing status of the kitchen in the world's fairs' model homes indicates one more trend toward modernization over the course of the 1930s. In Chicago, only three out of eleven homes placed the kitchen at the front of the house, while the rest located the kitchen to the side or back; in San Diego, likewise, only one house had a kitchen in the front of the house. By 1939 many more homes featured kitchens in the front, even several of the conservative period-influenced styles in New York. "The kitchen is progressing from its traditional location on the view-commanding rear of the house to the side or front," *Architectural Forum* noted approvingly, and then singled out houses in which "The kitchen has been moved to the house's least desirable exposure—the front."[31] This shift anticipates the kitchen location of the typical postwar suburban ranch. Like the changing location and status of the living room, the moving of the kitchen suggests shifting concepts of privacy. In the nineteenth century, the kitchen was banished to the farthest corners of the house because of its smells and messes; it needed to be hidden, although it was not a place of psychological privacy like the bedroom. By the 1930s modern technology—in the form of running water, gas or electric ranges, and electric refrigerators—had made the kitchen a more palatable place, and the de facto privacy of the service zone became irrelevant. Not only did kitchens become discreet and efficient, but their modernity was now something to brag about. The International Nickel Company, maker of the countertop alloy Monel Metal, furnished work surfaces for all of the kitchens in New York's Town of Tomorrow (including the Smartline Table, used in the kitchen of the Motor Home). Their publicity materials from the fair illustrate the emerging attitude that kitchens were to be seen by more people than just the housewife, and their beauty something to take delight in: "Monel *is* lovely to look at—*and it stays that way*—actually becoming more beautiful with use. It's a solid metal, like sterling silver. It's chip-proof, smooth and easily kept spick-and-span. . . . Every Monel-topped piece of equipment is painstakingly designed to give lasting service, to save steps and effort, to fit into a bright, happy ensemble, as carefully matched as a string of pearls."[32] The reader—and consumer—is meant to surmise that any kitchen that evokes associations to sterling silver or pearls is a kitchen that should not be hidden. The modern kitchens of 1939 were no longer considered private, and their emerging location at the front of the house reflects that changing attitude.

The kitchen was not just more beautiful in 1939, however—it was also the site of more activities than its nineteenth-century ancestor. Crane Company asked visitors to the New York fair, "What do you expect in a kitchen? An efficient place to work? Step-saving, energy-conserving

153

convenience?" They then reminded consumers that the modern kitchen was also a social center: "Many families eat one or more meals every day in the kitchen. . . . Growing children sometimes like a place to study near where mother is working. Nothing appeals more surely to the guests who come in for the evening than refreshments served in a kitchen designed for that purpose. . . . With the kitchen the 'showroom' of the house, it is amazing how guests will gravitate to it. Many of today's most successful parties have been held in the kitchen."[33]

The model kitchen of the 1930s had, in fact, become a part of the public zone of the house: like the Victorian parlor, the modern kitchen was located at the front of the house, was the place to impress visitors, and was an alternative socializing venue. What does this trend tell us about the American family who occupied the modern kitchen? Were they as modern as their kitchen? First, the 1930s kitchen suggested radically less formal standards for the house. That the kitchen, a place of household work, became acceptable as a site for entertaining, introduced an unprecedented mixing of public and private life; it evoked the same fluidity and dynamism as the new living room spaces of the San Francisco homes.[34] Second, the 1930s kitchen implied that the status of the housewife had been significantly altered from earlier generations. She (or her servants) no longer toiled in obscurity. Rather, her kitchen now housed an arsenal of appliances, ready to keep up with the Joneses and do the work of the house with unprecedented efficiency. Magic Chef ranges called out to the American housewife at the New York fair with this tantalizing image: "There's absolutely no reason why you should spend hours in the kitchen every afternoon in order to serve wholesome, tangy meals in the evening. Thousands of women . . . thanks to Magic Chef . . . are serving tempting, savory meals to their families after having been at the beach, playing cards, romping with the children, or just plain reading in their easy chair."[35]

Although this advertisement suggests that the housewife had, by the 1930s, an easier workload and greater respect within the house, historians have argued that such changes in the armature of housework did little to actually reduce the number of hours a woman spent cleaning and cooking. If she now had better appliances, she also had increased standards of cleanliness to maintain and

more tasks for which she alone (without the help of servants or children) was responsible.[36] In keeping with this analysis, I propose that housework was still fundamentally private in the 1930s. While the housewife, perched in her status kitchen, was certainly more visible in 1939, her work was still invisible: she had to continually clean up any messes that would be evidence of her cooking—her *work*—in order to maintain the pearly glow of the Monel countertop. Her work literally hid behind such gleaming modern conveniences. Thus while the 1939 kitchen seemed to be more honest about housework, letting anyone from the public see its command center, in the end it maintained older levels of discretion and, indeed, privacy about the actual mess of domestic life.

Because of the persistence of historical styles in New York's model homes (such as the center-entrance Colonial Revival–type house), San Francisco's houses emerge as probably the most modern shown in a 1930s fair. The San Francisco homes did often have dining rooms, a concession to tradition, but they also had living rooms and kitchens that bucked older trends in privacy and formality and led to dynamic, fluid domestic stages. Because of these qualities, the architectural critic for *Pencil Points,* Talbot F. Hamlin, argued that the San Francisco houses should be taken as models for "the future of suburban house development."[37] Describing the dominant type of home in the San Francisco fair as indebted to "the old California ranch tradition of free rambling planes," he praised the houses for their "direct simplicity, [and] straightforward planning." Furthermore, he believed that these houses would be of great appeal to American families, arguing that "after all, the foundation of any house architecture must be, first and foremost, the livability of the buildings which it creates. The American family will demand in its house free and open space, but it will also demand the possibility of complete privacy for its members. It will demand a minimum of wasteful, merely connective area. It will, I am confident, also, more and more develop a taste for houses without applied stylisms and with a charm that is at least half modesty."[38] In his assessment of the qualities of the San Francisco homes, and in his claim that they should and would become prototypes for future suburban development, Hamlin predicted the nature of the housing boom that would not begin for another decade. That the efficient yet dynamic

154

forms of the postwar suburban ranch were presaged in the 1939 fairs (both San Francisco and New York, in varying degrees) testifies to the emergent modernism of their designs.

Conclusion: Questioning Privacy

This essay has been predicated on a large-scale thesis about public and private spaces. The thesis goes something like this: the model homes of the 1930s fairs offered examples and prescriptions for how American families should design and outfit their homes, and on a deeper level, how they should conduct their private lives; the millions of visitors who walked through these houses imbibed the prescriptions, took them home, and gradually changed their houses to conform to these models. Of course we do not know how visitors to the fairs actually responded to the homes—the most we can do is speculate. The fairs were huge public spectacles, and the corporate- and government-sponsored buildings were large public statements about technology, science, and the future progress of society at large. The model homes, in contrast, were small experiences, rooted in the present, in the confines and challenges that characterize daily domestic living. What was it like, as a visitor, to leave behind grand public sentiment and stumble into a modest, private house? What was it like to encounter the private in such a public place? The possible collision of public and private experiences imbues the model homes with a particularly acute volatility as prescriptive vehicles.

On the one hand, the model homes might have been highly seductive experiences. Their true-to-life scale and intimate details created a completely immersive environment: visitors might quickly lose all references to the world beyond the present model house and instead submit themselves to its fantasy of warmth, sociability, and up-to-date appliances. Robert Rydell has discussed world's fairs as hegemonic forces, and the model homes might be an instance of hegemony at its most pernicious. By proposing a standard of domestic life, the model homes invaded the most private area of our mental life: how we envision our families, how we want to conduct our daily lives. If the fairs prescribed trends for society at large, the model homes provided settings and tools to live out our private dramas, and thus affected how we think of ourselves even when no one else is supposed to be watching.

On the other hand, perhaps the experience of entering a private home with the chaos of the fair outside was a bit jarring. Not only might it have been difficult to shift from being a public spectator to being a private dweller, but the homes themselves may have been compromised in their ability to conjure up true domestic privacy. In New York visitors had to pay an extra ten-cent admission to the Town of Tomorrow (and Keck's House of Tomorrow in Chicago charged its own separate concession), but crowds around and within the houses were still on the order of hundreds per day, quite different from the typical suburban lawn and street. Photographs make clear that furniture was sometimes arranged to accommodate crowds rather than demonstrate ideal configurations, and the tchotchkes and accessories that would typically enliven a home were often absent (presumably because of the difficulty of securing such small items). Thus the model homes may have been, at best, poor approximations of private life, and their persuasive capacities far less than I have assumed.

Yet if the model homes were flawed in their ability to conjure up private living experiences, they still may have been influential to the millions of visitors who crossed their thresholds. The historian Warren Susman described world's fairs as liminal spaces—spaces that are not anchored firmly in the past, present, or future, but rather hover just outside of, or parallel to, the patterns of one's quotidian existence.[39] In a liminal space, he argued, the visitor is more open to suggestion and change precisely because she is close to her life but not confined by it. Within the larger liminal space of the fair, it may not have mattered how immersive and convincing the model homes were; instead, they simply provided a space that reminded visitors of home, without actually being home, and suggested particular patterns of daily existence. The appeal of those patterns was less dependent on how well they were illustrated in the homes, and was more a product of the general mindset cultivated by the fair.

Ultimately, the model homes of the 1930s world's fairs were ambiguously private structures: they occupied a physically public space and alluded to private life even as they accommodated thousands of visitors. The lives they depicted were likewise complex. Over the course of the decade, the homes prescribed differing attitudes toward consumption, formality, and familial privacy. Each house demonstrated some mix of nineteenth-century standards and twentieth-century innovations, but in each house the mix differed. Indeed, these homes provide models where such classic binaries as period style and modern, formal and informal, and public and private are destabilized. They illustrate the complexity of transition, and demonstrate that the march toward a modernized American home was circuitous and gradual at best.

Notes

I would like to thank Laura Burd Schiavo for her support and insights about this topic. I would also like to thank Robert W. Rydell and Richard Guy Wilson for comments on an earlier draft of this essay.

1. The key text on the fairs of the 1930s is Robert W. Rydell, *World of Fairs: The Century of Progress Exhibitions* (Chicago: University of Chicago Press, 1993). See also Robert W. Rydell, *All the World's a Fair: Visions of Empire at American International Expositions, 1876–1916* (Chicago: University of Chicago Press, 1984); Robert W. Rydell, John E. Findling, and Kimberly D. Pelle, *Fair America: World's Fairs in the United States* (Washington, D.C.: Smithsonian Institution Press, 2000), chapter 3.

2. The doorway mechanism was described in "The Modern Houses of the Century of Progress Exposition," *Architectural Forum* 59 (1933), 61: "The kitchen door is opened and closed by an invisible ray that operates by interruption of the beam."

3. In their drive to present an ideal domestic setting, the model homes of the fairs can be linked to broader efforts at social standardization present at the 1930s fairs. One notable instance of this mentality was the "typical family" competition held for the 1940 New York fair, in which states nominated "typical families" to win a free week at the fair. Unsurprisingly, these families were all Caucasian and American-born, and most had two children. Robert Rydell has argued that the uniformity of these "typical families" reveals the challenges that the form of the American family was actually facing at this point in time. While all of the model homes discussed in this essay presume some combination of cohabitating adults and children, the value of various family members changed over the course of the decade, as we shall see. See Rydell, *World of Fairs,* 56–58, and Christina Cogdell, *Eugenic Design: Streamlining America in the 1930s* (Philadelphia: University of Pennsylvania Press, 2004), 123.

4. Lawrence Levine, "American Culture and the Great Depression," *Yale Review* 74 (1985): 223.

5. Talbot F. Hamlin, "California Fair Houses," *Pencil Points* 20 (1939): 293.

6. Kristina Wilson, *Livable Modernism: Interior Decorating and Design During the Great Depression* (New Haven: Yale University Art Gallery and Yale University Press, 2004).

7. For a discussion of the stylistic variation on view at the Chicago Fair, see Monica Obniski, "Exhibiting Modernity Through the Lens of Tradition in Gilbert Rohde's Design for Living Interior," *Journal of Design History* 20 (2007): 227–242.

8. Lisa D. Schrenk, *Building a Century of Progress: The Architecture of Chicago's 1933–34 World's Fair* (Minneapolis: University of Minnesota Press, 2007), chapter 5; Brian Horrigan, "The Home of Tomorrow, 1927–1945," in *Imagining Tomorrow: History, Technology, and the American Future,* ed. Joseph Corn (Cambridge: MIT Press, 1986), 137–163.

9. Wilson, *Livable Modernism,* 55.

10. For a critical history of the importance of spaciousness in American middle-class homes, see Sandy Isenstadt, *The Modern American House: Spaciousness and Middle-Class Identity* (Cambridge: Cambridge University Press, 2006), chapter 3.

11. While I have not found records to confirm the attribution of the designs, several pieces in the room clearly match items offered in the Herman Miller catalogues of the later 1930s, including the round glass-top coffee table before the fireplace, the square glass-top coffee table

before the sectional couch, the couch itself, the chairs at the card table, the radio, the upholstered armchairs before the fireplace and in the lower right of the photograph, and the side table also in the lower right. See *Herman Miller 1939 Catalogue: Gilbert Rohde Modern Design* (Atglen, Pa.: Schiffer, 1998).

12. "A Notebook at the Fair," *House Beautiful,* July–August 1939, pp. 34–35; "Design for Living," *House Beautiful,* May 1933, pp. 210–211, 229–230. A characteristically tepid review of the New York homes can be found in *Arts and Decoration:* "No one ought to go to the Fair feeling that because the interiors are not as sensational as Dali . . . the houses are not Modern from the standpoint of liveability. Esthetically the picture may not be finally solved, nor will it ever be, but progress has been made. It is slow, but it is true to the tempo of acceptable living"; Otto Teegan, "Houses in Our Towns of Tomorrow," *Arts and Decoration* 50 (1939): 8.

13. Talbot F. Hamlin, "Some Fair Comparisons," *Pencil Points* 20 (1939): 644.

14. Le Corbusier, *Towards a New Architecture,* trans. James I. Dunnett (Cambridge: MIT Press, 1987), 279.

15. Emily Genauer, *Modern Interiors: Today and Tomorrow* (New York: Illustrated Editions, 1939), 12, 19, 24.

16. *ABC of Modernage Furniture* (New York: Modernage Furniture, 1933), located in the Corporate Archives, Herman Miller, Inc., Zeeland, Michigan. See also advertisements in magazines throughout the 1930s, such as that from the *New Yorker* that claimed, "We'll show you how smartly you can 'go modern' within ANY budget!" *New Yorker,* April 18, 1936, p. 56.

17. For Kiesler's showroom, see "'Space House' Exhibited," *New York Times,* October 17, 1933; "Architect Designs a Space House," *House and Garden,* December 1933, p. 8f; "One Living Space Convertible into Many Rooms," *House Beautiful,* January 1934, p. 32. The Modernage pamphlet from 1933 refers, unhelpfully, to "designers of its own staff" but does not name any. *ABC of Modernage Furniture,* n.p. My thanks to Phyllis Ross and Christopher Long for sharing their thoughts on Modernage with me.

18. "Modern Houses Top N.Y. Fair," *Architectural Forum* 71 (1939): 63, 66.

19. For several examples of houses furnished thus, see the Garden House, Celotex House, and Fire-Safe House, ibid., 68, 71.

20. For plans and renderings of these houses, see "Exposition Model Homes," *Pencil Points* 20 (1939): 279, 290.

21. Ibid., 285.

22. For plans and renderings of these houses, see ibid., 272, 274.

23. Gwendolyn Wright, *Building the Dream: A Social History of Housing in America* (New York: Pantheon, 1981), chapters 6 and 9; also Clifford E. Clark, *The American Family Home, 1800–1960* (Chapel Hill: University of North Carolina Press, 1986), chapter 5.

24. Wright, *Building the Dream,* chapters 9 and 11.

25. The compressed space of the modern dining room is discussed in Wilson, *Livable Modernism,* 60–61. See also Gwendolyn Wright, *Moralism and the Model Home: Domestic Architecture and Cultural Conflict in Chicago, 1873–1913* (Chicago: University of Chicago Press, 1980), chapter 8; Clark, *The American Family Home.*

26. "Building Types: Dining Rooms," *Architectural Record* 85 (1939): 101.

27. Levine, "American Culture and the Great Depression," 198.

28. Norman Bel Geddes, "The House of Tomorrow," *Ladies' Home Journal,* April 1931, pp. 12–13.

29. Examples of this type of floor plan organization were the Johns-Manville Triple Insulated House, Garden Home, Celotex House, Kelvin Home, and Electric Home. See "Modern Houses Top N.Y. Fair," 67–70.

30. A partial list of other model houses with this type of floor plan: Happy Valley Estates Model Home, Santa Cruz Host Home, Sleepy Hollow, and Sunnybrae Model Home. See "Exposition Model Homes," 267, 275, 277, 278.

31. "Modern Houses Top N.Y. Fair," 63, 67.

32. *Monel at the New York World's Fair* (New York: International Nickel, 1939), World's Fair Collection, Manuscripts and Archives, Yale University Library.

33. *Family Planned Kitchen* (New York: Crane, 1939), 2, 5. World's Fair Collection, Yale University Library.

34. Gwendolyn Wright has proposed that the newly social space of the modern kitchen is related to a nostalgia for the idea of the homestead kitchen; Wright, *Building the Dream,* 253–254.

35. *The Range of Tomorrow Brings You Shorter Cooking Hours* (New York: American Stove, 1939), World's Fair Collection, Yale University Library.

36. Ruth Schwartz Cowan, *More Work for Mother: The Ironies of Household Technology from the Open Hearth to the Microwave* (New York: Basic, 1983). Sarah Fayen, as an undergraduate at Yale College, wrote an excellent senior thesis on the symbolism and design of the modern kitchen at the New York World's Fair, arguing that the housewife was actually more confined than ever before by these supposedly liberating kitchens; Sarah Neale Fayen, "The 1939–40 New York World's Fair: Reviving the Kitchen as the Heart of the Home," senior thesis, Yale College, 1998.

37. Hamlin, "California Fair Houses," 295.

38. Ibid., 293, 296.

39. Warren Susman, "Ritual Fairs," *Chicago History* 12 (1983): 6.

Spectres of Social Housing, San Diego, 1935

Matthew Bokovoy

During the depths of the Great Depression, San Diego hosted the California-Pacific International Exposition in Balboa Park, a rambling fourteen hundred–acre urban space with scrubby green Bermuda grass, eucalyptus trees, steep arroyos, and shallow ravines. The exposition opened on Memorial Day 1935 to initial crowds of more than 250,000 per week. During difficult financial times, it was remarkable that the sponsors of expositions could justify the expenditure of millions of dollars to stage ephemeral and seemingly frivolous events. San Diego's promotion of a world's fair did have precedent. The city had hosted an exposition in 1915–1916 to promote the special cultural qualities of the city and region and to offer hope to its citizens about San Diego's future. For a city of approximately 147,000 residents in the 1930s, there was no time better for again uplifting the collective morale of the city, state, and region.

The 1935–1936 San Diego fair was the first public venue at which the Federal Housing Administration exhibited its novel programs promoting modern housing in the United States. The exposition opened its gates on May 29, 1935, eleven months after the passage of the National Housing

Act. The FHA devised outreach initiatives called Better Housing Programs in municipalities across the United States. The goal was to stimulate private enterprise and generate increased housing starts throughout the home-building industries through a nationwide advertising campaign for home ownership. Among these initiatives, San Diego's Better Housing Program exhibit at the 1935 fair stood front and center, featuring the Palace of Better Housing and two related exhibitions, Modeltown and Modernization Magic, along El Prado, the main avenue of the fair. The San Diego Better Housing Program educated 3.2 million visitors to the fair about FHA loan programs, the cultural aspects of modern housing, and inner-city and rural home rehabilitation programs (fig. 1).

The message from the Palace of Better Housing at the fair supported the innovative wings of home building that pioneered mass production of housing and the real estate industry to resolve chronic housing shortages that had plagued the United States, and especially southern California, during the 1920s. The California real estate industry and other corporate interests believed prosperity arose from industry's leadership in delivering new suburban

Within the illustration:

PALACE OF BETTER HOUSING

NEARING COMPLETION

Larger and more comprehensive than any exhibit ever conceived or contemplated by the Better Housing Program of the Federal Housing Administration. This animated and extremely interesting government exhibit will clearly and concisely tell the story of the benefits to be derived from the National Housing Act.

The Federal Housing Administration Presents

"Modeltown & Modernization Magic"

at AMERICA'S EXPOSITION « » 1935

California Pacific International Exposition
San Diego, Cal.—May 29 to Nov. 11

The F. H. A. Exhibit will be in *conjunction* with and a *part of*
THE PALACE OF BETTER HOUSING

THE NATION'S GREATEST HOUSING EXPOSITION FOR 1935

fig. 1 Brochure, Modeltown and Modernization Magic exhibit, Federal Housing Administration, 1935. California-Pacific International Exposition, San Diego, 1935–1936. Special Collections, San Diego Public Library.

homes and modern amenities to America's middle class, and that San Diego represented the brightest hope for revolutionary changes in the American housing industry during the Great Depression. These industry leaders viewed federal initiatives in southern California, such as investments in public infrastructure, employment programs, and real estate recovery, as keys to future prosperity. FHA publicity materials assured fair visitors that the Better Housing Program exhibition was "designed to visualize the countless ways the public may benefit from the National Housing Act," and its supporters declared that the publicity "would do more to electrify the building industry and the people of the United States than million[s] [of] dollars put into printed propaganda." James Moffet, the director of the FHA, made a similar claim: the model housing campaign would "visualize phases of the National Housing Act, now clouded under legal and technical verbiage."[1]

The FHA's promises about housing emerged as a central theme of Depression-era world's fairs that united a faith in growth and home building with belief in a brighter national future. Speaking to the promise of better times for the region and the country, the *Official Guide* stated the fair's purpose: "to give the visitor a glimpse, a pre-vision of what the future holds for the Far West" as the federal government financed such projects as "Boulder Dam, its All-American Canal, its Grand Coulee Project, and a host of other activities that mark a new era." The board of directors of the exposition proclaimed that the fair expressed the "fullest example of co-operation with the federal government in its efforts to bring about recovery," and forecast that "the depression is over—our faces are forward —we are looking ahead to the great achievements of mankind in the next twenty years." The involvement of the FHA and the participation of other New Deal agencies, as well as such corporations as Ford Motor Company, General Motors, and the Standard Oil Corporation of California, in the California-Pacific International Exposition was in keeping with the vision of the executive committee of the fair, which maintained that the exposition would "inspire national confidence and a higher appreciation of American institutions, stimulate business and industry, and assist the government in bringing a more abundant life to its peoples."[2]

The San Diego fair envisioned the transformation of everyday life in the United States, a notion of material plenty that scholars have termed a "culture of abundance." The culture of abundance promised that the productive capacities of the industrial economy and the rising standard of living achieved from 1900 through the 1920s could eliminate scarcity and want and provide the goods and services to meet the social needs and frivolous desires of ever more Americans. It was premised on the belief that the United States had made the shift to a level and a democratization of consumerism never achieved by previous generations. People from all walks of life, workers and white-collar professionals, political radicals and businessmen, and government bureaucrats and intellectuals, believed that new applications of science and technology to industry and a focus on scientific planning should serve human ends to provide the "good life" to the American people. The form that vision would take as the nation emerged from the turmoil of the Great Depression became a vital question. Businessmen and federal bureaucrats proposed policies to relieve unemployment, restart the economy, and support private enterprise. Many workers and intellectuals hoped the state would promote wider access to goods and services, including decent housing, and a greater redistribution of national wealth approaching the socialist democracies of western Europe. Despite the variety of proposals to steer the country out of recession, it mattered to politicians and elites only that the American people believe in the notion of abundance.[3]

Where the FHA operated primarily to assist the banking and construction industries to increase community and housing construction, the local talent used to design the exhibition cannot be underestimated, one instance among many where states and locales assisted the shape of New Deal agency policies and initiatives. Scholars of the 1930s recently have focused upon regional and local variations of policy implementation while taking their lens off of developments in Washington, D.C., in order to understand the decentralized nature of the New Deal. In the process, they have uncovered many visionary policy alternatives that arose at the regional and local level that existed briefly during the 1930s. This story of the FHA in San Diego illustrates the decentralized nature of New Deal agency promotions that relied upon regional and local experts to implement agency policies. The regional coordinators of the Better Housing Program invited southern California architects to design Modeltown, one of the displays associated with the fair's Better Housing Pavilion. The architects, including such luminaries as Richard Neutra and Reginald Johnson, imagined something grander—an entire community and town of modern housing—which might be understood as another, more progressive version of the culture of abundance. They conceived Modeltown around the idea of the European "garden city." This archetype of the planning profession resembled the modernized rural, small town with a population of ten thousand to thirty-two thousand residents that had captured the imaginations of western European architects since the early nineteenth century. The pattern of development promoted a functionally zoned, mixed-use, and self-sustaining community, with a "civic center, business district, public parks, playgrounds, industrial, and residential sections." They explored regional and environmental variations in national housing standards to reimagine how Americans experienced the concept of community throughout the country. Modernization Magic showed audiences how inner-city homes could be rehabilitated, rather than demolished, through FHA programs of building modernization. Modeltown and Modernization Magic thus offered something truly original and visionary within FHA promotions.[4]

Given the power of the FHA and federal government to promote home ownership after World War II, we might well attend to the aberration, indeed contradiction, of the implication of housing exhibits at the fair. The FHA exhibits echoed the brisk debate of the era about whether federally supported housing policies were equal and just. Modeltown and Modernization Magic represent local efforts—paths not taken in federal housing policy. Would the innoative Modeltown homes help shape a more racially and economically inclusive "culture of abundance"? It stood as a real possibility despite more powerful economic interests represented within the FHA and the southern California real estate industry.[5]

The FHA Idea at the World's Fair
The housing program at the fair expressed the goals of the larger Federal Housing Administration effort. During the booming economy of the 1920s, real estate development had been the economic backbone of the United States, the American West, and San Diego. At the onset of the Depression, new housing starts in San Diego County decreased drastically in 1931 to well below one thousand. National investment in new construction and rehabilitation of old structures dropped roughly 92 percent between 1928 and 1933. Previous programs of government–private sector cooperation symbolized the laissez-faire economics of the pre-Depression era. In contrast, the FHA programs met this downturn by creating legal and financial incentives for the entire home-building industry. The coauthors of the FHA's National Housing Act, Winfield Riefler and Miles Colean, Secretary of Labor Frances Perkins, Assistant Secretary of the Treasury Marriner Eccles, the investment banker and industrialist William A. Harriman, and Vice President Henry Wallace, charged the agency to stimulate home construction and real estate recovery without direct federal spending. By using federal policy to support private enterprise, the FHA embraced the experimentation and eclecticism of the "second" New Deal. Designed primarily as a program to alleviate unemployment and generate business investment, the NHA was intended "to encourage improvement in housing standards and conditions, to facilitate sound home financing on reasonable terms, and to exert a stabilizing influence on the mortgage market." Riefler believed that the new programs were "directed toward unlocking the [economic] keys which have stopped practically all new residential construction," and that the agency's initiatives would "not disturb the relations between borrower and lender that exist in the market today."[6]

Builders and real estate brokers complied with FHA building standards to receive mortgage insurance rather than risk building homes that would be ineligible for the lucrative indirect subsidies of the agency. Federally insured mortgages offered safety and assurances to lenders, builders, and real estate brokers, and the housing industry welcomed such indirect subsidies into the housing market. FHA initiatives would revive home construction and real estate development by freeing investment capital to the home-building industry, its suppliers, and millions of Americans who tied their livelihood to this key sector of the national economy. FHA policies helped builders bypass the politics of local planning boards and insured banks and builders against losses through mortgage insurance. With the federal government as guarantor of the mort-

162

Matthew Bokovoy

gage financing market, banks and real estate agents were assured virtually risk-free investment potential.[7]

FHA officials maintained programs to increase mortgage lending, housing starts, and home ownership. The twenty-to-thirty-year amortized mortgage, fully insured by the agency, broadly offered Americans the possibility to pursue the "good life" in new suburban landscapes across the nation. The "pump-priming" of the national economy at the heart of New Deal fiscal policy through direct and indirect federal spending achieved rapid economic results. Compensatory liberalism as a fiscal policy required the federal government to expend its funds and run deficits during economic recessions, and to pull back on federal spending during economic booms. Indeed, suburban community builders increased permits and market share due to the interventionist role the FHA played in the national mortgage market. The FHA created an equity revolution for millions of white homeowners. According to the historian Kenneth Jackson, "No agency of the United States government has had a more pervasive and powerful impact on the American people over the past half-century than the Federal Housing Administration."[8]

Through organization at the regional and local level, yet guided by federal oversight, Better Housing Programs like that at the San Diego fair reached millions of Americans between June 1934 and January 1936. The first local campaigns created roughly $145 million to $210 million of business in 1934. By December of 1934, the FHA had organized 4,000 community campaigns in more than 1,100 municipalities. By March 1935, supported by the FHA's promotion of lending, borrowing, and spending, Better Housing Programs were active in 6,000 community campaigns in 2,000 locales, reaching 5.6 million people in areas containing roughly 65 percent of the country's population. For the fiscal year 1935, the Better Housing Program grew to 8,857 local committees, reaching territory with an estimated population of 88 million people. Reports from 3,691 canvassing committees indicated that they had made 11,900,000 door-to-door calls, with 2,180,000 pledges worth $570 million. The agency spent $1.3 million and reached Americans through 52 million direct mailings. The door-to-door canvassing alone, notes the historian David Freund, generated 1 million pledges for home-improvement jobs. Set firmly within the public policy and administrative

capacity of the federal government, the programs were virtually identical to the spirit of government and industry cooperation under the federal Housing Division during the 1920s and were less antagonistic to industry than other New Deal business legislation meant to discourage monopoly. The administrative and policy emphasis of the Federal Housing Administration privileged the business and finance end of housing and community building, with little official discussion within the agency for the state's role in developing social housing and planned communities. The historian Mark Weiss explains that the FHA was "run to a large extent both by and for bankers, builders, brokers" with predominantly real estate and finance backgrounds and no enthusiasm for radical social transformation.[9]

Not surprisingly, then, industry leaders in construction and real estate warmly welcomed the FHA's powerful interventionist role because the agency supported their interests and gladly participated in the San Diego exposition. A banking industry associate of Waldo Tupper, director of exhibits for the fair, said that "Modeltown is so unusual in its direct selling of FHA loans by Banks that an exception should be made" by Bank of America to provide funds for advertising at the fair. The building-supply and construction industries looked favorably upon the Better Housing Program. An associate of Alfred B. Swinerton remarked, the "more I think of the Oil Companies financing this [Better Housing Program exhibit] the better I like the idea, and I can see where it would definitely tie into their program." He suggested that "$50,000 apportioned among the oil companies would be a trifling amount, for the good will and actual business to result therefrom." While planning the 1936 season of the fair, exposition board members J. David Larson and Hart Miller notified a colleague of the special meeting in Washington, D.C., arranged by FHA officials. The meeting brought together the "presidents or the heads of most of the large industrial firms of the country." "These firms went on record to the effect that they would be space buyers" for the 1936 season and "would support the FHA in any program it endorsed." Ford Motor Company, General Motors Corporation, and Standard Oil of California committed to the final season.[10]

The brief national economic recovery during 1935–1936 created optimism in southern California for New Deal programs. FHA Director James Moffet visited San Diego in

Pop Goes the Future
Cultural Representations of the 1939–1940 New York World's Fair

Robert Bennett

Throughout the 1930s as the United States confronted the daunting challenges posed by the Great Depression, several American cities sponsored world's fairs that played a significant role in articulating the nation's response to this period of crisis. Functioning as "collective social displays," "cultural icons," and "ideological constructs," these fairs helped define and promote new cultural values and material practices that sought to "restore popular faith in the vitality of the nation's economic and political system."[1] With their deeply entrenched commitments to scientific rationality, technological progress, modernist aesthetics, industrial design, increasing consumer prosperity, and a positive view of corporate capitalism, these fairs both expressed and helped consolidate the emerging cultural logic of 1930s American modernism. Combining recent advances in technology and modernist design with optimistic narratives of material progress and prosperity, America's Depression-era fairs expressed a new, or at least a newly minted, form of utopian modernism streamlined to fit the sensibilities of the age. With its bold aspiration to design a brave, new "World of Tomorrow," the 1939–1940 New York World's Fair in particular represented some-

thing like a culmination of this cultural and historical period, producing what Terry Smith aptly describes as "the ultimate expression of new corporate modernity for mass consumption—the Modern made simple, marvelous, and total."[2]

While historians and cultural critics broadly concur that the 1939–1940 New York World's Fair expressed the techno-rational ideology and machine-age aesthetics of 1930s American modernism, many commentators have questioned the fair's seemingly simplistic relationship to modernism. Despite acknowledging the general critical consensus about the fair's essential modernist features, critic after critic has noted—at least in passing, if not at length—one way or another in which the fair's utopian optimism was significantly complicated, if not fatally undermined, by various ideological and cultural countercurrents.[3] Over time, these alternative accounts of the fair have gathered increasing momentum as cultural critics, historians, and creative writers have begun reinterpreting the fair's relationship to modernism in more nuanced and more complex ways. However sincerely the fair's designers may have envisioned it as a relatively straightforward modernist utopia, numerous commentators have questioned whether the fair's attempt to produce a "simple, marvelous, and total" version of the modern ultimately proved unconvincing or contradictory, perhaps even producing as many postmodern skeptics as modernist true believers.[4] As Jean-François Lyotard explains in *The Postmodern Condition,* one of the central defining features of postmodern culture is its pervasive "incredulity toward metanarratives."[5] The fair's planners might have confidently entrusted the planet's future to enlightened highway engineers and progressive industrial designers, but various dissenting voices have remained unconvinced by, or even profoundly skeptical of, the fair's utopian modernism. In many ways, this steadily increasing chorus of critics who— for one reason or another—reject the fair's unbelievable modern *credulity* provides us with an early example of where and how the seeds of postmodern *incredulity* can emerge out of the failed ruins of oversimplified and mythic forms of modernist utopianism.

Virtually all accounts agree that the 1939–1940 New York World's Fair played a significant role in synthesizing and popularizing the diverse currents that shaped 1930s American modernism. Celebrating designers, architects, and engineers as the "true poets of the twentieth century," the fair displayed everything from refrigerators and washing machines to soda shops and industrial production methods redesigned according to futuristic variations on machine-age American modernism.[6] From the stark, abstract geometry of its Theme Center—Harrison and Fouilhoux's Trylon and Perisphere (fig. 1)—to its sleek Bauhaus-inspired locomotives, tear-shaped automobiles, and simulations of rocket travel, the fair repeatedly displayed both a bold faith in technological progress and a penchant for streamlined modernist designs. As Smith explains, the fair drew heavily upon the "ideology," "practice," and "developed imagery" of 1930s industrial design to help bring "together all of the elements of U.S. modernity into a striking, generalized, and ambiguous visualization of . . . a 'usable future.'" Robert A. M. Stern adds that the fair helped synthesize a "remarkably cohesive message concerning the American reaction to European Modernism, the triumph of corporation-based industrialism, and the suburbanization of the landscape on a vast scale."[7] In short, the fair functioned as a kind of conceptual crucible

where the aesthetic practices and political ideologies of 1930s American modernism could be forged into a more or less coherent form.

In few places was the fair's modernist ideology more evident than in its bold, futuristic vision of how American cities should be reconstructed according to modernist architectural and urban forms. As Janet Abu-Lughod has noted, it is "amazing to recognize how central 'the city' was to the 1939 vision of tomorrow," while Stern describes the fair as seeking "vigorously, and in some cases desperately, to present distinctive architectural and planning schemes."[8] Everywhere fairgoers went, they encountered diverse demonstrations of the fair's quasi-religious faith in modernist architecture, techno-rational urban planning, and progressive highway engineering. Not only was the fair full of exhibits that displayed new trends in architecture and urban planning, but many of these exhibits either implicitly or explicitly suggested that rebuilding American cities would produce broader social benefits such as reducing pollution and crime or promoting greater social harmony and personal happiness. From Walter Dorwin Teague and Frank J. Roorder's City of Light exhibit—a three-story-high, city-block-long, dynamic model of a day in the life of New York City complete with thunderstorms, functioning elevators, speeding cars and subways, and 130,000 lights that turned on and off—to the directors Willard Van Dyke and Ralph Steiner's almost propagandistic urban documentary, *The City,* fairgoers encountered numerous displays that celebrated the virtues of well-planned cities, often explicitly advocating more decentralized urban forms. In several exhibits, fairgoers could even enter into the fair's futuristic World of Tomorrow, touring full-scale model suburban homes filled with the "latest technological innovations" in the Town of Tomorrow or riding in radio-controlled automobiles through models of the "latest highway design[s]" at the Ford Motor Company's Road of Tomorrow.[9] In different ways and with different degrees of vigor —or desperation—these exhibits repeatedly reminded fairgoers that the fair's utopian World of Tomorrow would be constructed by a new generation of modernist architects and urban planners who would create the rationally planned and technologically advanced homes, skyscrapers, and superhighways of the future.

More specifically, it was two of the fair's most popular exhibits—Henry Dreyfuss's Democracity and Norman Bel

fig. 1 Trylon and Perisphere at night. New York World's Fair, 1939. Digital file © Eric K. Longo/Collection of Eric K. Longo.

Geddes's Futurama—that most clearly articulated and most aggressively defended the fair's new modernist urban paradigm. Centrally located inside the Theme Center's Perisphere, Democracity (fig. 2) displayed a sprawling model of a vast, decentralized urban landscape that used superhighways to connect a dense urban Centertron with several suburban Pleasantvilles and light-industrial Millvilles. Brilliantly synthesizing the fair's central ideological commitments, Democracity's urban model demonstrated how recent advances in science, technology, and industrial design could be used to reconstruct the spatial and social geography of urban landscapes. As Stern explains, Democracity "encapsulated . . . several of the fair's central themes: the viability of creating social order and stability through careful urban planning; a predilection for Streamline architecture and design; and the recognition of the imminent hegemony of the automobile."[10] To further reinforce its bold utopian vision, Democracity presented its urban model through an elaborate multimedia spectacle that included both a "symphonic poem—a chorus of a thousand voices reaching out to the heavens," and bold visual images of the "interdependent society of today" projected overhead: "at ten equi-distant points in the purple dome loom marching men—farmers, stamped by their garb; mechanics with their tools of trade. As the marchers approach they are seen to represent the various groups in modern society—all the elements that must work together to make possible the better life which would flourish in such a city as lies below."[11]

With a dramatic symphony rising to "diapasonal volume" in the background, these projected images grew to "mammoth size" as they marched across the ceiling until the show concluded with a climactic "blaze of Polaroid light."[12] Clearly, Democracity's urban model represented not simply advances in rational urban planning but also a much broader statement about how scientists, engineers, and industrial designers could work together to produce a new utopian society, while Democracity's multimedia spectacle attempted to impress upon fairgoers the larger significance of its social vision.

Not to be outdone, Bel Geddes's 35,738-square-foot Futurama (fig. 3) used a series of several hundred dramatic dioramas to depict how 1960s America could be reconstructed through a combination of "wondrous changes and improvements . . . in our national highways," the construction of "breath-taking architecture," and the application of "modern and efficient city planning."[13] As with the Disney theme-park rides that Futurama would later inspire, visitors viewed Futurama's urban dioramas while riding past them in "magic" moving chairs equipped with individual speakers that narrated descriptions of each scene. With its massive scale, elaborate details, moving chairs, totalizing perspective of looking down on a miniaturized world, and ten thousand moving cars that sped across its various dioramas, Futurama's spectacular rhetorical techniques threatened to overshadow the substance of its urban vision. To top it all off, Futurama literally interpolated fairgoers into its urban ideology at the conclusion of the ride, where visitors were shown a diorama of an ideal urban intersection of the future; presented with a button boldly proclaiming, "I Have Seen the Future"; and then—as if in fulfillment of the button's prophesy—deposited onto the Intersection of Tomorrow, a life-size simulacra of the final intersection they had just seen.

At their conceptual core, both Democracity and Futurama were largely driven by a neo-Corbusian logic that advocated reconstructing architectural and urban spaces according to the "pure geometry" of "mathematical forms," "logical productions," "geometrical cells," "right angles," and the "straight line, inevitably; for the construction of buildings, sewers and tunnels, highways, pavements."[14] As many critics have noted, both exhibits displayed models of decentralized skyscraper cities that were thinly veiled variations on the abstract, geometrical modernism of Le Corbusier's Ville Radieuse and Plan Voisin (fig. 4). Both models envisioned an urban core of widely spaced, towering skyscrapers connected to garden suburbs through vast networks of commuter highways. While their skyscrapers may have softened Corbusier's pure geometry with curvilinear, streamlined surfaces, and their sprawling, decentralized suburbs attempted to adapt European modernism to American culture's preference for open spaces, both models essentially proposed modernist solutions to urban and architectural design problems. In fact, Democracity's and Futurama's urban designs ultimately sought to extend Corbusier's ideal of the modernist home as a "machine for living in" across entire megalopolitan regions, turning the urban landscape itself into a

180

Robert Bennett

fig. 2 Democracity exhibit, Theme
Center. Henry Dreyfuss, designer.
New York World's Fair 1939–1940.
Wurts Brothers Collection, National
Building Museum/Museum of the
City of New York.

fig. 3 Viewers in "sound chairs," Futurama exhibit, General Motors Building. Norman Bel Geddes, designer. *Futurama* (Detroit: General Motors, 1940). Collection of Donald Albrecht.

fig. 4 Voisin Plan for Paris, 1925. Le Corbusier, designer.

vast, finely tuned, and intricate machine. As Joseph P. Cusker explains, the fair's "model of the future . . . encompassed a larger field of view. The city, the region, and the nation as a whole were to be made over as part of the effort to create a national character in harmony with its industrial base."[15]

At the same time that the fair's urban models were firmly grounded in orthodox modernist principles, they were also influenced and broadened by an ecumenical range of European and American modernist precedents, including the decentralized, open spaces of Ebenezer Howard's Garden City and Frank Lloyd Wright's Broadacre City; the towering expressionistic skyscrapers depicted in Hugh Ferris's architectural renderings in *The Metropolis of Tomorrow* (1929) or exemplified by Bruno Taut's Stadtkrone (1919); and the cinematic science fiction fantasies of Fritz Lang's *Metropolis* (1927) or David Butler's *Just Imagine* (1930), a comedic, musical revision of Lang's dystopian film (fig. 5). In fact, Carol Willis argues that Stephen Gooson and Ralph Hammeras's stage set for *Just Imagine*—a "225-by-75-foot model of a glittering metropolis" with "lofty towers of up to 250 stories, nine levels of multilane traffic systems complete with moving cars, personal airplanes, and aerial traffic cops"—represents one of the most explicit precursors of "the extravagant models and dioramas created by industrial designers for the 1939 New York World's Fair."[16] Given Bel Geddes's own background in set design, his flair for the theatrical, and both models' use of moving cars, complex multilayered traffic schemes, and futuristic modes of traffic surveillance, one can reasonably conclude that Gooson and Hammeras's campy theatrical set provides as appropriate a reference point as does the rigorous geometry of Corbusian modernism for understanding Futurama. Combining the "technological efficiency" of "European Modernist tendencies" with the "highly theatrical futurism" of "American industrial designer's invention," both the fair in general and Democracity and Futurama in particular developed a rather convenient "marriage of modernism and the vernacular of Broadway."[17] While neo-Corbusian modernism provided the central foundation for the fair's urban ideology, different exhibits creatively reinterpreted and adapted, with varying degrees of success, orthodox modernist practices for a dynamic new American context.

183

fig. 5 Movie set for the science fiction musical *Just Imagine*, directed by David Butler, 1930.

Despite the fair's attempt to confidently project new American variations on European modernism, several critics were quick to challenge its utopian idealism. The fair was widely popular among both critics and the general public, but several prominent intellectuals expressed grave concerns about its often totalizing and simplistic conceptualization of modernism. In his dedication of the fair's Palestine Pavilion, for example, Albert Einstein seriously questioned the fair's blind faith in scientific reason and social engineering, arguing that the fair merely projected the "world of men like a wishful dream" and celebrated modern civilization's "creative forces" while denying its "sinister and destructive ones which today more than ever jeopardize the happiness, the very existence of civilized humanity."[18] Lacking Europe's more immediate experiences with the darker side of modern technology, the fair's Americanized modernism tended to fetishize technology as a simple panacea and promote naïve machine-age fantasies. Similarly, E. B. White's review of the fair for the *New Yorker* satirized Futurama's utopian vision as bathed "in purple light, going a hundred miles an hour around impossible turns ever onward toward the certified cities of the flawless future." White redefined the fair's futuristic "road to tomorrow" as a "long familiar journey" through corporate America's "Mulsified Shampoo and Mobilgas, through Bliss Street, Kix, String-O-Sol, and the Majestic Auto Seat Cover."[19] In the process of adapting European modernism to the streamlined aesthetics of American industrial design and Jeffersonian agrarianism, the fair also tended to strip European modernist practices of their occasionally leftward-leaning proletarian social agendas, turning them instead into tools for corporate advertising, rampant consumerism, and entertaining multimedia spectacles. Instead of seeing the fair as a brave new modernist utopia, several perceptive critics reinterpreted it as the irrational exuberance of grand modern metanarratives and capitalist modes of production willfully blind to their own obvious failures and glaring contradictions. As the Frankfurt School theorists Max Horkheimer and Theodore Adorno argue in *Dialectic of Enlightenment,* modernist practices that fail to consider the "destructive aspect of progress" can produce a "blindly pragmatized thought" out of touch with modernism's "transcending quality and its relation to truth."[20]

In addition, the fair's dystopic historical moment—sandwiched between periods of international economic and geopolitical crisis—only heightened both fairgoers' and critics' sense that the utopian modernism was "riddled by an odd sense of anomie in the midst of optimism, a mood quite understandable given the nation's tentative recovery from the Depression and its anxiety as it watched Europe going to war."[21] For Robert Rydell, the fair's optimistic ideology is belied by both its dystopian historical context and its blatant attempt to ideologically mask its larger political agenda:

Obscene is not quite the right word, but the discrepancies between the wealth and power, not to mention the streamlined glamour, manifest in exposition buildings and the grim economic conditions of the Depression can still jar the senses a full half century after the New York World's Fair closed its gates. The vast sums of money that went into these revelries of corporate capitalism underscored the differential impact of the depression on American social classes and highlighted the commitment of those atop America's economic pyramid to defusing the potentially explosive political situation that confronted them during the 1930s.[22]

The 1939–1940 New York World's Fair may have employed diverse modernist discourses, ideologies, and practices —ranging from the pure geometry of international style modernist urbanism and the streamlined machine-age aesthetics of 1930s American industrial design to a devout faith in technology and the benevolence of corporate and consumer capitalism—but account after account simply refuses to accept the fair's bright, shiny modernist facades at face value. Instead, many commentators have expressed at least some degree of ambivalence, if not open hostility, toward the fair's oversimplified utopian modernism, frequently reinterpreting it as both an illusion and a mask: the dreamy faux modernism of a reductive, spectacular fetishization of techno-rational instrumentality deceptively covering its blind subservience to the ideologies of corporate power.

Far from simply synthesizing and resolving the diverse currents of late-1930s American modernism, the fair projected an idealized solution that failed to resolve many of the period's larger historical complexities and contradictions. In *Narratives and Spaces,* David E. Nye succinctly summarizes this view, describing the fair not as "a micro-

184

cosm of 1930s America, but a corporate vision of what the future could be. Much is missing from the era of the New Deal, and the fair is at best a problematic symbol of American culture in the 1930s. Its themes, architecture, and organization lay entirely in the hands of an economic and cultural elite."[23]

Fatally flawed in its design, the fair's utopian modernism often proved more illusory than enduring and as ridiculous as it was compelling: its naïve faith in technology oversimplified the more complex reality of scientific reason and technological progress; its obvious pandering to corporate interests undermined its higher social aspirations; its elaborate multimedia spectacles entertained more than they enlightened; and ultimately its reductive and optimistic solutions rang hollow against its more complex and troubling historical context. At the very moment when the fair planners seemed to have convinced the American public that they had produced a synthesis of the aesthetic practices and political ideologies of 1930s American modernism, the geopolitical, economic, and epistemological foundations upon which the fair's modernist ideology was constructed were undermined both by American modernism's failure to resolve the cultural and political tensions of its own day and by the epochal changes that would soon be unleashed by the Second World War and its aftermath. In short, the fair's utopian modernist castles had been built if not on thin air, then at least on what would eventually come to be seen as the shifting sands of an emerging postmodernity.

In no place has this "gap between the fantasy World of Tomorrow and the real one that emerged after World War II" been depicted more clearly than in literary and cultural representations of the fair.[24] With the anomalous exception of David Gelernter's hagiographic historical romance, *1939: The Lost World of the Fair* (1995), cultural representations of the fair—both contemporary ones and those produced in the late twentieth century—have repeatedly depicted its utopian modernism with varying degrees of skepticism if not outright hostility. The most obvious and most contemporary manifestation of this is Matt Groening and David X. Cohen's animated sitcom *Futurama,* whose title is a highly ironic reference to Bel Geddes's exhibit and which ultimately develops a systematic refutation of the fair's utopian modernist ideology. The show's first episode

alone, "Space Pilot 3000," lampoons all of the core values promoted by the fair: scientific reason, technological progress, rational urban planning, social engineering, and corporate and consumer capitalism. Aside from the series title and the pilot episode, which parodically welcomes its viewers to its own "World of Tomorrow," Groening and Cohen's sitcom makes few explicit references to the 1939–1940 New York World's Fair, but its postmodern send-up of modernity in general broadly attacks the larger historical period, cultural sensibilities, and epistemological paradigm that the fair represented.[25] In "Space Pilot 3000," technology is used for such benevolent purposes as suicide booths, and corporations are depicted as intergalactic behemoths with tremendous power but little concern for human life. Even the sitcom's campy, retrofuturistic Googie, or Populuxe, architecture ironically pokes fun at the serious futurist aesthetics of modernist architecture, streamlining, and 1930s industrial design. Ultimately, the episode's final ironic twist is revealed when its protagonist, a pizza-delivery boy named Fry, travels a thousand years into the future only to be reassigned as an interplanetary delivery boy for an intergalactic corporation. In Groening and Cohen's *Futurama,* the scale and scope of technology and corporations progresses tremendously over the course of a millennium, but social and economic relations change little, and the fundamental existential predicaments of alienated modern subjects remain essentially the same.

While it is tempting to dismiss Groening and Cohen's parody as the product of more than a half-century of proliferating postmodern skepticism, their sitcom's dystopianism can be seen more accurately as the direct descendent of the first literary representation of the fair itself. Even before the fair closed its gates, Eando Binder's short story "Rope Trick" (1939) employed the genre of dystopian science fiction to challenge the fair's blind faith in science and technology. Depicting a pair of time travelers voyaging to the year 2039, the same futuristic year in which Dreyfus set his Democracity, Binder's story explores how the "great scientific achievements," "robots," "two hundred fifty stor[y]" skyscrapers, "elevated traffic spans," and "superhighways they vaguely planned in 1939" might actually be realized in the future.[26] Offering conflicting interpretations of how the fair's urban designs would even-

185

tually be realized, one character describes the futuristic world of 2039 as a "magnificent, glorious, breathtaking . . . wonder-city," while the other one sees it as the "same old world" where things "ain't so hot" because there "ain't no justice."[27] While the first character simply notices how many of the fair's technological wonders and urban designs have "come true," the other character more perceptively realizes that this technological progress has failed to produce the corresponding social transformations that the fair had predicted would result from its new urban designs.[28] Binder seems to predict that instead of helping create some perfect democratic society, the fair's cities of the future will lead to an increasingly prisonlike state where order can be maintained only through pervasive incarceration, arbitrary justice, surveillance systems, police force, and psychiatric hospitals rather than through simple advances in highway engineering.

Extending Binder's dystopian themes still further, Jack Womack's science fiction novel *Terraplane* (1988) also uses the 1939–1940 New York World's Fair to critique American culture's often uncritical belief in technological progress. Reversing the temporal direction of Binder's story, Womack's novel depicts twenty-first-century time travelers who return to New York City in 1939 in an attempt to reverse the actions of DryCo, a giant multinational corporation that has sent its own agents in time machines back in history to assassinate Roosevelt and Churchill in hopes of undermining opposition to Hitler during World War II. Womack's novel, however, not only depicts late-1930s New York City as a society with pervasive racism, xenophobia, segregation, injustice, and violence, but it also explicitly rejects the fair's utopian futurism. When a character from 1939 asks one of the time travelers to assess how "accurate" Futurama's predictions would prove to be, the time traveler responds with a "combination of laughter and tears" before criticizing Futurama for getting absolutely "nothing" correct.[29] Instead of producing a world of "better houses and apartments," Womack's time traveler explains that "what [will] come from such projects" is "miracles, yes, all God's wonders. The poison ocean rising higher each year, the thin air ashine with the sun's cancerous rays, the earth sodden with the blood of the billions killed upon it. The sound of orphans at play in the littered, rotting streets, born alone to die alone."[30] From this dystopian perspective, Womack depicts the fair's utopian modernism both as an ideological mask that conceals the

186

fig. 6 Aerial view showing first two thousand houses, Levittown, Hicksville, New York, 1947. Levitt and Sons, developers (1947–1951). Culver Pictures, Inc.

Robert Bennett

economic and political problems of its own day and as a flawed model that will produce a toxic future of environmental destruction, endless warfare, and blighted cities.

While these dystopian narratives use hyperbole to make their point, their basic critique of the fair's failed urban vision roughly parallels the fair's actual historical legacy. As Binder's story anticipates and Womack's novel chronicles, the fair's urban model did significantly influence the spatial reconstruction of post–World War II American cities, but it also largely failed to achieve its larger utopian social objectives. Stripped of its most extreme technological gadgetry—such as rocket transportation and radio-controlled cars—the fair's urban vision both anticipated and helped produce the essential paradigm of post–World War II American urbanism. The suburban architecture of Levittown (fig. 6), the urban housing projects of Stuyvesant Town (fig. 7), and the international style modernist architecture of corporate skyscrapers such as Lever House (fig. 8) were all influenced—at least in their broad principles, if not in their exact details—by the kinds of architectural and urban practices that the fair had promoted. Gelernter may be overstating the case when he declares that the fair's "utopian promises came true" in the "years following the Second World War" as postwar American cities largely "realized the heart" of Democracity's "utopian World of Tomorrow [which] amounts, in essence, to the modern suburbs," but he is essentially correct that the dominant trends in post–World War II American urbanism largely followed the urban practices presented at the fair.[31] At least in its general, essential characteristics, the world of tomorrow envisioned by the fair's designers eventually became the cities of today.

Where Gelernter errs, however, is not so much in his hyperbole as in his unqualified celebration of post–World War II suburbanization as an unproblematic realization of America's democratic ideals. In siding unreservedly with the fair's modernist urban ideology, Gelernter dismisses with little substantive argument an entire generation of post–Jane Jacobs architectural and urban critics who have repeatedly and ferociously criticized the real consequences of postwar urban redevelopment. By the early 1960s the fair's general faith in technological progress, and its modernist urbanism in particular, had increasingly come under attack on multiple fronts. While only isolated, prescient critics had seriously challenged the fair's utopian vision in its own day, by the 1960s a new generation of architec-

187

fig. 7 Stuyvesant Town and Peter Cooper Village, New York, 1948. Irwin Clavan and Gilmore Clark, architects (1943–1949). Photograph by Fairchild Aerial Surveys, Inc. Courtesy of the New York State Archives.

next page
fig. 8 Lever House, New York, ca. 1952. Skidmore, Owings and Merrill, architects (1951–1952). Photograph by Ezra Stoller. Ezra Stoller © Esto. All rights reserved.

tural and urban theorists had begun turning en masse against the kind of modernist urbanism that the fair had promoted. In her scathing critique of the "principles and aims that have shaped modern, orthodox city planning and rebuilding," *The Death and Life of Great American Cities,* Jane Jacobs lambastes the fair's modernist paradigm as a "dishonest mask of pretended order" that could be "achieved [only] by ignoring or suppressing the real order that is struggling to exist and be served."[32] Moreover, when Jacobs criticizes modernist urban planners for fallaciously basing their urban models on "principles derived from the behavior and appearance of towns, suburbs, tuberculosis sanatoria, fairs, and imaginary dream cities —from anything but cities themselves," she clearly includes both the 1939–1940 New York World's Fair and its imaginary communities high on her list of suspect models.[33] Seconding Jacobs's critique of modernism's "dullness,"

"regimentation," and "monotony, sterility and vulgarity," Robert Venturi, in *Complexity and Contradiction in Architecture,* similarly rejects modernism's "bland architecture," "blatant simplification[s]," and "puritanically moral language," while Colin Rowe and Fred Koetter, in *Collage City,* denounce modernism's "sterile scientific rigour" and "lamentable lack of tolerance."[34] By the mid-1960s America's newly reconstructed modernist cities had erupted in urban riots, and by the early 1970s modernist buildings and cities literally had begun to be unbuilt: the demolition of the Pruitt-Igoe housing development in St. Louis marked the beginning of the end for the fair's urban paradigm. As Binder's and Womack's dystopian narratives suggest, the fair's futuristic cities of modernist skyscrapers, sprawling suburbs, and vast highways would be built, but they would also come to be seen as failing to achieve many of their larger social objectives. The fair's utopian cities would be constructed in postwar America, but out of their failed ruins would emerge new antimodernist and postmodernist sensibilities that would reject modernism's pure geometry for more realistic and more complex alternatives.

While Binder, Womack, and Groening and Cohen all use dystopian science fiction to criticize the fair's failed utopian modernism, other writers such as E. L. Doctorow and Miles Beller use varying degrees of revisionist historical fiction to critique the fair from a slightly different perspective. Instead of simply proclaiming their radical skepticism toward the fair's modernist ideology, both Doctorow's *World's Fair* (1985) and Beller's *Dream of Venus (Or Living Pictures)* (2000) focus more on peeling back and probing beneath the fair's bright, shiny modernist facades to expose the hidden and flawed political ideologies that motivated the fair. Far from depicting either 1930s America or the fair in a dystopian manner, Doctorow's novel looks back upon both the fair and its larger historical context with a certain amount of respect and nostalgia. Not only does the novel's entire plot revolve around the narrator's eagerly anticipated visit to the fair, but the narrator generally describes the fair with a reverential awe, proclaiming himself "incredibly happy" and "trembling with joy" when he first sees the Trylon and Perisphere.[35] In particular, the narrator reserves his most lavish praise for the fair's bold utopian urban models, describing Democracity as a "totally planned planetary city of the future" that is "designed to

Robert Bennett

eliminate all problems and difficulties" and proclaiming Futurama the "most fantastic sight I had ever seen, an entire city of the future" where "everything was planned" and "people lived in these modern streamlined curvilinear buildings, each of them accommodating the population of a small town."[36] When he later exits Futurama onto the life-size Intersection of Tomorrow, he describes himself as feeling so "dazzled" that he "actually wobbled on [his] feet."[37] At least in his first encounter with the fair, Doctorow's narrator stands awestruck before its various utopian cities, literally experiencing them as an expression of what Nye describes as the technological sublime. While this particular manner of representing the fair neither explicitly criticizes nor entirely rejects the fair's modernist vision, it does suggest that the fair's modernist aspirations were perhaps more fantastic and spectacular than realistic and sustainable.

Despite this initial sense of amazement, Doctorow's novel ultimately goes on to qualify, if not outright reject, its narrator's uncritical response to the fair's utopian illusions. While the fair initially causes the narrator to "forget everything that wasn't the Fair as if the Fair were all there was, as if going on rides and seeing the sights, with crowds of people around you and music in your head, were natural life," he eventually recovers from this quixotic inversion of reality and illusion to recognize that Futurama's utopian models are not real, but rather merely the "largest most complicated toy ever made."[38] Less awestruck on his second visit to the fair, Doctorow's narrator even begins to notice "everywhere signs of decay": the Perisphere's bright, white "paint was peeling," while the "officials who ran the exhibits seemed less attentive to the visitors, their uniforms not quite crisp."[39] It is the narrator's parents, however, who most explicitly expose the fair's diverse shortcomings, noting that "no one in the world has the money to buy" the homes displayed at the Town of Tomorrow and criticizing the Westinghouse Time Capsule for containing nothing representative of the "Indians on reservations," the "Negroes who suffered from race prejudice," or the "great immigrations that had brought Jewish and Italian and Irish people to America."[40] Even the mesmerizing Futurama fails to impress the narrator's father, who dismisses it as a blatant advertisement for General Motors and a deceptive act of political manipulation: "General Motors isn't going to build the highways, the federal gov-

ernment is. With money from us taxpayers. . . . So General Motors is telling us what they expect from us: we must build them the highways so they can sell us the cars."[41] Ultimately, Doctorow's novel depicts the world's fair less as a failed modernist utopia than as an unrealistic modernist fairytale: it might have had the power to momentarily enchant children, but it lacked any ability to endure in the harsh daylight of reality or seriously engage mature, thinking adults. In the novel's final chapter, the narrator decides to bury his own personal time capsule, and Doctorow uses this scene to articulate his final critique of both the fair and the larger ideology of 1930s American modernism. Just before the capsule is buried, the narrator's friend adds his "old prescription pair of eyeglasses" with a "cracked" frame to teach future generations "something about our technology when they look through the lenses."[42] However dazzlingly the fair may have presented itself upon first glance, Doctorow's novel ultimately depicts both the fair and its underlying modernist ideology as fundamentally "cracked" — childish, manipulative, unrealistic, and "everywhere showing signs of decay."

Beller's novel even more explicitly attempts to peel back the fair's "faux stone floors" and "chrome-plated walls" in order to reveal how underneath its superficial modernist surfaces the fair was little more than "carny come-on stuccoed onto pasteboard and chicken-wire."[43] Extending Doctorow's revisionist history into a full-blown act of historiographic metafiction, Beller's blatantly postmodern novel completely rejects the "gleaming buildings and celibate street corners" that the fair tried to pass off as the "semblance of a timeless city," depicting Futurama instead as merely a "multi-leveled lie, a conspiracy of design and architecture" and an "airstream moderne version of Coney Island."[44] Like the rest of the fair, Futurama is "not prompted by high-blown ideals" but rather by nothing "more than commerce American-style": "When the seat finally clicked back into place, Zeke and the other voyagers were face-to-face with an intersection in Adams City, a major U.S. metropolis of 1960. Though the future belongs to all, Bel Geddes and his crew had little doubt it would be as American as Coca-Cola, Kelvinator, and Buster Brown shoes; from Malibu to Mali a planet cast in Hollywood's image animated by one-line epiphanies minted by Madison Avenue. . . . Futurama was a stage set, an elaborately expensive one, nothing more than an entertainment."[45]

While the Middle Ages might have had "honest faith in something called science," Beller's novel argues that the fair perverted science in the "service of teasin' and scintillatin,'" producing merely "stupid gadgets and dumb gizmos" promoted by "baggy-pants vaudevillians and saggy-tit grinders, hustling for a buck. . . . Forget the cosmic questions. Science better give us mindless fun."[46] Peeling back the fair's shiny but superficial streamlined facades, Beller's novel ultimately discovers what Helen A. Harrison describes as the fair's "ultimate compromise" between its "theory and practice. Conceived as a demonstration of the triumph of enlightened social, economic, and technological engineering, it was in actuality a monument to merchandising."[47]

Viewed from this perspective, the fair and its urban models represented not so much a failed modernist utopia as a kind of faux modernism—professing allegiance to scientific reason, technological progress, and sleek modernist aesthetic forms, but ultimately committed at a deeper level to an alternative set of conflicting values more closely aligned with corporate power, consumer advertising, and entertaining multimedia spectacles. Rejecting the fair's urban utopias as something ranging between an illusory "complicated toy" and a deceptive "conspiracy in architecture and design," both of these revisionist historical fictions dismiss the fair's utopian modernist ideology as little more than a streamlined facade. If the fair did forge a new form of corporate modernism, these novels insinuate that its often uncritical and submissive deference to corporate power largely overpowered its often superficial and half-hearted commitments to modernism. More corporate than modernist, Doctorow and Beller suggest, the fair's attempt to synthesize a coherent utopian ideology for the future out of modernist traditions of its recent past would ultimately prove insufficient, insincere, incomplete, and ineffective.

Taken collectively, all of these cultural representations of the fair present a sophisticated, albeit harsh, analysis of the fair's complex relationship to modernism. On the one hand, Binder's and Womack's dystopian science fiction narratives blame the fair's failures on the internal contradictions, erroneous assumptions, and oversimplifications found within modernism itself, while Doctorow's and

Beller's revisionist historical fictions criticize the fair for failing even to take its own modernism seriously, allowing instead for baser corporate and consumer interests and spectacular popular entertainments to corrupt its higher modernist ideals. Alternating between depicting the fair's modernism as a self-contradictory failure, an unrealistic illusion, and an ideological mask covering up less idealistic motivations, these narratives may not offer a fair and balanced view of the fair, but they have significantly influenced how later generations have come to understand and evaluate the event. For future generations raised on Groening and Cohen's sitcom, as for the fair's contemporaries who read Binder's short story or White's *New Yorker* review, it is more difficult to take the fair as seriously because these alternative narratives predispose readers to view it with various degrees of antimodern or even postmodern skepticism. That many contemporary historians and a new generation of postmodern architectural and urban theorists have largely come to share these writers' skeptical attitudes toward the fair may partially reflect the fact that we now belong to a historical and cultural period in which the fair's particular brand of modernism has proven largely implausible.

At a deeper level, however, these skeptical narratives also teach us something essential and informative about the nature of the fair's modernist ideology itself, revealing various imperfections, ambiguities, and contradictions in the fair's flawed attempt to construct a usable future out of the existing modernist discourses and practices of its day. After all, critical responses to the fair—whether in literature, history, cultural criticism, or architectural theory—are by no means simply products of the postmodern present but date back to the time and place of the fair itself. Reminding us that the 1939–1940 New York World's Fair did not exist in some kind of pure, hermetically sealed modernist bubble, these alternative narratives help us recontextualize its modernist project as only one part of a more complex cultural dynamic whose tensions were heightened by the fair's transitional location between evolving historical and cultural periods. Without dismissing the fair's modernist sensibilities altogether, these critical narratives ultimately situate it within a broader conversation between diverse voices with differing degrees of faith or disbelief in its incredible utopian World of Tomorrow.

Robert Bennett

Notes

This essay is a revised version of "Constructing the Post-WWII Megalo-politan Subject: The Socio-Spatial Ideology of the 1939–40 New York World's Fair," the first chapter of my book, *Deconstructing Post-WWII New York City: The Literature, Art, Jazz, and Architecture of an Emerging Global Capital* (New York: Routledge, 2001): 27–51.

1. David E. Nye, *American Technological Sublime* (Cambridge: MIT Press, 1996), 210; Robert W. Rydell, *World of Fairs: The Century-of-Progress Expositions* (Chicago: University of Chicago Press, 1993), 1, 9.

2. Terry Smith, *Making the Modern: Industry, Art, and Design in America* (Chicago: University of Chicago Press, 1993), 407.

3. Prominent examples of this stance can be found in Warren Susman, *Culture as History* (New York: Pantheon, 1984); Rydell, *World of Fairs;* and Nye, *American Technological Sublime.*

4. Smith, *Making the Modern,* 407.

5. Jean-François Lyotard, *The Postmodern Condition: A Report on Knowledge* (Minneapolis: University of Minnesota Press, 1984), xxiv.

6. *Official Guidebook* (New York: Exposition Publications, 1939), 29.

7. Smith, *Making the Modern,* 409; Robert A. M. Stern, Gregory Gilmartin, and Thomas Mellins, *New York 1930: Architecture and Urbanism Between the Two World Wars* (New York: St. Martin's, 1995), 729.

8. Janet Abu-Lughod, *New York, Chicago, Los Angeles: America's Global Cities* (Minneapolis: University of Minnesota Press, 1999), 186; Stern, Gilmartin, and Mellins, *New York 1930,* 755.

9. Stern, Gilmartin, and Mellins, *New York 1930,* 742, 747.

10. Ibid., 752.

11. *Official Guidebook,* 45.

12. Ibid.

13. General Motors Corporation, *Futurama* (New York: General Motors Corporation, 1940), 5, 17–19.

14. Le Corbusier, *The City of To-morrow and Its Planning,* trans. Frederick Etchells (New York: Payson and Clarke, 1929), 22, xxii, xxvi, 25, 10.

15. Joseph P. Cusker, "The World of Tomorrow: Science, Culture, and Community at the New York World's Fair," in *Dawn of a New Day: The New York World's Fair 1939/40,* ed. Helen A. Harrison (New York: Queens Museum and New York University Press, 1980), 13.

16. Carol Willis, "Skyscraper Utopias: Visionary Urbanism in the 1920s," in *Imagining Tomorrow* (Cambridge: MIT Press, 1986), 124.

17. Stern, Gilmartin, and Mellins, *New York 1930,* 746; Nye, *American Technological Sublime,* 200.

18. Albert Einstein, "Address at Dedication of Palestine Pavilion at New York World's Fair," May 28, 1939, Einstein Archive Online, 28–490.00.

19. E. B. White, "They Come Home with Joyous Song," *New Yorker,* May 13, 1939, p. 25.

20. Theodor W. Adorno and Max Horkheimer, *Dialectic of Enlightenment,* trans. Frederick Etchells (New York: Payson and Clarke, 1929), xi, xii, xiv.

21. Stern, Gilmartin, and Mellins, *New York 1930,* 727.

22. Rydell, *World of Fairs,* 118.

23. Nye, *Narratives and Spaces,* 105.

24. Warren Susman, "Ritual Fairs," *Chicago History* 12, no. 3 (1983): 4–9.

25. The first issue of the printed comic strip version of Groening and Cohen's *Futurama,* however, makes this connection to the fair more explicit. After time-traveling a thousand years into the future, the story's protagonist, Fry, discovers a Partridge Family lunch pail full of cultural artifacts from the 1970s in an obvious parody of the Westing-house Time Capsule that was deposited at the 1939–1940 New York World's Fair.

26. Eando Binder, "Rope Trick," *Astounding Science Fiction,* April 1939, pp. 77, 79, 81.

27. Ibid., 81, 83.

28. Ibid., 83.

29. Jack Womack, *Terraplane: A Futuristic Novel of New York, 1939* (New York: Tom Doherty Associates, 1988), 151.

30. Ibid., 152.

31. David Gelernter, *1939: The Lost World of the Fair* (New York: Avon, 1995), 49, 71.

32. Jane Jacobs, *The Death and Life of Great American Cities* (New York: Vintage, 1961), 3, 15.

33. Ibid., 6.

34. Jacobs, *Death and Life,* 4, 7; Robert Venturi, *Complexity and Contradiction in Architecture* (New York: Museum of Modern Art, 1966), 22, 25; Colin Rowe and Fred Koetter, *Collage City* (Cambridge: MIT Press, 1978), 6, 132.

35. E. L. Doctorow, *World's Fair* (New York: Plume, 1985), 252.

36. Ibid.

37. Ibid., 253.

38. Ibid.

39. Ibid., 282.

40. Ibid., 284.

41. Ibid., 285.

42. Ibid., 288.

43. Miles Beller, *Dream of Venus (Or Living Pictures): A Novel of the 1939 New York World's Fair* (Beverly Hills: C. M. Publishing, 2000), 7, 20.

44. Ibid., 21, 7, 20.

45. Ibid., 8, 173, 19–20.

46. Ibid., 24.

47. Helen Harrison, Introduction to *Dawn of a New Day: The New York World's Fair, 1939/40,* ed. Helen Harrison (New York: New York University Press, 1980), 2.

Coda
Reflections on Modernism and World's Fairs An Interview with Richard Guy Wilson

Conducted by Robert W. Rydell and Laura Burd Schiavo

LBS Let me begin by reviewing the exhibition Designing the World of Tomorrow, which opens at the National Building Museum in Washington, D.C., in October 2010. This is the first time that any museum exhibition about world's fairs has really looked at the design vocabulary of multiple fairs held in the United States during the Great Depression. What's exciting about this exhibit is that it's a real opportunity to get out of the habit of thinking that there was one world's fair in the 1930s (usually the 1939 New York World's Fair) or maybe two (the 1933 Century of Progress Exposition). Clearly, world's fairs were held across the United States during the Depression, and we think it's important for our audience to think about what it might have meant that tens of millions of visitors attended six fairs across the country in the span of seven years and saw modernistic designs, in many cases for the very first time. What the fairs did in a very public way was put modernism on view and associate it with ideas about the family, about the home, about urban planning, and about the role of science and industry in the future of the United States.

One of the things I'd like visitors to the National Building Museum exhibition to understand is that modernism as

it unfolded at the fairs was something to experience in a public setting and that it's different to experience these ideas in public rather than sitting at home with the Internet, which is I think the way most people learn new ideas today. [LAUGHTER] And I think it's important for our museum audience to understand what modern public space and public culture meant.

What are your thoughts?

RGW The world's fairs of the 1930s were certainly extremely important for introducing modernism to the American public. The fairs were not simply an architectural phenomenon that fairgoers were experiencing but also they were filled with exhibits that embodied modernism. These ranged from exhibits of kitchen design and furniture design to early demonstrations of television. The fairs provided the laboratories for infusing modernism into many facets of American life.

Remember that a good portion of America in the 1930s did not have electricity. The application of electricity at the fairs to so many parts of life like communication, transportation, and advertising was stunning. And this is part of the story of modernism that really needs more work, namely the overlay of modernism with science and technology and the power of American business and American corporations. If there is one thing that seems to me to really come alive in these fairs, and you might say, reaches a climax with the 1939-1940 New York World's Fair, it is the corporate pavilions. These stand-alone corporate structures were relatively new and underscored the growing power of corporations in creating a public image that shaped modern, post-Depression American culture.

RWR So the basic point is that modernism at the fairs is pretty complex and involves more than architecture.

RGW Yes. And let's not forget that there were traditional elements in these fairs. And we, as historians—and this is one my rants [LAUGH]—we're looking for a story. We have to categorize things, we have to put them in a nice neat package and make some sort of a logical categorization of the past. So we tell the story of progress from "traditional" forms of design to "modernistic" forms and we forget the nuances, contradictions, and tensions. For instance, at the Century of Progress Exposition, amid all

of its seemingly modernistic buildings, there was an American Colonial Village, designed by Thomas Tallmadge. Tallmadge, I might note, was a follower of Frank Lloyd Wright and Louis Sullivan and also wrote a history of American architecture that promoted their views. But here he is doing a Colonial Village! What was that doing there? Most books on the fairs don't spend much time on this exhibit because it just doesn't fit with the standard narrative flow that insists on telling the story of architecture and design as a series of distinct and separate eras. Too often, we historians, in our rush to periodize things, say, "This is it," and the blinders go on. How do you account for the persistence of tradition in these laboratories of modernism? It would be fascinating to go back and just see what is said in the press about this Colonial Village thing [fig. 1].

RWR So do you think that the fairs, just taken as a collective now, represent a distinctive American modernism, as contrasted with what was going on in Europe?

RGW Yes, I think we [Americans] still had an inferiority complex, we were looking over our shoulder at Europe and saying: "How do we stack up with them?" Another

THE COLONIAL VILLAGE

fig. 1 Colonial Village, 1934. Century of Progress Exposition, Chicago, 1933–1934. Lake County (Illinois) Discovery Museum, Curt Teich Postcard Archives.

opposite
fig. 2 Poster, Exposition internationale des arts décoratifs et industriels modernes, color lithograph on paper, Charles Loupot, Paris, France, 1925. © 2008 Artists Rights Society (ARS), New York/ADAGP, Collection: Powerhouse Museum, Sydney. Purchase 1986.86/1412.

Coda

way of also thinking about this competitive streak is if you look back at the European fairs—even beginning with London's [the 1851 Great Exhibition of the Works of Industry of All Nations, commonly known, for its noted architectural wonder, as the] Crystal Palace Exhibition—the European fairs very frequently were more edgy in terms of architecture and were more interested in promoting certain modernist ideas. Think about Antwerp and Milan in 1902; they were very modernist.

RWR So this is why the 1925 Paris Exposition des arts décoratifs was so important?

RGW Yes. The 1925 Paris exposition was extremely important and was lurking there in the background of American world's fair planners in the 1930s just as the Paris 1889 World's Fair was lurking there in the background for the 1893 Chicago World's Columbian Exposition. But we have to be careful how we read the 1925 fair. When we teach about this exposition, what is it that you pick out of this exposition to ask students to look at? When I teach about this fair, I like to show in class two posters that were used. One shows a nymph with a gazelle jumping through

the fields, very sexy and decorative. But the other poster, which you don't see so often, depicts factories with heavy smoke coming out their smokestacks [fig. 2]. Very frequently in the books all you see is the gazelle poster and you don't see the factory. To be sure, there are connections between the gazelle representation and the modernistic designs that suffuse the Bon Mârche Pavilion, but the factory poster suggests that French industrialists were onto modernism as well. And this is the point that the United States Commission to that fair made in its report to Congress [*Report of Commission Appointed by the Secretary of Commerce to Visit and Report upon the International Expositions of Modern Decorative and Industrial Art in Paris, 1925*], namely that European, especially French, manufacturers were much less intimidated by modernism than their American counterparts.

LBS So, going into the 1930s, it's safe to say that America's architectural designs were pretty traditional?

RGW Very bluntly, most American architecture was traditional; some of our greatest classical building projects were done in these years. Look at Federal Triangle just down the street [from the National Building Museum]. Remember that the National Gallery of Art was not completed until 1941. Three years after that the Jefferson Memorial was completed. You can go into any city across this country and look at the architecture of buildings completed during the interwar years and the federal courthouses, post offices, and most of the local governmental buildings were very traditional.

LBS This might be why Herbert Hoover thought there was nothing modern about American design when he refused to send an official U.S. exhibit to the 1925 Paris fair? [LAUGHTER]

RGW Yes, in many ways America was very traditional or conservative; this is jumping ahead a few years to make a point, but in 1949 the American Institute of Architects did a poll that asked Americans, "What building gives you a thrill?" It wasn't skyscrapers or movie theaters. The number one building was the Folger Shakespeare Library. Now, does anybody even know the Folger today? [LAUGHTER]

195

An Interview with Richard Guy Wilson

This indicates just how powerful the undertow of tradition was in American architecture.

RWR So what about the fairs of the 1930s?

RGW The planners of the 1933 Chicago fair determined that their fair would look different. And in some respects it did. Look at the use of building materials and lighting. And on the surface, a building like the U.S. Government Building appears very different, especially when we remember that at the 1931 Paris Colonial Exhibition the official U.S. Pavilion took the form of a Mount Vernon replica. Now, the government could have just put a Mount Vernon at Chicago three years later. But they opted for a design that has elements of what has come to be called art deco. But the structure has traditional elements: the symmetry, a dome and the hierarchical composition. Isn't this an old building in a new dress? The architects have put on more lipstick. But I'm not convinced that this is a wholly modernistic design. When you say that a building is modern, what is meant?

LBS Isn't this the question that Frank Lloyd Wright raised and that led to such a furor in the early 1930s about his exclusion from the architectural team that designed the Century of Progress Exposition?

RGW The case of Frank Lloyd Wright is complex. First, Frank Lloyd Wright couldn't work with anybody. He was impossible to work with. Second, the designs for exposition buildings that he proposed were typical Wrightian extravaganzas. Wright was great at designing with no budget in mind. The architects who worked on the Century of Progress had to be tethered to reality and to work within budget. After all, when the exposition opened, the country was in the worst year of the Great Depression.

RWR But Wright goes ballistic and says the modernism at the 1933 fair is a sham. What do you make of this?

RGW Well, maybe architecturally there is some truth to that. But he certainly never looked at the exhibits [figs. 3, 4]. He isn't looking at what people would experience at the fair. And the other thing, of course, was the new

materials. I'm not convinced that he really understood all of the materials like plywood that well. Frank Lloyd Wright would make a wonderful contemporary literary scholar, making outrageous statements and his audience would have to accept some of them. [LAUGHTER]

LBS Let's talk a bit more about the meaning of *modern*.

RGW The term *modern,* as we all know, is one of the most ambiguous, one of the most contentious words in the English language for those who deal with the visual and design arts. For instance, do we capitalize it? Or leave the *m* lowercase. Do we add *isms* or italics or an *e*? Is it a great, wonderful umbrella type of term that everybody just agrees to use? Or is it associated with particular ideologies? I think the core idea underpinning *modern* during the time period of this exhibit was that there is a better life—a utopia—and that through design we can create a much better world. In other words, there is a reform element here.

RWR So would it be accurate to think of belief in the "modern" as being analogous to religious belief? Or an ideological one?

196

RGW Yes, definitely, modernism was akin to a dogma. In the 1920s and 1930s there appears what might be called modernist converts. I can speak to this personally, since I was born in a Rudolph Schindler house in Los Angeles. And I've often puzzled why in the hell my parents went in that extreme of a direction in the 1930s. But there's something about modernism as a set of beliefs that people had to be converted to. And so you do have this type of a conversion factor going on at the fairs—an effort to convert large numbers of people to think about the "modern" in new ways.

And one way this happens is to make the buildings at fairs look different. These buildings do look very different. And so, is it just a covering over, as Wright says? The point is they do look different. Let's take a chair: a [Charles and Ray] Eames chair is just a chair, okay? [LAUGHTER] Right? Its function is the same as a Queen Anne chair. But they do look different. And they do feel different. How something looks is extremely important. To go back to the conversion or religious dogma aspect, a belief takes hold in a lot of people's minds that life can be improved, and this was no small accomplishment given the economic disaster of the 1930s and the Great Depression.

LBS How did the corporations fit into this?

RGW The idea that somehow we can improve life is common on both sides of the Atlantic during the 1920s and '30s. Look at Le Corbusier—it becomes his cause: life can be better. But in America, and this might be typical, corporations embrace this idea. They take it over. Who becomes the savior in the midst of this horrendous economic calamity? The new high priest is the industrial designer. You can make an argument that the industrial designer and the advertising guys really do save corporate and capitalist America. And the exhibit makes clear you can see evidence of their handiwork everywhere at these fairs.

RWR So this brings us back to modernism as religion?

RGW We can carry metaphors too far, but in some ways the debates about modernism become quite parochial, tied into separate schools and sects. It is similar to: "I know the truth. I know what modernism is, and you're with me or you're against me." Certainly this is what was going on with the Museum of Modern Art vis-à-vis the streamlined

197

Gulf Exhibit at the World's Fair, A Century of Progress, Chicago, Ill.

industrial designers. These sectarian debates appeared at the fairs and they are part of a broader proselytizing effort to convert a mass audience to new waves of thinking about the meaning of "modernity" and the future.

LBS Let's turn to the industrial designers for a moment and their relationship to architects and the corporate underwriters of these exhibitions.

RGW There was a huge impact of these fairs on the future of American architectural and design practice, especially on the individual architects and designers. We tend to just treat the [Norman] Bel Geddeses and [Henry] Dreyfusses or the individual architects of the fairs. What is seldom examined is that the fairs of the 1930s produced major changes in the way architectural firms practiced. Like the corporations, they too moved horizontally and vertically, incorporating different design elements under one roof. By the end of the 1930s, the [architectural] firm of Skidmore, Owings, and Merrill becomes full service, with branches in different cities. And so, in a sense, clients don't have to go any longer to separate industrial designers, interior designers, architects, and landscape architects to get your job done. What Skidmore, Owings, and Merrill say is: "We're going do the whole job for you." Just as corporations were modernizing their images, so were architectural firms.

LBS So how did the modern ideas and gadgets featured at fairs actually get into the mainstream of American culture? People, millions of them, went to these fairs. What happened next?

RGW Let's examine the houses for a minute. Model homes were very important exhibits at these fairs. The way that modernism entered the American homes [was] through the back door and the garage door. It did not come through the front door. People did not sit in chromium tubular chairs in their living room. In the kitchen you got your chromium tubular furniture and appliances that roll around and make it look like an operating room. The same can be said about the bathroom. It's also open to modernist appliances. The same holds true for garages that become parking lots for highly stylized modern auto-

mobiles. People get ideas about modern gadgets and new designs for transportation, but it's through the back door and the garage door that modernism enters into the mainstream of American life.

LBS But not so many of these model houses of the future were built, right? Do the houses have to have been replicated to "matter"?

RGW Certainly no houses were built that looked like George Keck's House of Tomorrow at the Century of Progress Exposition, but the California ranch house that was on view at the 1939 San Francisco fair is a different story. One could make a pretty good case that the modern suburban California-style ranch house caught on because of the Golden Gate International Exposition.

LBS So, when people think of modernism and the fairs of the 1930s, they generally think of the 1939 New York World's Fair with its Trylon and Perisphere. Do you think it's important to think about regional variations in modernism?

RGW Indeed. But let me tell you a story about the origins of the Trylon and Perisphere. In the early 1980s I interviewed Wally [Wallace K.] Harrison, one of the original designers of the 1939 fair. Wally and the other members of the design team were charged with coming up with an iconic structure for the fair. Chicago in 1893 had its Ferris wheel, Paris its Eiffel Tower; Chicago in 1933 had its Skyride. What would work for New York? The idea came to Wally on a trip through the South and looking at southern cities. That's when he realized that the images that best captured urban America were the big water tanks in the different cities. [LAUGHTER] Really! He goes back to New York and with his design team they come up with this abstracted water tank. It becomes an almost cubistic painting or sculpture that is inflated to gigantic proportions.

The Trylon and Perisphere dominate the posters of the New York World's Fair, and if you compare those to, say, some of the posters from 1933, with the U.S. Government Building, the Trylon and Perisphere are more modern in the sense that they are asymmetrical. They are more cubistic in comparison to the symmetry of the U.S. Government Building.

198

RWR Speaking of iconic structures, you get the Eiffel Tower, and in Chicago, you get the Ferris wheel and maybe the Skyride of 1933. And then the Trylon and Perisphere. Is there any generalization you can make about what gives these structures their longer shelf life that makes them so appealing? Is it just PR that drives them forward, or is there something intrinsic in the design?

RGW In all four cases they symbolize modern technology or modern structure ability. The fascinating thing about the Trylon and Perisphere is that the designers did not see the need to show the membranes there, whereas in the others the membranes are very much there. And in a sense, it is even more abstract than the others. People tend to forget that the Eiffel Tower was the triumphal tower celebrating the march of science. Around the base of it you've got roundels with the names of famous French scientists. Nobody ever looks at that anymore, but there was a purpose to that structure, and a very clear one. One could argue that the Ferris wheel and Skyride were sort of gimmicks to produce spectacle.

RWR And what about regional variations in the modernistic designs of these fairs?

RGW There are regional variations such as the San Diego fair. Richard Requa, a well-known architect at the time, but now largely forgotten, said this about his preparations for work on the 1935 exposition [quoting from a reissue of Richard Requa's *Inside Lights: On the Building of San Diego's Exhibition, 1935*]: "One of the surprising and impressive facts I learned from this study is that the principal elements, or fundamental features of our so-called modern styles of architecture had all been admirably employed in the creation of the prehistoric buildings of America. There was a striking similarity in the arrangement of masses and the use of horizontal lines, and the employment of geometrical design, in the ornamentation. And in its application and a few well-selected spots, particularly for doorways, friezes and parapets." So, in California, you get this interest in linking the design schemes of the Mayans, the Aztecs, Native Americans, and modern Americans. Requa indicates that a broad-based history of design and decoration will show the same compositional prin-

ciples existing in many cultures and civilizations. So you can read the Mayan buildings or Aztec buildings as being protomodern, but they also contain neotraditional elements. A lot of it comes down to the decorative elements. And certainly we are very interested in these sorts of abstract geometries that had a meaning to the Aztecs and the Incas.

So at the San Diego fair, you get this very interesting amalgam of ancient-cum-modern styles that will complicate anyone's reading of the meaning of modernism between the wars.

RWR and **LBS** Any final thoughts about the fairs, modernism, et cetera? We're happy to give you the last word.

RGW The fairs that appeared in the United States in the 1930s represented many different elements, and certainly those who attended them came away with different impressions. For instance, some visitors doubtless were made comfortable by "Elmer," the typical middle-aged, midwestern American offered as the poster child of the 1940 version of the New York World's Fair. Others probably better remembered entertainment aspects of the fairs, for instance, the sideshows featuring everything from strippers to miniaturized foreign villages. But from a perspective of seven decades later the modernist elements appear to be the most important. Not just the buildings but the displays put on by the corporations that convinced the American public that owning a late-model automobile and the superhighway was the way to a better life. Similarly, appliances from dishwashers to televisions would rule in the future.

An Interview with Richard Guy Wilson

Selected Bibliography

Ater, Renée. "Creating a 'Usable Past' and a 'Future Perfect Society': Aaron Douglas's Murals for the 1936 Texas Centennial Exposition." In *Aaron Douglas: African American Modernist,* edited by Susan Earle, 95–113. New Haven: Yale University Press, 2007.

Becker, Ron. "'Hear-and-See' Radio in the World of Tomorrow: RCA and the Presentation of Television at the World's Fair, 1939–1940." *Historical Journal of Film, Radio, and Television* 21, no. 4 (2001): 363–364.

Benton, Tim. "Building Utopia." In *Modernism: Designing a New World,* ed. Ian Christie, Tim Benton, Christopher Wilk, and Mark Jones, 149–224. London: Victoria and Albert Museum, 2006.

Bokovoy, Matthew. "The FHA and the 'Culture of Abundance' at the 1935 San Diego World's Fair." *Journal of the American Planning Association* 68, no. 4 (2002): 371-386.

_____. *The San Diego World's Fairs and Southwestern Memory, 1880–1940.* Albuquerque: University of New Mexico Press, 2005.

Bush, Donald J. *The Streamlined Decade.* New York: G. Braziller, 1975.

Carpenter, Patricia F., and Paul Totah. *The San Francisco Fair: Treasure Island, 1939-1940.* San Francisco: Scotwall, 1989.

Cawelti, John C. "America on Display: The World's Fairs of 1876, 1893, 1933." In *The Age of Industrialism in America,* ed. Frederic Copil Jaher, 317–363. New York: Free Press, 1968.

Cogdell, Christina. *Eugenic Design: Streamlining America in the 1930s.* Philadelphia: University of Pennsylvania Press, 2004.

Cohen, Barbara. *Trylon and Perisphere: The 1939 New York's World Fair.* New York: Abrams, 1989.

Cooms, Robert. "Norman Bel Geddes: Highways and Horizons." *Perspecta* 13 (1971): 14.

Draper, Joan E. *Edward H. Bennett: Architect and City Planner.* Chicago: Art Institute of Chicago, 1982.

Duranti, Marco. "Utopia, Nostalgia, and World War at the 1939-40 New York World's Fair." *Journal of Contemporary History* 4 (2006): 663–683.

Findling, John E. *Chicago's Great World's Fairs.* Manchester: Manchester University Press, 1994.

Findling, John E., and Kimberly D. Peppe, eds. *Historical Dictionary of World's Fairs and Expositions, 1851–1988.* Westport, Conn.: Greenwood, 1990.

Ganz, Cheryl R. *The 1933 Chicago World's Fair: A Century of Progress.* Urbana: University of Illinois Press, 2008.

Greenhalgh, Paul. *Ephemeral Vistas: The Expositions Universelles, Great Exhibitions, and World's Fairs, 1851-1939.* Manchester: Manchester University Press, 2000.

_____. *The Modern Ideal: The Rise and Collapse of Idealism in the Visual Arts from the Enlightenment to Postmodernism.* London: Victoria and Albert Museum, 2005.

Harris, Neil. *Cultural Excursions: Marketing Appetites and Cultural Tastes in Modern America.* Chicago: University of Chicago Press, 1990.

_____. "Expository Expositions: Preparing for the Theme Parks." In *Designing Disney's Theme Parks,* ed. Karal Ann Marling, 19–28. Paris: Flammarion, 1997.

Harrison, Helen A., ed. *Dawn of a New Day: The New York World's Fair, 1939–1940.* New York: Queens Museum and New York University Press, 1980.

Heller, Alfred E. *World's Fairs and the End of Progress: An Insider's View.* Corte Madera, Calif.: World's Fair, 1999.

Hilton, Suzanne. *Here Today and Gone Tomorrow: The Story of World's Fairs and Expositions.* Philadelphia: Westminster, 1978.

Horrigan, Brian. "The Home of Tomorrow, 1927–1945." In *Imagining Tomorrow: History, Technology, and the American Future,* ed. Joseph Corn, 137-163. Cambridge: MIT Press, 1986.

Jakle, John. *City Lights: Illuminating the American Night.* Baltimore: Johns Hopkins University Press, 2001.

Johannesen, Eric. *Cleveland Architecture, 1876–1976.* Cleveland: Western Reserve Historical Society, 1979.

Johnson, Stewart J. *American Modern, 1925–1940: Design for a New Age.* New York: Abrams, 2000.

Kihlstedt, Folke T. "Utopia Realized: The World's Fairs of the 1930s." In *Imagining Tomorrow: History, Technology, and the American Future,* ed. Joseph J. Corn, 97–118. Cambridge: MIT Press, 1986.

Kuznick, Peter J. "Losing the World of Tomorrow: The Battle over the Presentation of Science at the 1939 New York World's Fair." *American Quarterly* 46 (1994): 341-373.

Lerner, Mel, Herbert Rolfes, and Larry Zim. *The World of Tomorrow: The 1939 New York World's Fair.* New York: Harper and Row, 1988.

Levine, Lawrence. "American Culture and the Great Depression." *Yale Review* 74 (1985): 223.

Marchand, Roland. *Creating the Corporate Soul: The Rise of Public Relations and Corporate Imagery in American Big Business.* Berkeley: University of California Press, 1998.

_____. "The Designers Go to the Fair, I: Walter Dorwin Teague and the Professionalization of Corporate Industrial Exhibits"; and "The Designers Go the Fair, II: Norman Bel Geddes, the General Motors 'Futurama,' and the Visit to the Factory Transformed." Both in *Design History: An Anthology,* 89-121. Cambridge: MIT Press, 1995.

Mattie, Erik. *World's Fairs.* New York: Princeton Architectural Press, 1998.

McGovern, Charles F. *Sold American: Consumption and Citizenship, 1890–1945.* Chapel Hill: University of North Carolina Press, 2006.

Meikle, Jeffrey L. *Twentieth-Century Limited: Industrial Design in America, 1925–1939.* Philadelphia: Temple University Press, 1979.

Morshed, Adnan. "The Aesthetics of Ascension in Norman Bel Geddes's Futurama." *Journal of the Society of Architectural Historians* 63, no. 1 (2004): 74-99.

Museum of the City of New York. *Drawing the Future: Design Drawings for the 1939 New York World's Fair.* New York: Museum of the City of New York, 1996.

Neuman, Dietrich. *The Architecture of the Night: The Illuminated Building.* New York: Prestel Verlag, 2002.

Nye, David E. *American Technological Sublime.* Cambridge: MIT Press, 1996.

_____. *Narratives and Spaces: Technology and the Construction of American Culture.* New York: Columbia University Press, 1997.

Obniski, Monica. "Exhibiting Modernity Through the Lens of Tradition in Gilbert Rohde's Design for Living Interior." *Journal of Design History* 20 (2007): 227–242.

Ragsdale, Kenneth B. *The Year America Discovered Texas: Centennial '36.* College Station: Texas A&M Press, 1987.

Reinhardt, Richard. *Treasure Island: San Francisco's Exposition Years.* San Francisco: Scrimshaw, 1973.

Rydell, Robert. *All the World's a Fair: Visions of Empire at American's International Expositions, 1876–1916.* Chicago: University of Chicago Press, 1984.

_____. *World of Fairs: The Century-of-Progress Expositions.* Chicago: University of Chicago Press, 1993.

Rydell, Robert W., John E. Findling, and Kimberly D. Pelle. *Fair America: World's Fairs in the United States.* Washington, D.C.: Smithsonian Institution Press, 2000.

Schrenk, Lisa D. *Building a Century of Progress: The Architecture of Chicago's 1933–34 World's Fair.* Minneapolis: University of Minnesota Press, 2007.

Slade, Thomas M. "'The Crystal House' of 1934." *Journal of the Society of Architectural Historians* 29, no. 4 (1970): 350–353.

Smith, Terry. *Making the Modern: Industry, Art, and Design in America.* Chicago: University of Chicago Press, 1993.

Stern, Robert A. M., Gregory Gilmartin, and Thomas Mellins. *New York 1930: Architecture and Urbanism Between the Two World Wars.* New York: St. Martin's, 1995.

Susman, Warren. *Culture as History: The Transformation of American Society in the Twentieth Century.* New York: Pantheon, 1984.

_____. "Ritual Fairs." *Chicago History* 12, no. 3 (1983): 4–9.

Tilman, Jeffrey T. *Arthur Brown Jr.: Progressive Classicist.* New York: Norton, 2006.

Van Wesemael, Pieter. *Architecture of Instruction and Delight: A Socio-Historical Analysis of World Exhibitions as a Didactic Phenomenon.* Rotterdam: Uitgeverij 010, 2001.

Weingartner, Fannia, and Henry Ford Museum and Greenfield Village. *Streamlining America: A Henry Ford Museum Exhibit.* Herald Series. Dearborn, Mich.: Henry Ford Museum and Greenfield Village, 1986.

Wilson, Kristina. *Livable Modernism: Interior Decorating and Design in the Great Depression.* New Haven: Yale University Press, 2004.

Wilson, Richard Guy, Diane H. Pilgrim, Dickran Tashjian, and Brooklyn Museum. *The Machine Age in America, 1918–1941.* New York: Brooklyn Museum in association with Abrams, 1986.

Selected Bibliography

Contributors

Robert Bennett is assistant professor in the English Department at Montana State University and author of *Deconstructing Post-WWII New York City: The Literature, Art, Jazz, and Architecture of an Emerging Global Capital*.

Matthew Bokovoy is acquisitions editor for Native American and Indigenous Studies and the history of the American West for the University of Nebraska Press and a former editor of the *Journal of San Diego History*.

Robert Alexander González is assistant professor in the School of Architecture at Tulane University, founding editor of the international journal *Aula: Architecture and Urbanism in Las Américas,* and author of *Designing Pan-America: U.S. Architectural Visions for the Western Hemisphere.*

Neil Harris is the Preston and Sterling Morton Professor Emeritus of History and Art History at the University of Chicago. He is the author of numerous books, including *The Artist in American Society: The Formative Years, 1790–1860; Humbug: The Art of P. T. Barnum; Cultural Excursions: Marketing Appetites and Cultural Tastes in Modern America; Building Lives: Structural Rites and Passages; Chicago Apartments: A Century of Lakefront Luxury;* and *The Chicagoan: A Lost Magazine of the Jazz Age.*

Robert W. Rydell is professor of history in the Department of History and Philosophy at Montana State University. His books include *World of Fairs: The Century-of-Progress Expositions; All the World's a Fair: Visions of Empire at American International Expositions, 1976–1916; Fair America: World's Fairs in the United States,* with John E. Findling and Kimberly D. Pelle; and Frederick Douglass, Ida B. Wells, I. Garland Penn, and F. L. Barnett, *The Reasons Why the Colored American Is Not in the World's Columbian Exposition: The Afro-American's Contribution to Columbian Literature* (editor).

Laura Burd Schiavo is assistant professor of museum studies at George Washington University, contract curator at the National Building Museum, and author of *Washington Images: Rare Maps and Prints from the Albert H. Small Collection,* with James Goode.

Lisa D. Schrenk is associate professor of architecture and art history at Norwich University and author of *Building a Century of Progress: The Architecture of Chicago's 1933–34 World's Fair.*

Kristina Wilson is assistant professor of art history at Clark University and author of *Livable Modernism: Interior Decorating and Design in the Great Depression* and *The Modern Eye: Stieglitz, MoMA, and the Art of the Exhibition, 1925–1934.*

Richard Guy Wilson holds the Commonwealth Professor's Chair in Architectural History at the University of Virginia. His books include *The Machine Age in America; Thomas Jefferson's Academical Village; Colonial Revival House;* and *Harbor Hill: Portrait of a House.*

203

Photo Credits

Index

209